CAN ANIMALS BE MORAL?

CAN ANIMALS BE MORAL?

Mark Rowlands

OXFORD
UNIVERSITY PRESS

OXFORD
UNIVERSITY PRESS

Oxford University Press is a department of the University of Oxford.
It furthers the University's objective of excellence in research,
scholarship, and education by publishing worldwide.

Oxford   New York

Auckland   Cape Town   Dar es Salaam   Hong Kong   Karachi
Kuala Lumpur   Madrid   Melbourne   Mexico City   Nairobi
New Delhi   Shanghai   Taipei   Toronto

With offices in

Argentina   Austria   Brazil   Chile   Czech Republic   France   Greece
Guatemala   Hungary   Italy   Japan   Poland   Portugal   Singapore
South Korea   Switzerland   Thailand   Turkey   Ukraine   Vietnam

Oxford is a registered trademark of Oxford University Press in the UK and certain other countries.

Published in the United States of America by
Oxford University Press
198 Madison Avenue, New York, New York 10016

Library of Congress Cataloging-in-Publication Data
Rowlands, Mark.
Can animals be moral? / Mark Rowlands.
p.   cm.
ISBN 978-0-19-984200-1 (alk. paper)
1. Ethics—History.   2. Animals (Philosophy)
3. Emotions in animals.   4. Animal psychology.   I. Title.
BJ1031.R69 2012
179'.3—dc23   2011051638

1 3 5 7 9 8 6 4 2

Printed in the United States of America
on acid-free paper

For Emma

CONTENTS

PREFACE

When I became a father for the first time, at the rather ripe old age of forty-four, various historical contingencies saw to it that my nascent son would be sharing his home with two senescent canines. There was Nina, an incontrovertibly ferocious German shepherd / malamute cross, and Tess, a wolf-dog mix who, though gentle, had some rather highly developed predatory instincts. I was a little concerned about how the new co-sharing arrangements were going to work. As it turned out, I needn't have worried at all. During the eighteen months or so that their old lives overlapped with that of my son, I was alternately touched, shocked, amazed, and dumbfounded by the sorts of care, solicitude, toleration, and patience they exhibited toward him. They would follow him from room to room, everywhere he went in the house. Crawled on, dribbled on, kicked, elbowed, and kneed: these occurrences were all treated with a resigned fatalism. The fingers in the eye they received on a daily basis would be simply shrugged off with an almost Zen-like calm. In many respects they were a better parent than I. If my son so much as squeaked in the middle of the night, I would instantaneously feel two cold noses pressed against my face: get up, you negligent parent—your son needs you!

To some—perhaps to many—this is an unpromising way to start this book. Discussing animals with this sort of naked, shameless affection is a fault that will almost certainly lead to anthropomorphism and other cardinal sins of that ilk. When we talk about animals, in any serious academic sense, we must be appropriately dispassionate. There is game that is played when animals are discussed in a philosophical or scientific context. The game is: don't give them anything more than you absolutely have to. Cognitive abilities—assume only the bare minimum required to explain their behavior. Emotional sensibilities—ditto. Above all else: don't get attached to them. Many assume that, as far as animals are concerned, this is the only game in town. I disagree. But I am more than willing to play the game. Thus, when the book begins in earnest, I assure you I shall be more clinical, more sterile.

So, I thought I had better get mention of Nina and Tess out of the way early on. But I did have to mention them. After all, credit where credit is due. Care, solicitude, toleration, and patience are, ostensibly, moral emotions. At least, when they are attributed to humans we have little hesitation that in supposing that they are moral emotions—emotions that have identifiable moral content. And so it was, during those foggy, sleepless nights of my early fatherhood that the idea for this book started to grow slowly within me. Nina and Tess are both dead a few years now, but live on in this book. My thanks to both of them.

While I am on the subject of credit that is due, I would like to acknowledge my enormous intellectual debt to the work of, in purely alphabetical order, Marc Bekoff and Frans de Waal. On occasion, in the pages to follow, I shall criticize some of their claims and arguments. But these are the sorts of disagreements it is possible to have only with someone with whom one agrees on so very much. Without their groundbreaking work, this book would not have been written.

The question, "Can animals be moral?" is one that has, among philosophers at least, engendered an almost blanket denial. There are exceptions, but they are few and far between. This is curious, for addressing the question quickly plunges one into some of the central issues, problems, and, more significantly for my purposes, disputes of philosophy. In attempting to address this question in any serious way, one quickly becomes enmeshed, enveloped, and frequently bedazzled by some of the most difficult debates in philosophy: free will, autonomy, normativity, consciousness, self-consciousness, rationality, motivation, action, the nature and status of moral properties, and many more. Each of these topics has, of course, engendered a multiplicity of profoundly opposed views, endorsed by deeply entrenched opponents. It is, in many ways, odd that a near universal dismissal of the possibility of moral action in animals should emerge from this sort of widespread disharmony.

It is not remotely possible, in a work of this sort, to do all these— or even any—of these topics justice. It is certainly not possible to dig too many people out of camps in which they have become very comfortable—often for good reasons. Instead, I have restricted myself to two goals. First, I try to show that the blanket dismissal of the possibility of moral action in animals cannot be sustained because it rests on certain assumptions that are controversial and would be rejected by many, often the majority, of philosophers. Essentially, the blanket dismissal requires that one be willing to pitch one's tent in certain philosophical camps—camps in which many, perhaps most, philosophers would not be seen dead. Second, and equally important, I shall try to show that there are indeed good reasons to eschew these camps. Of course, I harbor no illusions that this book will be the last word on the question of whether animals can act for moral reasons. But if I have done my job properly, it will at least be *a* word.

I presented the central arguments of this book at various venues, including the Indiana University, Yale University, the University of

Chicago, and the biennial conference of the Spanish Society for Ethics and Political Philosophy. I would like to thank all involved parties for an opportunity to try out these arguments. In particular, my thanks go to Colin Allen, Gary Ebbs, Radhika Govindrajan, Kirk Ludwig, Martha Nussbaum, Timothy O'Connor, Antonio Casado da Rocha, Sandra Shapshay, and Allen Wood. Thanks also to Colin McGinn and Daniel Hampikian for useful comments.

Most of all, my thanks to my family. Thanks to my sons, Brenin and Macsen, who have made life more fun than I could have never imagined during my fatherless years. My thanks also to Hugo, for accompanying me on our long runs in the Miami heat (a difficult thing to do when you are wearing a big fur coat), when I devised and revised (and redevised and rerevised) the ideas and arguments that make up this book. And thanks to my wife, Emma, for once again putting up with me while I threw myself—body, mind, and spirit— into yet another book. This book, like all of my other books since our paths first crossed, is dedicated to her.

Mark Rowlands

Miami

CAN ANIMALS BE MORAL?

Animals, Emotions, and Moral Behavior

MORALITY TALES?

Eleanor, the matriarch of her family, is dying. Unable to stand, Grace tries to help her, lifting and pushing her back to her feet. She tries to get Eleanor to walk, nudging her gently along. But Eleanor stumbles, and then falls again. Grace appears very distressed, and shrieks loudly. She persists in trying to get Eleanor back to her feet, to no avail. Grace stays by the fallen figure of Eleanor for another hour, while night falls. Eleanor lives through the night, but dies the next morning, around 11:00 a.m. Shortly after her death, Maui arrives: she touches Eleanor's body and stands by it, gently rocking to and fro. Eventually, Eleanor's family arrives. They simply stand quietly around the body of their fallen matriarch. After a while, they are ushered away by the members of another family—although Eleanor's young daughter is allowed to remain with her mother's body. The daughter will, apparently, not recover from her loss, and three short months later will be dead too.

If the figures that played out this grim tableau were human, we might have little hesitation in attributing to them emotions of a certain sort. The efforts of Grace, we would probably be willing to accept, were motivated by her compassion for Eleanor and sympathy for her plight. Shock and sadness, we might accept, explain the behavior of Maui in the presence of Eleanor's corpse. The rapid demise of Eleanor's daughter following her mother's death, we would almost certainly be willing to accept, was the result of her enormous grief. However, none of the characters that animate these scenes are human. Eleanor is the matriarch of the First Ladies family of elephants. Grace is a younger, unrelated member of another family of elephants, the Virtues family. Maui belongs to the Hawaiian Islands family. The family that ushered away Eleanor's family, while permitting her young daughter to remain, is known as the Biblical Twins family.[1]

Grace is not unusual among elephants. A young female elephant suffers from a withered leg and can put little weight upon it. A young male from another herd charges the crippled female. A large female elephant chases him away and then, revealingly, returns to the young female and gently touches her withered leg with her trunk. Joyce Poole, who described this event, concludes that the adult female was showing empathy.[2]

Indeed, neither is Grace unusual among nonhuman animals (henceforth "animals") more generally. Binti Jua, a gorilla residing at Brookfield Zoo in Illinois, had her fifteen minutes of fame in 1996 when she came to the aid of a three-year-old boy who had climbed onto the wall of the gorilla enclosure and fallen twenty feet onto the concrete floor below. Binti Jua lifted the unconscious boy, gently cradled him in her arms, and growled warnings at other gorillas that tried to get close. Then, while her own infant, Koola, clung to her back, she carried the boy to the zoo staff waiting at an access gate.[3]

Continuing with the simian theme: Knuckles has cerebral palsy. He is the only known chimpanzee with this condition, one that leaves

---

1. Ian Douglas Hamilton, Shivani Bhalla, George Wittemyer, and Fritz Vollrath, "Behavioural Reactions of Elephants Towards a Dying and Deceased Matriarch," *Applied Animal Behaviour Science* 100 (2006), 67–102. This case was cited by Marc Bekoff and Jessica Pierce, *Wild Justice: The Moral Lives of Animals* (Chicago: University of Chicago Press, 2009), pp. 103–4.

2. Joyce Poole, *Coming of Age with Elephants: A Memoir* (New York: Hyperion, 1996).

3. Cited in Bekoff and Pierce, *Wild Justice*, pp. 1–2.

him impaired both physically and mentally, and unable to function as a normal member of his chimpanzee group. The other chimpanzees in his group treat him quite differently from the way in which a young male would normally be treated. For example, Knuckles rarely has to contend with the intimidating displays of aggression typically directed at younger males by their older peers. Even the alpha male tolerates Knuckles, and often grooms him gently.[4]

Frans de Waal relates the story of Kuni, a female bonobo chimpanzee residing at Twycross Zoo in England.

> One day, Kuni captured a starling. Out of fear that she might molest the stunned bird, which appeared undamaged, the keeper urged that she let it go.... Kuni picked up the starling with one hand and climbed to the highest point of the highest tree where she wrapped her legs around the trunk so that she had both hands free to hold the bird. She then carefully unfolded its wings and spread them wide open, one wing in each hand, before throwing the bird as hard as she could towards the barrier of the enclosure. Unfortunately, it fell short and landed on the bank of the moat where Kuni guarded it for a long time against a curious juvenile.[5]

Anthropologist Barbara King relates the story of Tarzan, a chimpanzee whose sister, Tina, had been killed by a leopard. The dominant male of Tina's group sat with the body for five hours. He kept away the young chimpanzees, with one exception: Tarzan was allowed to approach. He sat at his sister's side, pulled her hand, and touched her body.[6]

4. Bekoff and Pierce, *Wild Justice*, pp. 97–98.
5. Frans de Waal, *Bonobo: The Forgotten Ape* (Berkeley: University of California Press, 1997), p. 156.
6. Interview with Barbara King, *Primatology.net*, January 31, 2007: http://primatology.net.2007/01/31/on-god-gorillas-and-the-evolution-of-religion.

Perhaps most famous of all among stories of chimpanzee grief is the story of Flint, described by Jane Goodall and reported in *National Geographic Magazine*, among many other places. When Flint's mother, Flo, died, Flint withdrew from other chimps. He climbed a tree to the nest he shared with his mother. He declined to eat, seemingly lost the will to live, and died less than a month after his mother.[7]

Grief, however, does not appear to be an exclusively simian trait. Marc Bekoff describes an event in the life of a coyote pack that he studied in Grand Teton National Park:

> One day Mom left the pack and never again returned. She had disappeared. The pack waited impatiently for days and days. Some coyotes paced nervously about, as if they were expectant parents, whereas others went off on short trips only to return empty-handed. The traveled in the direction she might have gone, sniffed in places she might have visited, and howled as if calling her home. For more than a week some spark seemed to be gone. Her family missed her. I think the coyotes would have cried if they could.[8]

Of course, other emotions also seem to be exhibited by canids. On a busy highway in Chile, a dog has been hit by a vehicle and lies unconscious in the middle of the road. Another dog weaves in and out of the traffic, and manages to drag the dog to safety.[9]

There is also the case of Angel, an eighteen-month-old golden retriever owned by the Forman family of Boston Bar, British Columbia.

---

7. See, for example, the article "Do Animals Have Feelings?" by Aline Alexander Newman, *National Geographic World*, June 2001, p. 28. See also http://www.janegoodall.ca/chimps-we-know-f-flo.php.

8. Marc Bekoff, *Minding Animals: Awareness, Emotions, and Heart* (Oxford: Oxford University Press, 2002).

9. See http://www.youtube.com/watch?v=-HJTG6RRN4E. My thanks to Brendan Manley for drawing my attention to this.

Angel saved ten-year-old Austin Forman from the attentions of a cougar, even though she almost died doing so.[10] Both cases seem to involve concern for the welfare of another allied with great courage.

None of these observations are particularly novel. Nor are they restricted to elephants, simians, and canids. As long ago as 1964, Stanley Wechkin, Jules Masserman, and William Terris demonstrated that hungry rhesus monkeys would not take food if doing so subjected another monkey to an electric shock. The monkeys refused to pull a chain that delivered them food if doing so gave a painful shock to a companion. One monkey persisted in this refusal for twelve days.[11] Similar results were obtained when the experimental subjects were not monkeys but rodents. In 1959, Russell Church demonstrated that rats would not push a lever that delivered food if doing so caused other rats to receive an electric shock.[12] In a similar vein, in 1962, George Rice and Priscilla Gainer showed that rats would help other rats in distress. In their experiment, one rat was suspended by a harness, which would cause it distress that it manifested by squeaking and wriggling. Another rat could lower the suspended rat by pressing a lever, and this is what it, in fact, did.[13]

CONCERN AND THE MORAL EMOTIONS

These are all examples of the sorts of cases sometimes cited as evidence for the claim that some nonhuman animals can experience,

10. See http://www.telegraph.co.uk/news/worldnews/northamerica/canada/6933888/ Canadian-familys-dog-saves-11-year-old.
11. S. Wechkin, J. H. Masserman, and W. Terris, "Shock to a Conspecific as an Aversive Stimulus," *Psychonomic Science* 1 (1964), 17–18.
12. R. Church, "Emotional Reactions of Rats to the Pain of Others," *Journal of Comparative and Physiological Psychology* 52 (1959), 32–34.
13. G. Rice and P. Gainer, "'Altruism' in the Albino Rat," *Journal of Comparative and Physiological Psychology* 55 (1962), 436–41.

and be motivated to act by, emotions of a certain sort. The emotions in question include compassion, sympathy, grief, and courage. There is a general category under which these emotions can be subsumed: we might call it *concern* or *solicitude*.[14] In the behaviors described in the previous section, certain animals arguably show themselves to be concerned with the welfare or fortunes of others. One can be concerned with the welfare of others in many ways, positive and negative. One can rejoice in the happiness of another, or one can resent it. One can experience sadness or shock at the misfortune of another, or one can revel in it. Compassion, sympathy, grief, courage, malice, spite, and cruelty are all ways in which one can be concerned with the fortunes of others, and so are all forms of concern in this sense. But that an attitude should have, as its focus, the welfare or fortunes of another is, it seems, the hallmark of a moral attitude. If this is correct, then concern is a category of moral attitude. Therefore, if animals experience, and are motivated to act by, concern in its various forms, then it seems they are motivated to act by moral considerations— moral reasons, broadly construed. The cases described in the opening section, therefore, are often cited as evidence in support of the claim that animals can act morally: that animals are, in this sense, moral *agents*.

The examples cited above, in fact, barely scratch the surface of the available evidence that points in this direction, and this evidence is growing rapidly. In fact, in one sense, the evidence has been there for a long time, but was overlooked because of certain idiosyncrasies in the development of psychology and cognate disciplines in the middle

14. I might have chosen the word "care," thus closely aligning the view I wish to defend in this book with the version of the sentimentalist tradition in moral philosophy that has become known as "care ethics." I have chosen to use the word "concern," in part precisely to avoid aligning myself closely with that position. The case I am going to defend, while consistent— indeed, sitting very comfortably—with at least some versions of care ethics, does not depend on care ethics. That is, I shall not be developing a care ethical case for the idea that animals can act for moral reasons.

part of the last century. The dominance of behaviorism during that time meant that much data that could be described in terms of emotions, or regarded as evidence for the presence of emotions in other animals, had to be described in purely behavioral terms—aversion, reinforcement, and so on.

Someone who is skeptical of this evidence can be so in two logically distinct ways. First, one can deny that the evidence establishes the presence of the presumed emotional states in animals. While the evidence may be suggestive of certain sorts of moral emotions in animals, evidence that *suggests* the presence of an inner state of a certain sort does not *establish* the presence of such a state. Bernstein, for example, defends what he calls "the law of parsimony"—a version of Lloyd-Morgan's canon: "It is, of course, possible that animals have a sense of justice and morality.... In science, however, one must present evidence that a certain relationship is true and no plausible alternative is possible."[15] One should not explain an animal's behavior by postulating a moral emotion when another—nonmoral—explanation is available.

The plausibility or otherwise of these deflationary, nonmoral explanations is, of course, an open empirical question. But it would be a mistake to suppose that they are without problems. Some, for example, are almost laughably simplistic. For example, in the days following Binti Jua's "heroics," several deflationist accounts of her behavior were quickly offered. Some proffered that Binti Jua had been hand-raised by zoo staff and had been taught her mothering skills by these staff using a stuffed toy as a pretend baby. Maybe Binti Jua was just doing what she had been trained to do—believing that the unconscious boy was simply another stuffed toy. This "explanation," resting as it does on a refusal to accept that a gorilla is capable

15. I. M. Bernstein, "The Law of Parsimony Prevails," in Leonard Katz ed., *Evolutionary Origins of Morality* (Exeter, UK: Imprint Academic, 2000), p. 33.

of distinguishing a boy from a stuffed toy—something that, most will accept, a dog can do with a 100 percent success rate—is astonishingly, and one might suspect willfully, naive.

Moreover, there is a certain type of logical mistake that many proponents of these deflationary explanations tend to make: a form of *false dilemma*. Consider, for example, a deflationary account of the refusal of the rats to push the lever that supplies food if this results in an electric shock being delivered to a fellow rat. Some deflationary accounts argue that the rats refrained from pushing the lever not out of sympathy for their fellows, but because they found their distress cries unpleasant. Supporting this deflationary account is another experiment in which white noise was found to have an even greater deterrent effect than the squeals of conspecifics.[16] I am not suggesting that this deflationary explanation is necessarily false. Rather, I am interested in the pattern of reasoning that underlies it. The guiding assumption is that if it is the unpleasant quality of the distress squeals that drives the rats' refusal to push the lever, this precludes an explanation in terms of a moral emotion such as sympathy.

To see this, consider the probably apocryphal story of Abraham Lincoln, who ordered his carriage driver to stop and rescue two young birds that he spied were in distress. On being complimented for his kindness, he responded that it was, in fact, purely a matter of self-interest: He would not have been able to sleep at night thinking about those birds. There is a well-known error embodied in Lincoln's response. Why would the plight of the birds ruin Lincoln's sleep? It would do so only if Lincoln were, in some respects at least, a compassionate person. If he were callous or indifferent, then the birds' suffering would have no impact on his slumbers. Thus, the mistake is to suppose that Lincoln's acting in his own interest precludes his action having a moral explanation: to the extent that Lincoln's

16. Marc Hauser, *Wild Minds: What Animals Really Think* (New York: Henry Holt, 2000), p. 220.

interests are infused with moral concerns, it does no such thing. Similarly, if I were to encounter someone with severe injuries, my horror or shock—both of which are unpleasant—might drive me to find a way to alleviate her suffering. But this does not mean that I am not motivated by concern. On the contrary, in this case, shock and horror is the experiential form my concern takes. The rats may find the distress cries of their conspecifics unpleasant, and this may be what reduces their tendency to push the food lever. However, it is a non sequitur to suppose that this precludes a moral explanation in terms of their concern: finding the cries unpleasant may be, in this instance, the experiential form their concern takes.

I am not, of course, trying to defend this case as an unequivocal example of moral action on the part of rats. On the contrary, in this specific case, I suspect the jury has not concluded its deliberations. Hauser's discovery that white noise has a similar effect on the behavior of rats is relevant evidence. Perhaps even more so is the fact that rats exhibit habituation effects: they become habituated to the distress of their conspecifics and, accordingly, the frequency of their lever pushing increases. Nevertheless, neither of these behaviors is conclusive. I can be put off my dinner for a variety of reasons; the distress of my sons might be one, the loud music emanating from the neighbor's house might be another. And human moral deliberation is well known to be subject to habituation effects.

I have claimed that there are two possible skeptical attitudes one can adopt with regard to the sort of empirical evidence described in the opening section. The first form, which we have just addressed, denies that the evidence supports anything like the attribution of moral emotions to animals. For example, behavior that one might, naively, take to show the existence of a moral emotion, such as compassion for one's conspecifics, can be explained more parsimoniously in terms of distaste for an unpleasant sensation. One is free to regard this distaste as an emotional state if one insists. But it is not a form of concern: it does not focus on the welfare or fortunes of one's conspecifics but is purely self-oriented. Therefore, while this distaste might be an emotion, it does not qualify as a moral emotion. This form of skepticism, therefore, consists in replacing a postulated moral emotion with a nonmoral alternative.

The second form of skepticism is subtly different. In this form, a moral emotion is replaced not by a clearly nonmoral alternative, but by something that prima facie seems to be a moral emotion but, in fact, is not. This skeptical strategy can allow that Grace, for example, is the bearer of kindly, perhaps even compassionate, feelings toward Eleanor. But it denies that this emotion, when instantiated in Grace, qualifies as a moral emotion—in the way it typically would when instantiated in a normal adult human being. While similar to, perhaps even identical with, compassion in terms of its phenomenological profile—in terms, that is, of what it is like to have it—this profile is not a decisive determinant of its moral status. The emotion lacks a certain something that is required for it to qualify as a genuinely moral emotion. The first form of skepticism replaces a putative moral emotion with a clearly nonmoral *alternative*. The second form replaces a putative moral emotion with an apparently moral, but actually nonmoral, *facsimile*. While the first form of skepticism has been associated with scientists, the second has largely been the preserve of philosophers.

Whether the attribution of a given emotion to an animal is or is not justified is always an open, and sometimes a deeply complex, empirical question, where theoretical assumptions and confusions can decisively prejudice the conclusions we reach. It is a question that can only be answered by making extensive observations of behavior and bringing the best theoretical resources we have to bear on constructing a hypothesis that does the most justice to all of these observations. The hypothesis, it goes without saying, may ultimately prove incorrect. But, always, at any given time, we just do the best we can with the available evidence. None of this important work forms the subject matter of this book. The purpose of this book is not to garner further empirical evidence of the sort described in the opening section. This evidence sits in the background, and at times will inform the discussion as it unfolds. But it does not drive this discussion. Some assume that this evidence (and much more like it) demonstrates, in a reasonably incontrovertible fashion, that other animals are moral beings—they can be motivated to act by moral considerations. I shall assume only that the evidence makes a prima facie case for the claim that animals can be motivated to act by emotions—all species of concern—that have an identifiable moral content. This assumption is the point of departure for the arguments to be developed in this book.

The concerns of this book are primarily conceptual rather than empirical. The central question is: can animals be moral? That is: can animals act for moral reasons—act on the basis of moral emotions? Possibility claims are notoriously cheap. In one sense of "can," the answer to this question is clearly affirmative. Yes, if animals had minds like ours, they could act for moral reasons just as we do. But that is not what the question means. Rather it means: given that animals are not like us in certain important respects—given they are what they are and we are what we are—can animals act for moral reasons? This question is not answered by accruing new empirical evidence, for what is at issue here is precisely how the substantial body of evidence we already have should be interpreted. And satisfactory interpretation of this evidence requires that we ask and answer questions that philosophers often ask, but whose relevance and impact, I shall try to show, extends far beyond the narrowly philosophical. What is a moral emotion? That is, what is it for an emotion to have moral content? What are the problems with attributing such emotions to animals?

Can these problems be surmounted? What does it mean to be motivated by a moral emotion? Does it mean that the emotion causes behavior? Does it mean that it provides a reason for behavior? Is the difference between these two claims important? If so, why? Most important, perhaps, what are the problems with the idea that animals can be motivated, in the sense identified as relevant, to act by moral considerations?

The history of philosophy has reached a near unanimous decision on the central question of this book. *No*, animals cannot be moral. They cannot act for moral reasons, or on the basis of moral considerations. This answer has been reached because philosophers asked themselves all these other questions too, and arrived at certain specific answers. The answers they gave to these questions have played a major, even decisive, role in shaping not only how we think about other animals but also in how we think about ourselves. These answers are, I shall argue, for the most part, false. But that they are false does not mean they are wildly erratic or unreasonable. As we shall see, there are ostensibly persuasive—persuasive in the sense that almost everyone has been persuaded—reasons for supposing that animals cannot act morally and that, therefore, if they act on the basis of emotions, these emotions cannot be moral ones. Nevertheless, I shall argue that these ostensibly persuasive reasons are spurious. In part they are grounded in logic and argument. But in part they are based on confusions. And in part they have their roots in a persistent tendency of human thought to fall under the spell of a certain kind of magic—or, at least, magical thinking. The positive goal of this book is to show that animals can be motivated by moral concerns, and these concerns take the form of emotions that have identifiable moral content. The corresponding negative goals of this book are to show that the respectable reasons against this claim fall far short of compelling, to unmask confusions, and to banish the fruits of magical thinking.

HUME, DARWIN, AND DE WAAL: ANIMALS AS PROTO-MORAL

I shall argue that animals can act morally in the sense that they can act on the basis of moral emotions—emotions that possess identifiable moral content. These moral emotions provide moral reasons for animals to act; and acting on the basis of a moral reason is *sufficient* for acting morally. I do not claim moral emotions are *necessary* conditions of moral action. My position, therefore, does not entail that emotions or sentiments are the *only* sorts of moral reasons there are. I certainly would not object to the claim that there are moral reasons available to humans that do not reduce to emotions or sentiments. I suspect this means—but it does depend on how one interprets Hume—that I have only one foot planted in the Humean "sentimentalist" moral tradition. Nevertheless, I think it is a comfortable place to plant one's foot.

Hume's attitude toward animals is ambivalent. On the one hand, his list of what he called the *natural virtues* includes courage, perseverance, fidelity, industry, and friendliness, and Hume thought that animals could, at least arguably, possess these virtues. He also argued, significantly, that the status of these traits as virtues did not require that they be acquired or exercised voluntarily. On the other hand, Hume also claimed that morality is a distinctively human phenomenon: "Animals have little or no sense of virtue or vice; they quickly lose sight of the relations of blood; and are incapable of that of right and property."[17] In a similar vein, animals' "want of a sufficient degree of reason may hinder them from perceiving the duties and obligations of morality."[18] This apparent tension is resolved once we recognize that, according to Hume, morality involves more than the

---

17. David Hume, *A Treatise of Human Nature* (Oxford: Oxford University Press, 1978), p. 326.
18. Hume, *A Treatise of Human Nature*, p. 468.

natural virtues. The sentiments implicated in these virtues may provide the rudiments of morality, but that is all they can do. Our natural sentiments, and the virtues they underwrite, will tend to make us favor those close to us. Morality, in the full, human, sense requires that we develop artificial virtues, predominantly the virtue of justice, that allow us to make impartial, and therefore fair, judgments. While animals arguably possess the natural virtues, they do not possess the artificial virtues. Therefore, they are not moral beings in the sense that humans are.

Thus, in Hume we find two claims. First, animals possess the rudiments of morality—in the form of natural sentiments and the virtues that these underwrite. Second, animals fall short of being moral agents in the way that humans are. In them, we find the building blocks of moral agency, but not a fully developed human form of this capacity. This deficit is tied to their lack of reason. The same themes are reiterated in the work of Darwin. At the beginning of chapter 4 of *The Descent of Man*, Darwin writes:

> Any animal whatever, endowed with well-marked social instincts, the parental and filial affections being here included, would inevitably acquire a moral sense or conscience, as soon as its mental powers had become as well, or nearly as well developed, as in man.[19]

To the extent that the mental powers of animals are not "nearly as well developed as in man" animals do not possess a moral "sense or conscience." Darwin's account of the development of this moral sense has two strands. First, there is the idea of the social instincts. Second, there is the explanation of the moral conscience in terms of these instincts.

19. Charles Darwin, *The Descent of Man* (London: John Murray, 1871), pp. 149–50.

Darwin adopted a broadly sentimentalist account of morality, of the sort endorsed by Hume. The foundation of morality is provided by the social sentiments (Darwin refers to them as the "social instincts"). Empathy, sympathy, and compassion are stock examples of the social sentiments. Darwin, echoing Hume, thought of these sentiments as part of our natural history. It is natural for us to have these sentiments in the usual sorts of eliciting circumstances; and failure to have them in such circumstances is a sign that something has gone seriously wrong at the basic biological level. This assumption of a broadly sentimentalist account of morality has become common among those who, like Darwin, try to understand morality from an evolutionary perspective. It is sometimes thought that his reliance on the social sentiments commits Darwin to *group selectionism*—the claim that the unit of natural selection is the group. The thought that underpins this is the idea that the function of these sentiments is to promote the fitness of the social group—through, for example, the promotion of group solidarity—rather than the individual, for whom such sentiments can prove costly. However, there is, in fact, no commitment to group selectionism entailed by Darwin's account.[20] The social animals are those that have evolved to live in groups. Such animals are more likely to survive and propagate their genes in the context of the group than would be the case if they lived lives of isolation. That is, the group promotes the inclusive fitness of its individual members. Therefore, for those members it is desirable that the group prosper. In the case of some of these animals—the social mammals, birds—evolution hit upon a certain strategy for making this happen: feelings of affection, sympathy, and concern for members of the group. In other words the social

20. The issue of whether Darwin was, in fact, a group selectionist is, of course, another matter. I take no stand on this issue here. I merely point out that Darwin's account of the development of the moral conscience does not commit him to group selectionism.

sentiments hold the group together, and the group promotes the inclusive fitness of its individual members.[21]

The second strand of Darwin's position consists in the explanation of the moral conscience in terms of the social instincts. This explanation involves the idea of a clash of instincts—one animal can be pulled in different directions by competing instincts. This is especially true when a strong but relatively transient instinct clashes with a weaker but more permanent one. Darwin employs the example of a bird motivated to act in different ways by migratory and maternal instincts. The stronger, transient instinct (to migrate) wins, but in the failure to satisfy the weaker instinct we find the roots of regret, and so of a moral conscience. Or consider another, more gruesome, example.[22] One of the Gombe chimpanzees is observed simultaneously hugging *and* eating a baby baboon. As the baboon struggles and cries, the chimpanzee responds with distressed hugging, but then continues eating. The similarity between a baby baboon and baby chimpanzee is, it is reasonable to suppose, sufficient to cause motivational conflict in the chimp between the maternal and predatory instincts. In this case, the predatory instinct wins. Darwin's account of the origins of the moral conscience is brilliant, fascinating, and oddly neglected. Unfortunately, it has no direct bearing on the arguments to be developed in this book. Therefore, with some regret, I now set it aside. The other strand of Darwin's position, the social sentiments, is, however, central to the case I shall develop.

Darwin is quite clear that the possession of social sentiments by a subject is not sufficient to make that subject a genuinely moral agent.

21. Frans de Waal is also skeptical of the claim that Darwin's account is group selectionist. See *Primates and Philosophers: How Morality Evolved*, ed. Stephen Macedo and Josiah Ober (Princeton, NJ: Princeton University Press, 2006), p. 16.

22. Taken from Stephen Clark, *The Nature of the Beast: Are Animals Moral?* (Oxford: Oxford University Press, 1984), p. 34.

That is, he is quite clear that he does not wish to claim that animals can be, as he puts it, "moral beings":

> A moral being is one who is capable of comparing his past and future actions or motives, and of approving or disapproving of them. We have no reason to suppose that any of the lower animals have this capacity; therefore, when a Newfoundland dog drags a child out of the water, or a monkey faces danger to rescue its comrade, or takes charge of an orphan monkey, we do not call its conduct moral.[23]

The clash-of-instincts model yields only the rudiments of the moral sense. To explain moral conscience in its full-blown sense, we need to augment the cognitive powers of the individual: to possess a moral sense or conscience in its proper sense, the individual needs to possess the ability to explicitly think about and compare past and future actions or motives—and presumably, also, needs to exercise this ability on at least some occasions.[24] This claim is reiterated at the end of his book when Darwin sums up what he takes himself to have demonstrated in chapter 4:

> A moral being is one who is capable of reflecting on his past actions and their motives—of approving of some and disapproving of others; and the fact that man is the one being who certainly deserves this designation, is the greatest of all distinctions between him and the lower animals.[25]

There is, perhaps, a certain room for maneuver introduced by the phrase "the one being who *certainly* deserves this designation."

---

23. Darwin, *The Descent of Man*, pp. 170–71.
24. Darwin, *The Descent of Man*, p. 171.
25. Darwin, *The Descent of Man*, p. 933.

However, Darwin's view seems to be that it is very likely that only humans are moral beings. The roots of moral conscience and conduct may be found in other animals, but it is only in the human animal that we find real, full-blooded, moral action—action that is performed for moral reasons.

Frans de Waal also defends essentially the same position. The target of de Waal's arguments is what he calls the "veneer theory." This understands morality as veneer—a thin surface or crust that lies on top of a nature that is fundamentally selfish, competitive, and amoral. Thomas Huxley, identified by de Waal as the progenitor of this view, compared humanity to a gardener who has a difficult time keeping his garden free of weeds. Huxley saw human ethics as a victory over essentially amoral evolutionary processes.[26] Against this, de Waal argues that "the building blocks of morality are evolutionarily ancient."[27] The building blocks of our morality are part of our evolutionary legacy: they can be found in many of the social mammals, especially the great apes. However, de Waal stops short of the claim that morality itself can be found in nonhumans.

> In the course of human evolution, out-group hostility enhanced in-group solidarity to the point that morality emerged. Instead of merely ameliorating relations around us, as apes do, we have explicit teachings about the value of the community and the precedence it takes, or ought to take, over individual interests. Humans go much further in all of this than the apes, which is why we have moral systems and they do not.[28]

So de Waal, in the tradition of Hume and Darwin, argues that while the building blocks of morality can be found in other animals, it is

26. De Waal, *Primates and Philosophers*, p. 7.
27. De Waal, *Primates and Philosophers*, p. 7.
28. De Waal, *Primates and Philosophers*, p. 54.

only in humans that we find the genuine article. Like Hume and Darwin also, de Waal ties this difference to the increased cognitive powers of the sort that, in the case of humans, result in "explicit teachings about the value of the community and the precedence it takes, or ought to take, over individual interests"—a clear echo of Hume's emphasis on the artificial virtue of justice.

In Hume, Darwin, and de Waal, therefore, we find two common themes: (1) animals possess the rudiments of morality, but (2) they fall short of being moral agents in the way that humans are. However, (2) is clearly a red herring. I cannot imagine anyone who would wish to argue that animals are moral agents "in the same way that humans are." The question is not whether animals are moral agents in the same way as humans—normal, adult humans—but, rather, whether animals are, or can be, moral agents.[29] That is, the question is whether animals can act morally—act for moral reasons. An affirmative answer would require that we identify what it is, precisely, that animals do when we are tempted to describe them as acting morally, and then working out whether this is, all things considered, sufficient for moral action. If it is, they can act morally. If it is not, they cannot. The comparison with what humans do when we are tempted to say they act morally is simply irrelevant.

Putting this irrelevance aside, we can reinterpret the Hume/ Darwin/de Waal position as follows: (1) animals possess the rudiments of morality, but (2) they are not moral agents. Being a moral agent requires more than possession of the rudiments of morality. And all three are reasonably clear on what this something more might be: increased cognitive sophistication of the sort that allows one to acquire artificial virtues such as justice (Hume), compare past and

---

29. In chapter 3, I shall amend this formulation of the question. The correct question is whether animals can be moral *subjects*, not whether they can be moral *agents*. Pending elucidation and defense of the moral subject/agent distinction, I shall here employ the more familiar concept of a moral agent.

future events and motives and approve or disapprove of them (Darwin), or explicitly understand the value of community and the precedence it should take over individual interests (de Waal).

The target of this book now begins to present itself. I shall argue that none of these things are required in order for an individual to act for moral reasons. For an individual to act morally, I shall argue, it is not necessary that she have the ability to reflect on her motives or actions; nor does it require that she be able to explicitly formulate or understand the principles on which she acts, nor that she be able to adopt an impartial perspective of the sort required for a sense of justice. While the actual motivation of any given individual, human or otherwise, is always an empirical matter, I shall argue—*pace* Hume, Darwin, and de Waal—that there are no logical or conceptual difficulties to thinking that some animals can act morally.

BEKOFF AND PIERCE: THE MORAL LIVES OF ANIMALS

In their book *Wild Justice*, Marc Bekoff and Jessica Pierce defend a claim that is ostensibly stronger than that of Hume, Darwin, and de Waal. Their claim is that animals can exhibit moral—and not merely proto-moral—behavior. However, this difference is, I suspect, not as great as it seems. Bekoff and Pierce think of moral agency as species-relative: moral agency in a human is very different from moral agency in other species.[30] However, this species-relative conception of moral agency means that it is possible for Bekoff and Pierce to agree with Hume, Darwin, and de Waal on all the important facts, and merely choose to describe or categorize those facts in a different way. Hume, Darwin, and de Waal take human moral agency as the benchmark

30. Bekoff and Pierce, *Wild Justice*, p. 144.

and argue that animals fall short of this benchmark, and therefore fail to qualify as moral agents. Bekoff and Pierce, in effect, refuse to set a benchmark and then argue that animals can act morally even though they do not do so in the way humans do, because moral agency is relative. It is, perhaps, a little strong to say that Bekoff and Pierce agree on all the relevant facts pertaining to animal behavior with Hume, Darwin, or de Waal. But they certainly agree with them on the vast majority of relevant facts. And so one cannot help suspect that the divergence between Bekoff and Pierce's position and that of Hume, Darwin, and de Waal is largely terminological.

Bekoff and Pierce understand moral behavior as "a suite of inter-related behaviors that cultivate and regulate the complex interactions within social groups. These behaviors relate to well-being and harm. And norms of right and wrong attach to many of them."[31] Within this suite of behaviors, they claim, three behavioral clusters are identifiable.

> The *cooperation* cluster: altruism, reciprocity, trust, punishment, and revenge.
> The *empathy* cluster: empathy, compassion, caring, helping, grieving, and consoling.
> The *justice* cluster: sense of fair play, sharing, desire for equity, expectations concerning desert and entitlement, indignation, retribution, and spite.[32]

Although Bekoff and Pierce do not mention this fact, this tripartite distinction corresponds closely to three major traditions in moral philosophy. The necessity, when inhabiting a world red in tooth and claw, of cooperation and associated traits such as reciprocity, trust,

---

31. Bekoff and Pierce, *Wild Justice*, p. 7. I think this is inadequate as a definition of morality. It is, clearly, far too broad, but there are other deficits also. Some of these deficiencies will prove important as the discussion of this section develops.
32. Bekoff and Pierce, *Wild Justice*, p. 8.

punishment, and revenge is a major theme of Hobbesian contractualism. The importance of empathy, and of states such as sympathy, compassion, caring, and consoling made possible by empathy, is a defining characteristic of the Humean sentimentalist tradition. The primacy of justice and associated concepts such as fairness is a theme consistently defended in moral traditions inspired by Kant, including Kantian forms of contractualism of the sort propounded by John Rawls. So each of Bekoff and Pierce's three clusters has, in effect, its own significant philosophical representative: Hobbes, Hume, and Kant, respectively.[33]

Within each category, Bekoff and Pierce draw no clear distinction between behavior and its motivation. In the empathy cluster, for example, motivational states such as empathy and compassion are run together with behaviors like helping, grieving, and consoling. The cooperation cluster comprises largely behaviors. And the justice cluster seems to be made up largely of motivational states (a sense of fair play, expectations, etc.). This lack of clarity is exacerbated in sentences such as the following: "Empathy, as Preston and de Waal suggest, isn't a single behavior, but a whole class of behavior patterns that exist across species."[34] But empathy is not, in fact, a behavior at all—it is an emotional state or an ability that can motivate behavior. It is true that for each motivational state there might be a behavioral expression. So we might talk of empathetic behavior, for example. Nevertheless, it is important to draw the distinction between motivation and behavior in a clearer way than do Bekoff and Pierce. In this view I am in agreement with de Waal: "In discussing what constitutes morality, the actual behavior is less important than the underlying capacities. For example, instead of arguing that food-sharing is a

---

33. Colin McGinn (in conversation) first alerted me to the idea that each of these clusters might correspond to a moral tradition. The identification with Hobbes, Hume, and Kant, respectively, is mine.

34. Bekoff and Pierce, *Wild Justice*, p. 89.

building block of morality, it is rather the capacities thought to underlie food-sharing (e.g. high levels of tolerance, sensitivity to other's needs, reciprocal exchange) that seem relevant."[35] The question of whether an action performed by an animal qualifies as a moral action cannot be answered independently of an understanding of the motives the animal has for performing this action. This, I shall argue, vitiates Bekoff and Pierce's arguments with respect to both the cooperation and the justice clusters. They have, in fact, provided little reason for thinking that the behaviors they identify in these clusters count as moral.

Problems with the Cooperation Condition

Bekoff and Pierce, in line with standard practice, identify four distinct forms of cooperation: kin altruism, mutualism, reciprocal altruism, and generalized reciprocity. "Kin altruism" refers to a form of behavior that is costly for the actor (i.e., it decreases reproductive fitness) but beneficial for the recipient (i.e., it increases reproductive fitness), where the motivation of this behavior is provided by the fact that actor and recipient are genetically related. An example of kin altruism is provided by a study of alarm call behavior in Balding's ground squirrel by Paul Sherman. Alarm calls in the presence of a potential predator are obviously beneficial to the members of one's dray, but they are also potentially costly to the caller since they increase the chance of it being eaten. Sherman shows that males, who do not nest near genetic relatives, give alarm calls less often than females, who do nest near genetically related squirrels.[36]

---

35. De Waal, *Primates and Philosophers*, p. 16. Bekoff and Pierce (*Wild Justice*, pp. 59–60) cite this passage from de Waal, but I believe they have not paid sufficient attention to it.

36. Paul Sherman, "Nepotism and the Evolution of Alarm Calls," *Science* 197 (1977), 1246–53.

"Mutualism" refers to "a form of cooperation in which two or more individuals work together on a task that can't be accomplished singly."[37] For example, African wild dogs, lions, and wolves hunt in coordinated groups, and when they do so they do better than lone individuals in bringing down large prey. Essential to mutualism is the idea that the payback is immediate, or nearly so. All members of the pack get to eat when the kill is made, even if some eat before others.

"Reciprocal altruism" is distinguished from mutualism by the fact that the payback need not be immediate. If you scratch my back, then I'll scratch yours—but I might not do it until later. Perhaps the most famous example of reciprocal altruism is provided by anthropologists Dorothy Cheney and Robert Seyfarth, who showed that female savanna baboons spend the most time grooming females from whom they have received the most grooming. Cheney and Seyfarth also witnessed similar behavior in vervet monkeys.[38]

"Generalized reciprocity" is the providing of help to an unfamiliar and unrelated individual based on previous experience of having been helped by an unfamiliar individual. The existence of generalized reciprocity in nonhumans is extremely controversial. One possible example, cited by Bekoff and Pierce, is provided by zoologists Claudia Rutte and Michael Taborsky, who trained rats in a cooperative task of pulling a stick to obtain food for a partner. Rats who had previously been helped by an unknown partner were more likely to help others.[39] Another possible case, again cited by Bekoff and Pierce, consists in observations, conducted by Felix Warneken and Brian Hare at the Max Planck Institute, of chimpanzees spontaneously helping humans

37. Bekoff and Pierce, *Wild Justice*, p. 69.
38. D. Cheney and R. Seyfarth, *How Monkeys See the World* (Chicago: University of Chicago Press, 1990).
39. C. Rutte and M. Taborsky, "Generalized Reciprocity in Rats," *PLaS Biology* 5.7 (2007), e196.

retrieve a stick inside their enclosure (regardless of whether there was a reward).[40]

There is nothing surprising in the claim that animals exhibit kin altruistic and mutualistic behavior: this behavior is observationally well established and its mechanisms, in general terms at least, well understood. However, few have supposed that these sorts of behaviors qualify as moral. Kin altruism has a straightforward genetic explanation: since acting in this way would enhance propagation of genes that one shares, the gene for such behavior would spread through a community. The problem is not that a genetic explanation necessarily precludes a moral one: on the contrary, it is plausible to suppose that many moral behaviors have a genetic basis. This is particularly so in cases of behaviors caused by the moral emotions—the principal subject of this book. These moral emotions, as Darwin emphasized, are part of our natural history, and therefore clearly have a genetic basis. The problem, rather, is that, in the case of kin altruistic and mutualistic behavior, there is no reason to suppose that anything like moral emotions, or moral motivations more generally, plays any role in motivating the behavior. When wolves, for example, hunt together to bring down an elk, we can explain this in purely genetic terms without citing a moral motivation: a wolf with the cooperation gene is more likely to survive and reproduce than one without this gene. Therefore, the cooperation gene would spread. No reason has been given, in this case, to suppose that any intervening role is played by a moral emotion, sense of justice, or anything of that ilk. And without this motivation there is no reason to suppose that hunting together is an expression of wolf morality rather than simply something wolves do because it is beneficial to them. I shall not labor this point because Bekoff and

40. F. Warneken, B. Hare, A. Melis, D. Hanus, and M. Tomasello, "Spontaneous Altruism by Chimpanzees and Young Children," *PLaS Biology* 5.7 (2007), e184. Cited in Bekoff and Pierce, *Wild Justice*, p. 75.

Pierce, in effect, concede it: "Our proposal is that the moral animals are those capable of complex cooperative behaviors, and not just the simpler forms of kin-selected altruism and mutualism."[41] It is easy to see why Bekoff and Pierce would be tempted by this position. Reciprocal altruism and generalized reciprocity are more complex abilities that seem to require more complex explanations. Reciprocity in grooming behavior, for example, seems to require the ability to keep track of who has groomed whom—and we have now left straightforward genetic explanations of behavior behind. More complex motives need to be introduced, and these stand at least a chance of being motives that possess moral content. This being so, it means that Bekoff and Pierce, presumably, need to supply a stirring defense of the existence of reciprocal altruism and generalized reciprocity in animals.

However, their defense is rather disappointing, even supine. Responding to the sort of skepticism of reciprocal altruism and generalized reciprocity evinced by people such as Stevens and Hauser,[42] they write: "The jury is still out on the question of whether animals have the cognitive skills necessary for complex forms of reciprocity, and just what these cognitive capacities might be. After all, the scientific understanding of social cognition is still very young."[43] This amounts to nothing more than the claim that animals might have the necessary cognitive capacities to engage in reciprocal altruism, not that they do have those capacities—hardly the unequivocal defense required. In a similar, unacceptably tentative, vein, they add: "But reciprocal altruism is only one type of cooperative behavior, and other forms of cooperation may involve equally complex, though different, mental and emotional capacities. So even if

---

41. Bekoff and Pierce, *Wild Justice*, p. 83.
42. J. Stevens and M. Hauser, "Why Be Nice? Psychological Constraints on the Evolution of Cooperation," *Trends in Cognitive Sciences* 8 (2004), 60–65.
43. Bekoff and Pierce, *Wild Justice*, p. 80.

we conclude that only chimpanzees are capable of reciprocal altruism, this isn't the end of the story as far as wild justice is concerned."[44] However, in the absence of a specification of what those behaviors are and the grounds for thinking of them as moral, nothing has yet been done to advance the case for wild justice. If this is the state of play for reciprocal altruism, then things are far more tentative still for generalized reciprocity, whose existence is more controversial and would require far more complex cognitive capacities. To the extent that the existence of generalized reciprocity in nonhumans is questionable, and to the extent that the existence of even reciprocal altruism in nonhumans is limited, the case for "wild justice" built on this foundation will be questionable and limited. The claim that animals can act morally will, I think, have to be defended by other means.

Problems with the Justice Condition

Bekoff and Pierce's second cluster of purportedly moral behaviors comprises the justice cluster. They define justice as

> a set of expectations about what one deserves and how one ought to be treated. Justice has been served when these expectations have been appropriately met. Our justice cluster comprises several behaviors related to fairness, including a desire for equity and a desire... and a capacity to share reciprocally. The cluster also includes various behavioral reactions to injustice, including retribution, indignation, and forgiveness, as well as reactions to justice such as pleasure, gratitude, and trust.[45]

---

44. Bekoff and Pierce, *Wild Justice*, p. 83.
45. Bekoff and Pierce, *Wild Justice*, p. 113.

If it were applied to humans, the definition would, of course, be too broad. In particular, a "set of expectations about what one deserves and how one ought to be treated" does not add up to justice—at least as this is ordinarily understood—for the simple reason that one can have unjust expectations about what one deserves or how one ought to be treated. Bekoff and Pierce's discussion of the justice cluster is, I shall argue, vitiated by a failure to appreciate this point. Their conception of justice is so broad that, in effect, it renders their claim that animals exhibit justice vacuous.

The inadequacy of the Bekoff and Pierce conception of justice is evident in the way they respond to recent empirical work that seems to undermine the claim that animals have a sense of justice—that such a sense is unique to humans.[46] Jensen, Call, and Tomasello arranged for chimpanzees to play what is known as an "ultimatum game." In an ultimatum game, a divisible quantity—with humans it is typically a sum of money, with Jensen's chimpanzees it was raisins—is given to one individual. The individual is then asked to divide the commodity between herself and the other player (or players). The other player knows how much of the commodity is being offered, and has the choice of accepting or refusing the offer. If he refuses, neither of the players will receive anything. In humans, offers of 20 percent or less of the commodity are typically rejected. But chimpanzees accepted any offer from their partners, and apparently did not get upset by low offers. Jensen concludes that only humans have a sense of equity. Ironically, the chimpanzees were behaving more rationally—they were rational maximizers—but did not, Jensen and Tomasello conclude, exhibit a sense of justice.

Bekoff and Pierce's response is based on a point made by Robert Solomon and involves distinguishing "real" ideas of justice from what,

---

46. K. Jensen, J. Call, and M. Tomasello, "'Chimpanzees Are Rational Maximizers in an Ultimatum Game," *Science* 318 (2007), 107–9. The case is cited in Bekoff and Pierce, *Wild Justice*, p. 110.

following Solomon, they refer to as "bone-in-the-sky" conceptions of justice. Solomon writes:

> Some wolves are fair, a few are not. Some arrangements are fair (from the wolf's own perspective); some are not. Wolves have a keen sense of how things ought to be among them...justice is just this sense of what ought to be, not in some bone-in-the-sky theoretical sense but in the tangible everyday situations in which the members of the pack find themselves. Wolves pay close attention to one another's needs and to the needs of the group in general. They follow a fairly strict meritocracy, balanced by considerations of need and respect for each other's "possessions," usually a piece of meat.[47]

Bekoff and Pierce endorse Solomon's line. Thus, to use one of their examples, familiar from earlier work of Bekoff,[48] when animals play, they exhibit a sense of justice: "Animals exhibit fairness during play, and they react negatively to unfair play. In this context, fairness has to do with an individual's specific social expectations, and not some universally defined standard of right and wrong."[49]

The problem, however, is that if we define justice this broadly, the claim that animals possess a sense of justice, and that they exhibit this sense in their behavior, becomes rather unsurprising. Indeed, it seems to become trivial. Animals turn out to have a sense of justice only because the concept of justice has been defined in such a way that it is the sort of things animals can possess. In other words, that animals

---

47. Robert Solomon, *A Passion for Justice* (Lanham, MD: Rowman and Littlefield, 1995), p. 141.
48. See, for example, Marc Bekoff, *Animal Passions and Beastly Virtues: Reflections on Redecorating Nature* (Philadelphia: Temple University Press, 2006), section 3, "Social Play, Social Development, and Social Communication: Cooperation, Fairness, and Wild Justice," pp. 123–76.
49. Bekoff and Pierce, *Wild Justice*, p. 120.

have a sense of justice becomes a matter of stipulation rather than discovery. If we identify justice with any behavioral norm that happens to be in place in a social group, then who would wish to deny that animals have a sense of justice? That is, who would wish to deny that there are norms of behavior that regulate the interactions between members of a social group, and that an individual's violation of those norms can often lead to conflict? Without such norms and their enforcement, it is difficult to see how any social group could remain in existence. If there is a question about whether animals can act morally, this surely cannot be it. If it were, it would have been answered in the affirmative many years ago.

ANIMALS AS MORAL SUBJECTS

I have argued that neither the cooperation cluster nor the justice cluster provides a promising route for defending the claim that animals can act morally. However, the empathy cluster is, I shall try to show during the course of this book, far more promising. The case I shall develop turns on the moral emotions—emotions that possess identifiable moral content. These include emotional states such as sympathy and compassion, kindness, tolerance, and patience, and also their negative counterparts such as anger, indignation, malice, and spite. But it also includes states that Bekoff and Pierce are inclined to locate in other clusters—for example, a sense of what is fair and what is not. While the "justice" implicated in this sense may not add up to justice itself, what is important for my purposes is the motivational role this sense plays rather than its content. Acting on the basis of emotions such as these is, I shall argue, sufficient for acting morally. Therefore, to the extent that animals act on the basis of such emotions they act morally. More precisely, I shall defend the following claims:

(1)Animals can be moral *subjects.*

This claim—the central thesis of the book—requires a lot of unpacking. Much of this is the function of claims (2)–(5) below. Some preliminary unpacking will, however, be useful, even on pain of later reiteration. First of all, for reasons that will not become clear until chapter 3, I shall deny, with certain qualifications to be identified in chapter 9, that animals are moral *agents.* This, however, does not mean that they are unable to act morally. The category of a moral *subject* is introduced and defended as a category of beings that can act for moral reasons, but do not necessarily qualify as moral agents as this category is usually understood. All moral agents are moral subjects, but not all moral subjects need be moral agents. The primary thesis defended in this book is that animals can be moral subjects because, and to the extent, they act for moral reasons.

Second, the claim I shall defend is that animals "can" be moral subjects—and not, necessarily, that they are. There are no logical or conceptual obstacles to some animals being moral subjects. Whether a given animal is, in fact, a moral subject is an empirical matter. Animals are moral subjects to the extent they act on the basis of a certain type of motivation, and whether they act on the basis of such motivation is an empirical matter that this book does not address. Those who are swayed by the sorts of empirical cases described in the opening section, culled from a far larger selection of cases that can be found in the work of empirical scientists such as de Waal and Bekoff, will be amenable to the claim that animals are the subjects of these sorts of motivations. I have nothing empirical to add to the observations of others better qualified to observe. My business is that of the philosopher: conceptual analysis and clarification.

Third, to the extent animals can act for moral reasons, they can do so in the same sense—or, more precisely, *one* of the same senses—that humans can act for moral reasons. I shall argue, *pace* Hume,

Darwin, and de Waal, that animals can act morally. There is no reason to think of their behavior as proto-moral—that is, quasi-moral in some rudimentary sense but falling short of the genuine article. However, this is not because, *pace* Bekoff and Pierce, what it is to act morally varies from one species to another. Rather, I shall argue that there is a way of acting morally. Humans can act in this way. And animals can act morally in precisely this way. Humans have other ways of acting morally—they are sensitive to moral reasons that animals cannot entertain. Nevertheless, there is one category of moral reason that both animals and humans can possess, and acting on the basis of such reasons is sufficient for acting morally.

(2) To be a moral subject is to be *motivated* to act by moral *considerations.*

The remaining theses concern what it is, in this context, to be a moral consideration, and what it is to be motivated by such considerations. With regard to the first issue, I shall defend the following two claims:

(3) In the case of animals, these considerations take the form of *morally laden emotions* (or *moral emotions*).

First, the moral emotions in question are forms of *concern*, and include what we commonly take to be positive ones, such as sympathy, compassion, tolerance, and patience, and also negative or otherwise deficient counterparts like indifference, anger, malice, and spite. These are all ways in which one might be concerned with other individuals (or fail to exhibit the appropriate concern—indifference is, in this sense, a deficient mode of concern). Second, I shall argue:

(4) An emotion is morally laden if and only if it involves (in a sense to be clarified) a moral *evaluation* or *judgment.*

With regard to the issue of motivation, I shall defend the following:

(5)   Morally laden emotions motivate animals to act by providing *reasons* for those actions.

To say that animals are motivated by moral reasons is to say that their actions are not *merely* caused by whatever states cause them. Reasons may be causes—but they are also more than *mere* causes. A cause does what it does—it causes whatever it, in fact, causes. A reason motivates in virtue of its content. Because of this, the concept of a reason introduces an element of normativity that has no echo at the level of the mere cause. Roughly, if one has reason to A, and there are no countervailing reasons, then one *should* A—and this should is not something that can be captured in terms of the concept of statistical regularity. If one does not A, then, ceteris paribus, something has gone awry, and not merely (or, indeed, even) in the sense that it is statistically unlikely. Animals, I shall argue, are motivated to act by moral reasons, not merely causes. In short, the overall thesis to be defended is this: *Animals can be moral subjects in the sense that they can act on the basis of moral reasons, where these reasons take the form of emotions with identifiable moral content.*

The following two chapters will be concerned, primarily, with clarification of these theses. Chapter 2 isolates the relevant sense of the term "emotion" as it figures in theses (3)–(5). Emotions, in this sense, are identified with intentional states that possess both descriptive and prescriptive content. The chapter defends the practice of attributing emotions—and, more generally, states that possess intentional content—to animals, and also defends this practice against well-known objections. It also defines what it is for an emotion to be morally laden.

Chapter 3 draws and defends what will prove to be the crucial distinction between a moral *subject* and a moral *agent*. To be a moral subject is not the same thing as being a moral agent. A moral agent is morally responsible for, and so can be praised or blamed for, its actions. A moral subject is one that is motivated by moral reasons. The concepts of agent and subject are, therefore, as distinct as the concepts of motivation and evaluation. Nevertheless, there are powerful reasons for supposing that this distinction breaks down in the specifically moral case. That is, while the distinction between agent and subject is generally legitimate, it cannot be applied in the specifically moral case: there is no distinction between a moral agent and a moral subject. A significant part of this book will, in effect, be devoted to showing that the distinction can indeed drawn in the moral case: that the distinction between a moral subject and a moral agent is a legitimate one.

Chapter 4 examines the historical case against the claim that animals can be moral subjects—can act for moral reasons. This case has its origins in Aristotle, was developed crucially by Kant, and today forms the orthodox view of the nature of moral action. According to this view, a necessary condition of an action being moral is that the subject have, and at least sometimes exercise, the ability to critically scrutinize its motivations and actions.

The remaining chapters, 5 to 10, will try to undermine this orthodox view of moral action, and examine some of the implications of its rejection. The claim I shall defend is, as I indicated earlier, best expressed in modal terms: it is *possible* for animals to be motivated by moral reasons. Thus, it is *possible* for animals to be moral subjects. If animals are in fact motivated by other-regarding emotions (an empirical claim with, at the very least, growing evidential warrant), then there are no logical or conceptual obstacles to thinking of these emotions as morally laden ones—just as they are regarded, typically, when they occur in humans. This may seem a cautious claim—possibility claims are sometimes notoriously easy to defend. Thus, one might suspect that in defending only the modal claim I am unacceptably stacking the dialectical deck in my favor. But this is, in fact, not the case. The logical and historical case against the claim that animals can be moral subjects is one that almost everyone has found compelling. It is almost universally assumed, at least by philosophers, not only that animals are not moral subjects but, in addition, that they cannot be such subjects. And underlying this is not a simple prejudice but a powerful argument that turns, ultimately, on the connection between moral motivation and moral responsibility. Unpacking this argument is the task of the book. The details must wait until later. But when forthcoming they will establish that even in defending the possibility claim I very much have my work cut out for me.

Finally, to reiterate another point made earlier—reiterate perhaps unnecessarily, but experience suggests otherwise—the thesis to be defended in this book should be understood as involving an existential, rather than universal, quantification: there exist some moral reasons for action such that (some) animals can possess them. It goes without saying that, in the domain of moral decision and action, humans have capabilities that animals lack. Humans can reflect on their motivations. A human can ask herself if the motivation she has for what she does is a good one or bad one, whether she should embrace or resist it. Humans can formulate abstract principles that allow them to judge the rightness or wrongness of their motivations and actions. They can communicate these principles to each other. They can engage in practices of explaining and justifying their actions in terms of these reasons. No animal can do these things. And because of this, there are many moral reasons for action that humans can entertain and animals cannot. But that, I shall argue, does not preclude animals from being moral subjects. For none of these abilities are necessary conditions of acting for moral reasons. Animals are certainly not the subjects of the gamut of moral reasons that humans can entertain and upon which they can act. But they can, nonetheless, act on the basis of *some* moral reasons—*basic* moral reasons, as we might think of them. And when they do this, they are doing what we do when we act on the basis of these reasons: they are acting on the basis of genuinely moral reasons. As such, they are moral subjects. This is the thesis to be defended in the following pages. First, however, there are some preliminary issues to be addressed. What, precisely, is a moral or morally laden emotion? And under what conditions can we attribute such emotions to animals?

2

Attributing Emotions to Animals

THE PROBLEM

The previous chapter surveyed some of the empirical evidence suggesting that at least some animals should be regarded as possessing morally laden emotions—various forms of concern. It is noticeable that all the examples cited were of social mammals—elephants, gorillas, chimpanzees, monkeys, dogs, and rats. It is among the social mammals that the case for possession of moral emotions is strongest. However, when we consider emotions more generally, the class of bearers may well be augmented. Jaak Panskepp, for example, has argued on neurobiological grounds that basic emotions such as happiness, sadness, fear, anger, surprise, and disgust extend beyond the human realm, encompassing all mammals, in all likelihood birds, and possibly reptiles.[1] And in this at least, with the possible exception of reptiles, Panskepp's view coincides quite closely with common sense.

Nevertheless, attributions of emotions to animals are deeply problematic. At least they are if emotions are understood as states of a certain sort. And, perhaps unfortunately, that is precisely how I need to understand emotions if the dialectical purposes of this book are to be pursued. Thus, lined up against neurobiology, cognitive ethology, and common sense are certain broadly philosophical considerations. Many emotions are plau-

---

1. Jaak Panskepp, *Affective Neuroscience: The Foundations of Human and Animal Emotions* (Oxford: Oxford University Press, 1998). Panskepp does question whether surprise and disgust should be classified as genuine emotions rather than simpler types of motivational state.

sibly regarded as intentional states. That is, they are states that possess intentional or propositional content. Therefore, the attribution of emotions in this sense presupposes the attribution of propositional content. However, there are reasons for supposing this attribution will be problematic. In particular, there are reasons for supposing that the attribution of emotions to animals would often require the attribution to them of propositional content that they cannot, in fact, entertain. On these grounds, John Deigh, for example, has argued that thinking of emotions as states that possess propositional content excludes animals, infants, and young children lacking in language.[2] In this respect, Deigh is an occupant of a position carved out by Donald Davidson and Stephen Stich.[3]

This book defends the claim that animals are moral subjects in the sense that they can act for moral reasons. But reasons, unlike mere causes, are states with intentional content. Given that I think of these reasons as moral emotions, I am committed to the view that these emotions are intentional states: states individuated by their intentional content. And I, therefore, need to defend the possibility of attributing states with intentional content to animals. That is the primary purpose of this chapter. A bonus, I shall argue, is that the framework I develop to defend the possibility of such attribution also allows us to understand what makes an emotion a specifically moral—morally laden—one.

EMOTIONS AS INTENTIONAL STATES

The category of emotions is a large, mottled, and messy one. In common parlance, the term "emotion" can be used to pick out several

---

2. John Deigh, "Cognitivism in the Theory of Emotions," *Ethics* 104 (1994), 824–54.
3. Donald Davidson, "Thought and Talk," in S. Guttenplan ed., *Mind and Language* (Oxford: Oxford University Press, 1975), pp. 7–23; Davidson, "Rational Animals," in E. LePore and B. McLaughlin eds., *Actions and Events: Perspectives on the Philosophy of Donald Davidson* (Oxford: Blackwell, 1985), pp. 473–80; Stephen Stich, "Do Animals have Beliefs?" *Australasian Journal of Philosophy* 57 (1978), 15–28.

quite different kinds of state. A not insignificant amount of conceptual tidying, and where necessary pruning, is required before we even begin to address the question of whether animals can possess emotions. As is often the case, this process begins with ostension. These are the sorts of things we call emotions: happiness, sadness, fear, anger, surprise, disgust. These comprise Ekman and Friesen's (1989) class of "basic emotions."[4] Even here, there is notable variability in the types of state listed. But this is only the beginning. If we want to extend the list beyond the basic, we might add affection, anxiety, amusement, awe, cheerfulness, compassion, concern, contempt, contentment, delight, disappointment, elation, embarrassment, empathy, envy, exasperation, excitement, guilt, helplessness, hope, horror, indignation, irritation, jealousy, joy, longing, love, lust, nervousness, optimism, pleasure, pride, rage, remorse, satisfaction, shame, shock, stress, submission, sympathy, torment, trust, worry, and zest.

Three things are worth noting about even this cursory list. First, this is a list of things that are commonly *called* emotions. That something is called an emotion is, of course, no guarantee that is actually *is* an emotion. It may be that some of these terms do not denote emotions at all. Second, one name does not entail one named. It may be that some (or even all) of these terms are systematically ambiguous—used to pick out, in different contexts, different types of state. Third, more than one name does not entail more than one named. It may be that some or many of these words are redundant— merely different ways of picking out the same state.

The variety in the kinds of things commonly classified as emotions is reflected in the number of research programs that aim to explain what emotions really are. There are philosophical approaches

---

4. Ekman and W. V. Friesen, "The Arguments and Evidence About Universals in Facial Expressions of Emotion," in Hugh Wagner and Antony Manstead eds., *Handbook of Social Psychophysiology* (New York: John Wiley and Sons, 1989).

that aim to explain the nature of emotions via classical conceptual analysis, or some variant thereof. There are approaches in computational psychology that attempt to explain emotions in terms of higher-order functional profile.[5] There are neural network and dynamical systems accounts that try to explain emotions in terms of unfolding patterns of activity in artificial neural nets.[6] There are attempts to account for emotions in evolutionary terms.[7] Of course, these approaches are not necessarily mutually incompatible—indeed, one hopes that at least some of them are compatible—but they are, nevertheless, different.

We can begin to assign order to the above list by distinguishing two broad categories. The distinction turns on states that do versus states that do not take intentional objects. While the categories are themselves clear, it is far less clear which state goes into which category. Indeed, many of the states identified in the above list can, depending on how they are understood, belong to both; and this means that at least some of the terms that comprise our list are ambiguous.

The first category comprises what we might call *moods*. Moods need not take any particular intentional object. That is, they need not be about anything in particular. I might just be happy or sad, for no particular reason, and without any apparent justification. If my sadness is caused by a chemical imbalance, for example, then I need not be sad for any particular reason, and I need not be sad about anything in particular. In addition to happiness and sadness, anxiety,

5. I. Wright, A. Sloman, and L. Beaudoin, "Towards a Design-Based Analysis of Emotional Episodes," *Philosophy, Psychiatry, and Psychology* 3 (1996), 101–26; P. Thagard, *Coherence in Thought and Action* (Cambridge, MA: MIT Press, 2006).

6. C. Magai and J. Haviland-Jones, *The Hidden Genius of Emotions: Lifespan Transformations of Personality* (Cambridge: Cambridge University Press, 2002).

7. L. Cosmides and J. Tooby, "Evolutionary Psychology and the Emotions," in M. Lewis and J. Haviland-Jones eds., *Handbook of the Emotions* (New York: Guilford Press, 2000), pp. 91–115.

cheerfulness, elation, excitement, joy, nervousness, optimism, stress, and zest can all (though need not) be understood as moods.

On the other hand, many of these states are intentional—they have intentional content or take an intentional object. Smith is angry or indignant that Jones snubbed him—whether the snub is real or imagined. States like this have what is known as content, where the content is the meaning of the sentence that follows the "that"-clause. If Smith is angry that Jones snubbed him, then the content of Smith's anger is the meaning of the sentence "Jones snubbed me." This is the reason for Smith's anger, and, if certain circumstances obtain, it can also be its justification. The same sort of point can be made about states like compassion and sympathy. When one feels compassion or sympathy for an individual it is because one perceives that the individual has, in some way or another, suffered some misfortune. This misfortune provides the reason, and can provide the justification, for the sympathy or compassion. So, because they have this reason-giving, justification-specifying content, states like compassion or sympathy, anger or indignation, seem to be crucially different from moods such as happiness and sadness. Just to complicate matters further, however, there is a way of using the terms "happiness" and "sadness" that makes them much more akin to these content-involving states. Smith is happy that Jones apologized for snubbing him, for example. Happiness and sadness can be understood as moods; but they can also be content-involving states. The same is true of most of the items on the list. All of the items on the list admit of a construction—happy that, sad that, joyful that, nervous about, excited about, optimistic about, and so on—that seems to require us to think of them as intentional states rather than moods. In other contexts, however, they can clearly be moods.

When it comes to the classification of the emotions, nothing is simple, and nothing is obvious, and everything can be understood in more than one way. Paul Griffiths may be right when he argues that only Ekman and Friesen's six basic emotions constitute a natural kind.[8] But this is not germane to the concerns of this book. The task, at this stage, is simply to specify the concept of emotion involved in the thesis that this book defends: the claim that animals can possess moral emotions that provide reasons for their actions. For the purposes of this book, the relevant sense of emotion is the intentional, content-involving sense. The question to be addressed is whether animals can possess emotions that can be ascribed to them using a that-clause, or a variant thereof. This is not, of course, to deny that they can be the subjects of nonintentional moods. But the peculiarly problematic character of the attribution of emotional states to animals emerges only when we understand these states in the intentional, content-involving sense. And that is the sense of emotion implicated in the claim that animals can act for moral reasons.

ATTRIBUTING INTENTIONAL STATES TO ANIMALS: THE PROBLEM

The problems in attributing content-based states to animals revolve, in one way or another, around the identity of the content possessed by those states. Suppose, to use an example associated with Malcolm and developed by Davidson, that a dog—let us call him Hugo—chases a squirrel up a tree.[9] The squirrel disappears into the foliage and, unbeknownst to Hugo, escapes to another tree. Unaware of the squirrel's flight, Hugo barks obstinately at the foot of the tree. It is tempting to say that Hugo believes the squirrel is in the tree. But as

---

8. Paul Griffiths, *What Emotions Really Are: The Problem of Psychological Categories* (Chicago: University of Chicago Press, 1997).

9. Norman Malcolm, "Thoughtless Brutes," *Proceedings of the American Philosophical Society* 46 (1973), 5–20. Malcolm's example involved a cat rather than a squirrel. See also Davidson, "Rational Animals."

people like Davidson and Stich have argued, this attribution is problematic. As Davidson puts it:

> Can the dog believe of an object that it is a tree? This would seem impossible unless we suppose that the dog has many general beliefs about trees: that they are growing things, that they need soil and water, that they have leaves or needles, that they burn. There is no fixed list of things someone with the concept of a tree must believe, but without many general beliefs there would be no reason to identify a belief as a belief about a tree, much less an oak tree.[10]

The more general moral of these considerations is the following:

> We identify thoughts, distinguish between them, describe them for what they are, only as they can be located within a dense network of related beliefs. If we really can intelligibly ascribe single beliefs to a dog, we must be able to imagine how we would decide whether the dog has many other beliefs of the kind necessary for making sense of the first.[11]

Does Hugo, for example, believe the squirrel is a mammal, that it is warm-blooded, that it has a skeleton, and so on? All these beliefs are part of our concept of a squirrel, and so without them Hugo cannot share our concept. Therefore, the attribution to Hugo of the belief that there is a squirrel in the tree is problematic. More generally, the content of a belief, Davidson, argues, is dependent on its place in a network of logically related beliefs. Attribution of beliefs (and other propositional attitudes) is, therefore, a holistic enterprise. Roughly:

10. Davidson, "Rational Animals," p. 474.
11. Davidson, "Rational Animals," p. 475.

Attribution-holism: The attribution of a single belief or other propositional attitude to an individual requires, and only makes sense in terms of, the attribution of a network of related beliefs.

This attribution-holism precludes attribution of beliefs to individuals who do not share our belief network. Animals are such individuals.

At this point, it might be tempting to think that this problem arises only because we have overintellectualized the content of the state that drives Hugo's behavior. He is not thinking anything of the form "The squirrel is in the tree." Rather, his thoughts incline more to the demonstrative: "Got to get it, got to get it!" or variations on that theme. That is, we can specify the content of Hugo's belief in demonstrative terms. I think it is fairly clear that this suggestion will not work. We cannot make do simply with demonstratives: we need a *sortal*. What is it that Hugo has got to get? The squirrel? The tree? Off the ground? More air in his lungs? Quicker? To the extent these answers seem implausible, that is because we know the squirrel that is the object of Hugo's focus. The strategy of appealing only to demonstratives to explain the content of Hugo's intentional states assumes that we can explain Hugo's behavior on the basis of a bare (that is, representationally unmediated) causal contact with an object in the environment. But this will not work. To suppose that we can specify the content of Hugo's motivation in this purely demonstrative way assumes, in effect, that Hugo has no way of representing the object he has to get. This assumption is not only unwarranted; it leaves us with no possibility of explaining Hugo's behavior. Bare causal contact with the world explains nothing. To explain Hugo's behavior we need to know how he represents the object with which he is in causal contact. More generally, the problem of attributing content to animals stems from our failure to understand how they represent objects in the world, not from the fact that instead of representing objects in the world they make do with bare causal contact with those objects. But to understand how they represent objects we need to understand which sortals they use to categorize those objects. And this delivers us straight back in the hands of the Davidson-Stich argument: Which sortals would those be?

ASIDE: ON THE CONTINUING APPEAL, OR OTHERWISE, OF THE DAVIDSON-STICH ARGUMENT

In the eyes of many, the Davidson-Stich argument has not weathered the test of time particularly well.[12] This is because of the subsequent rise of direct reference models of meaning of the sort associated with Kripke,[13] Putnam,[14] and Burge.[15] Indeed, elsewhere I have employed direct reference considerations in replying to the Davidson-Stich argument.[16] My revisiting of the argument here is the result of two things. First, and most important, my concerns in this book are relatively novel ones: the attribution of moral emotions to animals. When I finally turn to this attribution I am going to need, for reasons that will become clear, the idea that there are certain circumstances (to be specified) in which it is legitimate to explain the behavior of an

---

12. I would like to thank Colin McGinn for reminding me of this (in conversation).

13. Saul Kripke, *Naming and Necessity* (Cambridge, MA: Harvard University Press, 1980).

14. Hilary Putnam, "The Meaning of 'Meaning,'" in K. Gunderson ed., *Language, Mind and Knowledge*, Minnesota Studies in the Philosophy of Science 7 (Minneapolis: University of Minnesota Press, 1975).

15. Tyler Burge, "Individualism and the Mental," *Midwest Studies in Philosophy* 4 (1979), 73–121.

16. Mark Rowlands, *Animal Rights: A Philosophical Defense* (Basingstoke, UK: Macmillan, 1998), chapter 7. See also the 2nd edition of this book for an updated version of this argument: *Animal Rights: Moral Theory and Practice* (Basingstoke, UK: Palgrave Macmillan, 2009).

individual by using content that this individual is incapable of entertaining. The reason for this is the subject of later sections. So the strategy to be employed with respect to Davidson-Stich is to give them everything they want—to assume, in effect, that direct reference models never emerged—and then show that their arguments still do not work. Establishing this will simultaneously allow me to identify the conditions under which it is legitimate to explain an individual's behavior by way of content that the individual is incapable of entertaining.

Second, I am not entirely convinced that the Davidson-Stich argument has worn as badly as many assume. There are two reasons why, with respect to animals at least, they still make a significant case to answer. To understand the first, consider an error made by Stich in the development of his argument. Stich understands content-identity as a similarity relation. The content of a mental state can be factored into three elements: causal-pattern similarity, ideological similarity, and reference similarity.[17] The details of these elements are unimportant here. What is important, however, is Stich's characterization of reference similarity. According to Stich, a pair of beliefs counts as reference-similar only if the *terms* the subjects use when they express the beliefs are identical. This, of course, makes reference-similarity a linguistic phenomenon, and precludes the beliefs of animals being assessed along this axis. This, of course, flies in the face of the generally accepted idea that mental states can be intentional in a way that does not reduce to the intentionality of linguistic items. Indeed, if there is a relation of derivation here, it almost certainly runs the other way. This appears to be a strange oversight on Stich's part.

Nevertheless, the claim that the mental states of animals can qualify as reference-similar will not, on its own, do all the work

---

17. Stephen Stich, *From Folk Psychology to Cognitive Science: The Case Against Belief* (Cambridge, MA: MIT Press, 1983).

required of it. Attributions of content based on reference-similarity will be indifferent to the mode of presentation of the object implicated in the attribution. But it is the mode of presentation of the implicated object rather than its reference that will play the major role in explaining the behavior of the individual to whom the content is attributed. And the mode of presentation will, at least on Stich's understanding of this, be constituted by causal-pattern and, particularly, ideological similarity.

The second reason has to do with the role played by both linguistic *convention* and the role of *experts* in the direct reference model—neither of which is applicable to the case of animals. For example, Burge argues that a subject—let us call him Oscar—can plausibly be regarded as possessing the concept of arthritis even through he is incapable of distinguishing arthritis from more general rheumatic ailments. If this is correct, then we cannot understand Oscar's concept possession in terms of the possession of his surrounding beliefs, as the Davidson-Stich argument assumes we can. However, the reason this concept can be attributed to Oscar depends crucially on the fact that he is embedded in a linguistic community that uses the term "arthritis" in a given way, and on the fact that Oscar is willing to defer to experts in his use of this term. Without these assumptions, the attribution of the concept of arthritis to Oscar cannot be sustained. Neither of these considerations is, it seems, applicable in the case of animals. Thus, it may be that there are significant, relevant differences between the circumstances of humans and animals vis-à-vis concept possession. And, while the Davidson-Stich model might provide an implausible account of human concept-possession, it might nevertheless be applicable to the case of animals.

If one is not convinced by this attempted rehabilitation of the Davidson-Stich argument, the important point to bear in mind is where the consideration of their argument is leading. For the dialectical purposes of this book, the important principle is that it is, in certain circumstances to be identified shortly, legitimate to explain the behavior of an individual by way of content that, we have reason to suppose, this individual cannot entertain. That is where I want to get. Consideration of the Davidson-Stich argument is the means I am going to use to get there.

ATTRIBUTING INTENTIONAL STATES TO ANIMALS: PART 1

My response to the Davidson-Stich argument has three strands. First: I shall argue that while *de dicto* ascriptions of content are prima facie problematic, there is—with certain qualifications to be identified shortly—no such corresponding problem with *de re* ascriptions. Second, while we might not be able to make a *de dicto* ascription of content to an animal, we have every reason to suppose that there exists a content that can, correctly, be employed in such an ascription. Third, and most important, as long as certain conditions—to be specified—are met, we can legitimately use the sentences with which we would make *de dicto* ascriptions of content to ourselves to explain the behavior of animals. This section is concerned with the first strand.

If the Davidson-Stich argument is correct, it would undermine the possibility of attributing intentional states not only to animals, but also to certain classes of human: young children and members of exotic cultures with very different belief systems. Macsen is two years old, and almost certainly does not believe that squirrels are mammals, that they are warm-blooded, that they possess skeletons, and so on. Nevertheless, when one of the many squirrels that populate his garden makes an appearance, he will point and vocalize loudly: "Squirrel!" What is it that he believes? Convinced by Davidson and Stich, we might be reluctant to attribute, to Macsen, the belief *that* there is a squirrel over there. Nevertheless, it seems we would be hard pushed to deny that he believes *of* a squirrel that it is over there.[18]

There are two distinct types of belief attribution that we can make to an individual: *de dicto* and *de re* attributions.[19] A *de dicto* ascription to an individual is made by way of an embedded that-clause—Jones believes that *p*—and such attributions are crucially dependent on the way in which the individual represents the object of the belief. It is *de dicto* ascriptions that are the targets of the Davidson-Stich argument. *De re* ascriptions of belief are immune to this argument because they are not sensitive to the way in which the object of the belief is represented. For example, Oedipus believes that Jocasta is his wife. This is a *de dicto* ascription of a belief to Oedipus. He certainly does not believe that his mother is his wife, at least not initially—that discovery came as a bit of a shock. The ascription to Oedipus of the belief that mother is his wife is, again, a *de dicto* ascription—and, in this case, the ascription would be false. Nevertheless, Oedipus's mother is, in fact, his wife. Therefore, we can truly make a *de re* ascription of belief to Oedipus: he believes *of* his mother that she is his wife. He does believe that Jocasta is his wife. Jocasta is, in fact, his mother. So, he does believe *of* his mother—of the individual person who is, in fact, his mother—that she is his wife even though he does not believe *that* his mother is his wife.

Therefore, while we might not be able to attribute the belief that there is a squirrel in the tree to Hugo, or the belief that there is a squirrel

---

18. Note that I say "it seems." This *de re* attribution is more problematic than it appears. I shall discuss this issue later. Note also that the same issue that arises with respect to the squirrel arises also with respect to the tree. We would have to de-reify that too. Thus the *de re* attribution would presumably be of the form: "With respect to the tree, the dog believes of the squirrel that it is in it." *De re* attributions quickly become horribly messy—which is, perhaps, one reason why we are more comfortable employing the *de dicto* alternative form. For ease of exposition, I shall ignore this complication in the discussion to follow.

19. Note that I claim there are two distinct types of belief *attribution*, not that there are two distinct types of belief. The claim that there exist two different types of belief, one *de dicto* the other *de re*, is implausible. The existence of two types of belief attribution is, however, relatively uncontroversial.

over there to Macsen, we can nevertheless legitimately make the corresponding *de re* attribution. Hugo believes *of* the squirrel that it is in the tree.[20] And Macsen believes *of* the squirrel that it is over there.

Philosophers have tended to privilege *de dicto* ascriptions of belief over their *de re* counterparts in a way that, I suspect, might not be reflected in common sense. Nevertheless, they have respectable reasons for this. The possibility of *de re* ascriptions of belief to animals might seem, to many philosophers, to be of little consolation. What we are trying to do in ascribing beliefs to Hugo, or Macsen, is understand their behavior. But this understanding is precisely what *de re* ascriptions do not supply. The *de re* ascription of belief to Oedipus has no implications for his behavior. It is only when we make the *de dicto* ascription—of the belief *that* his mother is his wife—that we arrive at the rather gory denouement. *De dicto* ascriptions of belief (when combined with similarly *de dicto* ascriptions of desire) can explain behavior; *de re* ascriptions cannot.

The reason is that *de re* ascriptions, notoriously, fail to reflect the *intensionality* of intentional ascriptions. That is, they do not explain the failure of substitution of co-referential terms in intentional contexts. This intensionality is, arguably, the hallmark of intentional ascriptions. Without it, we are unable to make sense of the claim, for example, that while Oedipus believes that Jocasta is his wife, he does not believe that his mother is his wife, even though Jocasta is his mother. The possibility of *de re* ascriptions of beliefs to animals might, therefore, seem to be a Pyrrhic victory at best.

Moreover, there are reasons for doubting that *de re* ascriptions of belief can be made independently of *de dicto* ascriptions.[21] When

20. Of course, in the case of this attribution to Hugo, we face the same problem with the *de dicto* ascription of the concept of a tree—indeed, that was the concept Davidson used in developing his case. I assume that the strategy developed in this and the following section can be applied to this concept also.

21. My thanks to Colin McGinn (in conversation) for drawing my attention to this.

Macsen points at a squirrel and shrieks "Squirrel!" he is simultaneously pointing and shrieking at, as Quine would put it, an undetached squirrel part and a squirrel stage. What justifies the *de re* ascription of the content "squirrel" to him rather than the content "undetached squirrel part" or "squirrel stage"? To justify the *de re* ascription of the first sort of content, it seems we would need to be in possession of specifically *de dicto* information concerning the mode of presentation of that with which Macsen is in causal contact. In the absence of this information, all we are entitled to say, it seems, is that there is a perhaps indefinite list of *de re* attributions that we might make to Macsen—one of which will prove to be correct.

Both of these objections, in their different ways, point to the need to buttress any putative *de re* ascription with a *de dicto* counterpart. This brings us to the second strand of the argument.

ATTRIBUTING INTENTIONAL STATES TO ANIMALS: PART 2

According to the Davidson-Stich argument, the *de dicto* attribution of beliefs to animals fails because of our inability to identify the content possessed by such states. Here it is necessary to distinguish two questions: (1) Is it possible for us to identify the content of the states we ascribe, in *de dicto* contexts, to animals? (2) Is there a content that is possessed by the intentional states of animals that can be correctly employed in such attribution? The first is an epistemic question, broadly construed; the second is an ontological question. I shall argue that while we might not be able to identify, certainly not without difficulty, the content of states we could employ in *de dicto* ascriptions of such states to an animal, we have every reason to suppose that there exist contents that can, correctly, be employed in such an ascription. To grasp these contents we need to understand the ways in which the animal represents the world. And to understand this, we need to understand the concepts in terms of which it so represents it. This is not something that can be done from the armchair, but requires detailed empirical investigation of the abilities of different animals, and scrupulous examination of what these abilities reveal, or likely reveal, about its conceptual repertoire. On any reasonable account of concept possession, however, there is every reason to suppose that at least some animals do possess concepts, and so that there exists a *de dicto* content-ascription that correctly describes the way a given animal represents the world.

To suppose that there is no content available for use in *de dicto* ascriptions is to suppose that animals do not represent the world. And that is a breathtakingly implausible assumption. Identifying this content is a difficult matter, and may be one that is ultimately beyond us. But it is not too difficult to see, at least in broad outline, how the project would proceed. A promising framework for understanding the conditions under which it is reasonable to suppose an animal possesses a concept has been proposed by Colin Allen.[22] Allen argues that it is reasonable to suppose that animal O possesses the concept of an X if:

(1) O systematically discriminates some X's from some non-X's.

(2) O is capable of detecting some of its own discrimination errors between X's and non-X's.

(3) O is capable of learning to better discriminate X's from non-X's as a result of capacity (2).[23]

Conditions (1)–(3) collectively specify when it is reasonable to suppose that an animal, O, possesses the concept of X. They do not

22. Colin Allen, "Animal Concepts Revisited: The Use of Self-Monitoring as an Empirical Approach," *Erkenntnis* 51 (1999), 33–40.

23. Allen, "Animal Concepts Revisited," p. 37.

constitute an analysis of what it is for an animal to possess the concept of X (just as the conditions under which it is reasonable to suppose that someone is a murderer do not add up to an analysis of the concept of a murderer). Allen is not entirely wedded to (3). But since the purpose of (1)–(3) is not to provide a necessary and sufficient condition for concept possession, this does not matter. Allen simply notes that the satisfaction of (iii) increases the reasonableness of supposing that animal O possesses the concept of X. The notions of "discrimination" and "detection," ones that might prove unacceptably vague if this were construed as an analysis of concept possession, are harmless here. That is, we can understand "O systematically discriminates some X's from some non-X's" to convey that O discriminates between X's and non-X's in a manner characteristic of the kind of creature that O, in fact, is. If O, for example, is sentient, then we can suppose that the discrimination in question is a conscious process, or has ramifications at the level of the creature's consciousness, and so on.[24] This framework applies most clearly to perceptual concepts.[25] With this in mind, let us return to Hugo's unfinished business with the squirrel.

---

24. This would allow Allen to avoid the objection that his conditions are too weak—satisfiable by computers, artificial neural networks, and so on. If these conditions were advanced as an analysis of concept-possession, Allen would, I suspect, be vulnerable to this sort of objection. However, it is not and so he is not.

25. Some might be tempted by the idea that the content of perception is nonconceptual. The dispute concerning conceptual versus nonconceptual content is, in my view, one of the more sterile disputes thrown up by recent philosophy of mind, largely because no condition that is both plausible and clear has been supplied for what is required for a content to count as conceptual. On one relatively clear account, it is the capacity to form beliefs about the content of a perception that renders the content of that perception conceptual. The underlying premise is that since the content of a belief is conceptual, the content of a perception can be the content of a belief only if that content is also conceptual. Allen's account of the conditions under which it is reasonable to possess a concept entails that this account is false—if we assume, as we should, that progressive improvement in discriminatory abilities does not require the ability to form beliefs about one's discriminatory abilities. For the purposes of this book, nothing turns on the question of whether the content of perception is conceptual or nonconceptual, and I shall henceforth ignore this issue.

To identify the concept or concepts in terms of which Hugo represents the squirrel, we need first look at his behavior with respect to squirrels. First: is there any behavioral evidence that Hugo discriminates between squirrels and other smallish furry mammals—rabbits, rats, cats, and so on? Perhaps there is no such evidence—and if so, this would make it unreasonable to suppose that Hugo possesses the concept SQUIRREL, and instead might incline us to the hypothesis that Hugo is operating with a broader conceptual category. We might, for example, investigate the idea that Hugo is operating with a broader, affordance-based representation: whereas we would distinguish squirrels, rabbits, rats, and cats, Hugo subsumes these under the category CHASEABLE THING. Or perhaps there is evidence that Hugo is operating with a narrower category. Perhaps when chasing squirrels there is behavioral evidence of an attempt to keep them away from trees. But when chasing rabbits there is evidence of a strategy of keeping them away from holes in the ground. In this case, this may be evidence for Hugo operating with a somewhat narrower affordance-based category: perhaps he distinguishes the category CHASEABLE THING THAT GOES UP from the category CHASEABLE THING THAT GOES DOWN.

If Hugo is capable of discriminating squirrels and rabbits, then we can, as Allen's framework suggests, investigate further. Hugo, let us suppose, sometimes makes mistakes: he sometimes attempts to get between squirrels and holes in the ground, and sometimes attempts to place himself between rabbits and the trees. If so, does he show any evidence of being able to detect these errors in discrimination? Does he show any improved detection of rabbits/squirrels over time—that is, do his errors of discrimination decrease over time?

These are the sorts of questions that need to be addressed in order to decide on the question of which concepts Hugo can reasonably be thought to possess. The answers to these questions will not be easy to determine: far from it. However, there is no reason to suppose they are unanswerable. Nothing in the Davidson-Stich argument counts against thinking that there are contents available with which *de dicto* ascriptions of intentional states can be made. At most, the Davidson-Stich argument shows that these contents might be difficult for us to identify—and, at the very least, their identification will require substantial empirical investigation.

This concludes part 2 of the argument. If the argument developed so far is correct then: (1) we can make legitimate *de re* ascriptions of content to animals (although, in the absence of a correct *de dicto* ascription, we may have to content ourselves with a set of possible *de re* ascriptions rather than one definitive ascription) and (2) there is no reason for supposing that there are no legitimate *de dicto* ascriptions of content we can make to animals. The third, and most important, strand of the argument consists in a partial rehabilitation of the *de dicto* ascriptions of intentional states to animals—ones that we might make in the absence of extensive empirical investigation into their behavior: the sort of attribution Hugo's owner makes when he says, "Hugo believes that the squirrel is in the tree." Very roughly, this practice, I shall argue, is not a way of attributing content to animals, but a (legitimate) way of explaining their behavior through the use of content that *tracks* whatever content they, in fact, possess.

ATTRIBUTING INTENTIONAL STATES TO ANIMALS: PART 3

I shall argue that we can legitimately use the sentences with which we would make *de dicto* ascriptions of content to ourselves to explain the behavior of animals. The use of such sentences is, in essence, a way of *tracking* the content whose ascription we would make if we knew how the animal represented the world. The term "tracking," as I shall understand it, denotes a relation between propositions:

(*Tracking*): Proposition p tracks proposition p^* *iff* the truth of p guarantees the truth of p^* in virtue of the fact that there is a reliable asymmetric connection between the concepts expressed by the term occupying the subject position in p and the concept expressed by the term occupying the subject position in p^*.

A propositional content, p, can therefore be employed as a way of explaining the behavior of an animal, even if p is not a content the animal entertains, or is even capable of entertaining, to the extent that p *tracks* a distinct propositional content, p^*, that can, in fact, be attributed to that animal. Of course, since, in the absence of extensive empirical investigation, we cannot be sure of the identity of p^*, p constitutes, in effect, our best guess as to the proposition that will track the propositional content we think we can legitimately ascribe to the animal.

Hugo, we were tempted to say, believes that the squirrel is in the tree. Swayed by the Davidson-Stich argument, we now suspect this belief-ascription is problematic. The concept of tracking underwrites the legitimacy of using propositions such as "The squirrel is in the tree" to explain Hugo's behavior. Suppose, simply for the sake of developing this point, that empirical investigation of Hugo's abilities suggests that he represents squirrels in fairly general affordance-based terms. That is, he distinguishes between things that are chaseable and those that are not, but makes no finer-grained distinctions within this category. He does not distinguish, for example, between chaseable things that go up and chaseable things that go down. If so, the most accurate content-ascription we could make to Hugo would be of the form, "The chaseable thing is up there." What is the relation between the content-ascription we were initially tempted to employ ("The squirrel is in the tree") and the one that empirical investigation, we have assumed for the sake of argument, shows is the accurate one?

The Davidson-Stich argument is based on the idea that our use of the term "squirrel" is (in virtue of our network of beliefs) anchored to us in a way that it is not anchored to a dog. The variation in content derives from this variation in anchoring context, and that is why we cannot use content-ascriptions appropriate to humans in nonhuman contexts. The answer to this problem, therefore, is to relativize content-ascriptions to contexts.[26] In other words, we should understand ascriptions of belief as functions from contexts to contents.

Let us begin with the idea of a nonanchored, context-free proposition, p. This proposition can be anchored to a context. I shall use the expression $[H: p]$ to denote p anchored to the human context, and $[C: p]$ to denote the same proposition anchored to the canine context. Both $[H: p]$ and $[C: p]$, therefore, are also propositions: they are anchored, context-bound propositions.[27] "H" and "C" denote human and canine contexts, respectively. In accordance with the Davidson-Stich argument, I shall assume that this comprises a network of related beliefs (perhaps together with certain affordance-related but

---

26. This is a trick I learned from Jerry Fodor's *Psychosemantics* (Cambridge, MA: MIT Press, 1987), chapter 2. Fodor's concern was with the idea of *narrow content* rather than content entertained by animals, and the understanding of ascriptions of narrow content as functions from contexts to contents was a way of accommodating the inexpressibility of narrow content. While there are differences between the case of narrow content and the content possessed by animals, I suspect the two cases are, in most important respects, analogous.

27. We can imagine that these anchored propositions are attributed by way of certain linguistic forms. Thus, let us suppose:

(1) "s" is true iff p

(2) H["s"] is true iff $[H: p]$

(3) C["s"] is true iff $[C: p]$

H["s"] should be read: the sentence "s" when used to express the content of a human's mental state. C["s"] should be read: the sentence "s" when used to express the content of a canine's mental state. Let us say that sentences, such as "s," are *applied* and that propositions (that is, propositional contents), such as p, are thereby *attributed*. $[H: p]$ is a proposition, but H["s"] is not a sentence. In other words, H["s"] is true *iff* $[H: p]$ should be read as follows:

(4) The sentence "s" can be used to describe the content of a human's mental state if and only if the proposition $[H: p]$ is true.

nondoxastic facts—for example what counts as chaseable for Hugo—a German shepherd—need not count as chaseable for, say, a Pomeranian). Therefore, if

p is the proposition that there is a squirrel in the tree,
p^* is the proposition that the chaseable thing is up there.

Anchored proposition $[H: p]$ will track the anchored proposition $[C: p^*]$ if and only if

(1) If $[H: p]$ is true then $[C: p^*]$ is true, and (2) this truth-preservation obtains because of a reliable asymmetric dependence between the concept expressed by the subject term of $[H: p]$ and the concept expressed by the subject terms of $[C: p^*]$.

That is:

(1) If $[H:$ the squirrel is in the tree$]$ is true then $[C:$ the chaseable thing is up there$]$ is also true, and this truth preservation obtains because of reliable asymmetric dependence between the concept expressed by "squirrel" (as anchored to a human) and the concept expressed by "chaseable thing" (as anchored to a dog, such as Hugo).

Of course, as I mentioned earlier,[28] the Davidson-Stich argument can be reiterated for other concepts contained in the sentence: Hugo does not possess the H-concept of a tree, for example. That is why in $[C: p^*]$ reference to the tree has been replaced with the demonstrative expression "up there." If we wanted to keep the reference to the tree, we could prosecute essentially the same strategy simply by

28. See footnote 20.

reformulating the sentence to put "tree" in the subject position (that is, in the somewhat Yoda-like form: "In the tree is where the squirrel is"). There is, then, a reliable asymmetric connection between being in a tree and being "up there." I shall, henceforth, ignore this complication. Let us consider (1) and (2) in turn.

According to (1), [H: p] guarantees (via the route specified in (2)) the truth of [C: p^*]. We can legitimately use [H: p] in our ascriptions of intentional states to Hugo even though p is not a propositional content Hugo does, or even could, entertain. We can do this because p tracks another propositional content that Hugo does entertain. And it does this because [H: p] guarantees the truth of [C: p^*] by the route specified in (2). This is not to say, to reiterate, that Hugo does, or even can, entertain the proposition [H: p]—in fact, that is what is being explicitly denied. Rather, the proposition [H: p] can be used to explain Hugo's behavior, and it can be used in this way because it tracks the proposition [C: p^*] that, let us suppose, Hugo does entertain.[29]

It is important to realize that there are other context-bound propositions whose truth [H: p] can also guarantee. Suppose Hugo does, in fact, discriminate within the category of chaseable things (and is capable of detecting his errors of discrimination in the way specified by Allen). Hugo distinguishes the chaseable things that tend to escape upward from those that tend to escape downward. Thus, there exists another context-bound proposition [C: p^{**}]—[C: the chaseable

---

29. We might compare this to what is, for the philosopher at least, the more familiar case of twin earth. The propositional content that water is drinkable is not a content that my twin could entertain. Nevertheless, there is a truth-preserving relationship of the appropriate sort between content that I entertain (that water is drinkable) and the content my twin entertains (that retaw is drinkable). If the former is true the latter must be true, and this is so because there is a reliable connection between (almost all) the properties of water and the properties of retaw. In virtue of this truth preservation by way of a specified route, I can use the propositional content that water is wet to explain my twin's behavior even though this is not a content he can entertain.

thing that goes up is up there]—and [H: p] guarantees the truth, by the route specified in (2), of [C: p^{**}]. Crucially, in order to legitimately employ the content [H: the squirrel is in the tree] in ascribing a belief to Hugo, we do not need to know whether [C: p^*] or [C: p^{**}] is true. In general, there will be a set of context-bound propositions $\{[C: p^*], [C: p^{**}] \ldots [C: p^{n*}]\}$ whose truth will be guaranteed by [H: p]. In order to legitimately use [H: p] to ascribe content-based states to Hugo, one does not need to be able to identify all the members of this set, nor, crucially, does one need to know which member of this set is correct. It merely needs to be true that one member of this set is correct, and that its truth is guaranteed by [H: p]. If it is reasonable to suspect that one member of this set is true, then it is reasonable to use [H: p] in ascribing an intentional state to Hugo.

That [H: p] simply guarantees the truth of [C: p^*] is not sufficient for p to track p^*. Also crucial is the *way* it does this. Suppose Hugo lives in a world where the world's most famous living concert pianist is a timorous person, fearful of dogs, and has the misfortune of living next door to Hugo. Hugo regards him as a chaseable thing. Then, it would seem, [H: p = the world's most famous living concert pianist is in the tree] guarantees the truth of [C: p^* = the chaseable thing is up there]. But, presumably, we would not, in this case, deem [H: p] to be a suitable proposition to employ when we try to explain the behavior of Hugo.[30] The key to resolving this problem is to understand that it is not simply that [H: p] guarantees the truth of [C: p^*] that is important. In addition, it must guarantee this truth in a certain way. This is the import of (2).

The phrase "in a certain way" amounts to this: there must be a reliable connection between the concepts expressed by the subject terms of [H: p] and [C: p^*]. There is no reliable connection between the concept of the world's most famous living concert pianist and

30. Thanks to Daniel Hampikian for a version of this objection.

that of a chaseable thing. It may be true that the present incumbent of that title is eminently chaseable, but that certainly was not true of his or her more robust, less dog-fearing predecessor. The reliable connection is presumably best captured in terms of a universal quantification. It is not true that, for all x, if x is the world's most famous living concert pianist then x is chaseable. His less timorous predecessor, let us suppose, was not. But it is true that for a dog such as Hugo (but maybe not for a Pomeranian: C is, in this way, different for Hugo than it is for a Pomeranian), for all x, if x is a squirrel then x is chaseable. This connection is a reliable one.

This apparatus provides us with a plausible way of explaining the behavior of both nonhumans and "nonstandard" humans (children, radically different cultures, etc.). In the case of a proposition, p, that a subject does not entertain, p can be legitimately employed in explaining the behavior of that subject (whether human or animal) when three conditions are satisfied:

(1) The ascription of p is the *de dicto* version of a *de re* ascription that is correct.[31]

(2) There exists a proposition p^* that the subject does entertain and the truth of $[H: p]$ (that is, p anchored to its context) guarantees the truth of $[C: p^*]$ (that is, p^* anchored to its context).

(3) p guarantees the truth of p^* by way of a reliable asymmetric connection between the concepts expressed in the subject terms of $[H: p]$ and $[C: p^*]$.

When we use $[H: p]$ to explain Hugo's behavior, we may be employing content that Hugo does not—indeed cannot—entertain.

---

31. Given my earlier comments on the problems with *de re* ascriptions, this may not necessarily be the *de re* ascription we initially envisaged.

Nevertheless, the use of this content is legitimate because it is, in effect, a way of "sneaking up" on the content that Hugo does entertain.[32] The legitimacy of employing [H: p] in ascribing content to Hugo can be understood in three stages. First, there is the question of whether the corresponding *de re* ascription is at least plausible—a candidate for the correct *de re* ascription. If [H: p] = [H: the squirrel is in the tree], the first question we have to ask is whether the corresponding *de re* ascription is, prima facie, plausible: is it plausible to suppose that Hugo believes *of* the squirrel that it is in the tree?[33] Second, is it plausible to suppose that [H: p] guarantees the truth of whatever context-relativized content [C: p^*] Hugo does entertain? Third, if so, does [H: p] guarantee the truth of [C: p^*] by way of a reliable asymmetric connection between the concepts expressed by the subject terms of p and p^*? If all three conditions are met, the use of [H: p] in explaining Hugo's behavior is justified. Our *de dicto* content-ascriptions are anchored to us. Conditions (1)–(3), in effect, provide a recipe for understanding how content-ascriptions anchored to a given context can be used across contexts in explaining behavior.

I am not suggesting, of course, that the account developed here is the only possible way of responding to the Davidson-Stich argument.[34] I develop this response largely because it contains one feature that will prove very valuable in the arguments to follow: the idea that it is, in certain circumstances, legitimate to explain the behavior of an

32. The expression "sneaking up" is borrowed from Jerry Fodor, who uses a similar strategy of relativizing contents to contexts to identify a criterion of identity for narrow content. See his *Psychosemantics*, chapter 2.

33. This is the case even though we may not be able to convert plausibility into truth in the absence of the required *de dicto* information. It may, conceivably, turn out that the correct *de re* ascription is that of a belief about a squirrel stage rather than a squirrel—although I suspect that, ultimately, we will be able to rule this out on empirical grounds. See, for example, Gareth Evans, "Identity and predication," *Journal of Philosophy* 72 (13), 343–63.

34. See David DeGrazia, *Taking Animals Seriously: Mental Life and Moral Status* (Cambridge: Cambridge University Press, 1996) for some alternatives.

animal by way of content that the animal cannot entertain. The focus, so far, has been on the ascription of cognitive states such as beliefs to animals. The value of this feature comes to the fore, however, when we switch focus from cognitive states to emotional ones. This is what I am now going to do.

ATTRIBUTING EMOTIONS TO ANIMALS

"I fear thee ancient mariner, I fear thy skinny hand, for thou art long and lank and lean as is the ribbed sea sand."[35] The attribution of the emotion of fear, either to oneself or to others, seems to involve two distinguishable components. First, there is a factual or cognitive content. You are, in fact, an ancient mariner, and your hand is, accordingly, skinny, and you bear a certain resemblance to the ribbed sea sand. Second, there is the evaluative component. You, ancient mariner, are the sort of thing that should be feared. Two things should be noted at this point. First, and this reiterates a point I made earlier, that two components of content can be distinguished does not entail that they are separable. It may be that the factual and evaluative contents are, in the emotion in question, united as an indivisible whole. I take no stand on this issue. Second, here is something else on which I take no stand: whether emotions can be reduced to judgments. I claim only that emotions *involve* judgments, and nothing more sanguine than that. This section, in effect, attempts (among other things) to specify the content of the term "involve" in this context. Emotions involve both factual and evaluative judgments; and this combination of the factual and evaluative is, accordingly, a characteristic feature of the attribution of emotions. When the emotions in question are morally laden ones, the type of evaluation takes on a specifically moral hue.

35. Samuel Taylor Coleridge, "The Rime of the Ancient Mariner."

Smith, let us suppose, is indignant that Jones snubbed him. The content of his emotion can, it seems, be specified by the first-person utterance: "Jones snubbed me." However, there is clearly more to Smith's indignation than this. Implicit in the emotion is Smith's idea that Jones was (morally) wrong to snub him. Without this evaluation, Smith's indignation is unexplained. Bound up with Smith's indignation is his belief that he has been hard done by: morally speaking, he deserved better. This combination of the factual and the morally evaluative is a defining feature of what I shall call the morally laden emotions. My fear of the ancient mariner involves a form of broadly prudential evaluation—the ancient mariner has not wronged me, but, I believe, he might. Smith's indignation involves a form of moral evaluation. All emotions involve evaluation. The morally laden emotions involve moral evaluation.

If emotions are, in general, a combination of the factual and the evaluative, this introduces a new wrinkle in understanding of the ascription of emotions to animals. The little dog, let us suppose, fears the big one. But how does it represent this dog? The Davidson-Stich argument can, of course, be reiterated for the factual component of the emotion, and the antidote to this argument is the same. The proposition "There is a big dog here" is one that can legitimately be used in explaining the dog's behavior even if it is not a proposition that the dog entertains as long as two conditions are met: (1) it is the *de dicto* form of a true *de re* ascription, and (2) the truth of the context-bound proposition [H: there is a big dog here] *tracks* (that is, guarantees, via a reliable connection between the concepts expressed in the subject-terms of each sentence), the truth of whatever proposition is, in fact, entertained by (and thus anchored to) the dog.

However, given that the emotion involves, in addition, an evaluative component, essentially the same problem will be reiterated here. It should be no surprise, therefore, that I am going to advocate the same strategy in this case also.

In connection with the evaluative component of the emotion's content, the analogue of the problem we faced with factual or cognitive content is this: we cannot incorporate the evaluative component of an emotion into that emotion's content in such a way as to make it a proposition that the subject of the emotion must entertain in order to have the emotion. Can the little dog understand the concept expressed by "should" or "warrant"—as it seems it would have to do in order to understand the proposition that it should fear the big dog, or that its fear of the big dog is warranted? If not, and if these concepts form part of the content of the emotion, how can it possess the emotion? The problem is, of course, exacerbated when we move from a prudential "ought" to a moral one. Can an animal understand the "ought" of moral obligation? If it cannot, and if moral emotions involve moral evaluation, how can it possess moral emotions?

The answer, I shall argue, involves the earlier distinction between the tracking of a true proposition and the entertaining of a true proposition. In this case, the propositions will be evaluative rather than factual ones. Emotions, if they are legitimate, track true evaluative propositions, but they do not require that the subject of an emotion entertain, or even be capable of entertaining, such a proposition.

To see how this strategy works in the case of emotions, consider what it means for an emotion to, let us say, *misfire*—which I shall understand as, roughly, the analogue of what it is for a belief to be false. I shall understand the category of misfires as a conjunctive one: an emotion misfires when it is either *misguided* or it is *misplaced*. This distinction follows from the idea that emotions have both a factual and an evaluative component. Smith is indignant because he believes Jones has snubbed him, but he is, in fact, mistaken. Jones didn't snub him at all. Let us say that Smith's indignation is, in this case, *misplaced*. An emotion is misplaced when it is grounded in a factual assertion that is, in fact, false. The other source of failure occurs when Jones, in fact, has every right to snub Smith—say because of Smith's obnoxious behavior during their previous encounter. Smith, as we might say, deserved no better from Jones in this case. Let us say that Smith's indignation, in this case, is *misguided*. The emotion is misguided because it is based on an assumption of entitlement that is, in fact, erroneous.

An emotion that is based on an evaluation that is nonmoral can also be misguided. I fear the ancient mariner and his skinny hand. But let's suppose he turns out to be a rather pleasant old chap, in an avuncular sort of way, one who bears me no ill will. In such circumstances, my evaluative judgment that he should be feared, that he warrants fear, would be erroneous, and my fear, accordingly, would be misguided.

The idea of an emotion being misguided allows us to understand the location in logical space of the evaluative component of the emotion. If an emotion, E, is not to be misguided, then a certain evaluative proposition, p, must be true. The truth of this proposition, as we might say, makes sense of the emotion. We need not think of emotions as reducible to evaluations. Nor, crucially, does the possession of a given emotion require the entertaining of the evaluative proposition. Rather, for any emotion, there is a certain evaluative proposition that must be true in order for the emotion to not be misguided.

In this sense, possession of an emotion tracks a true evaluative proposition. If an emotion is not misguided, then there exists a certain evaluative proposition, p, and p is true. The nonmisguided status of an emotion, therefore, guarantees the truth of a given evaluative proposition. When we have emotions, and they are neither misguided nor misplaced, these emotions, in this sense, track true evaluative propositions. For an emotion to track a proposition does not require that the subject of this emotion entertain, or even be capable of entertaining, it. Thus, this account avoids the charge of overintellectualization, and explains how emotions can be spread as widely through the animal domain as they are commonly taken to be.

This framework allows us to understand what it means for an emotion to be morally laden. An individual possesses a (nonmisguided) morally laden emotion when it is in a state that tracks a true evaluative proposition of a specific sort—a proposition that expresses a moral evaluation. This allows us to define the concept of a morally laden emotion as follows:

> An emotion, E, is *morally laden* if and only if (1) it is an emotion in the intentional, content-involving, sense, (2) there exists a proposition, *p*, which expresses a moral claim, and (3) if E is not misguided, then *p* is true.

This definition emerges as a relatively straightforward extension of the framework for understanding the attribution of emotions to animals—and that framework itself emerged as a relatively straightforward extension of the framework developed for understanding the attribution of states with intentional content to animals.

CONCLUSION

I am going to argue that animals can be moral subjects in the sense that they can act on the basis of moral reasons. These moral reasons take the form of moral emotions—emotions understood as intentional states that possess identifiable moral content. This chapter has been concerned with some essential preparatory work. First, if the arguments of this chapter are correct, then animals are the sorts of things to which content—and states individuated by this content—can be attributed. Indeed, we can legitimately explain the behavior of animals using the same sentences as the ones we use to ascribe content to ourselves—even if these sentences express propositions that animals cannot entertain. The legitimacy of this practice is grounded in the distinction between the tracking and the entertaining of a proposition. Using this framework, I argued that the behavior of animals may, legitimately, be explained by appeal to states that possess both factual and evaluative content. Finally, this framework was also used to supply an account of what it means for an emotion to be a morally laden one.

With this preparatory work in place, the next chapter clarifies the idea of a moral subject and begins to examine the formidable problems with thinking that animals can be such subjects.

3

Moral Agents, Patients, and Subjects

THE SHAPE OF THINGS TO COME

The primary thesis to be defended in this book is that some animals can be moral subjects in the sense that they can be motivated to act by moral reasons. These moral reasons take the form of morally laden emotions—emotions that have moral content. An emotion has moral content in the sense that, if it is not misguided, it guarantees the truth of a moral proposition. What makes a proposition a moral one is something that I shall not discuss. I shall assume we have a reasonable grasp on which propositions are moral ones and which are not. The first task of this chapter is to further elaborate the idea of a moral *subject*, and distinguish it from things with which it might be confused. In particular, I shall argue that the concept of a moral subject does not reduce to either of two more familiar concepts. First, it is distinct from the concept of a moral *patient*. Second, although the dialectical situation here is a lot more complex, a prima facie case can be made for the claim that the concept of a moral subject does not reduce to that of a moral *agent*. I shall make this prima facie case.

With this preliminary work complete, I shall then begin to examine the reasons that have engendered the almost universal belief that the concept of a moral subject collapses into that of a moral agent. If these reasons are cogent, then the prima facie case for the distinctness of the concepts of a moral agent and a moral subject crumbles. It is important for the concerns of this book that the distinction between moral subjects and moral agents does not collapse: I want to argue that animals can be moral subjects but not that they can be moral agents. Thus, in effect, the arguments developed in the second half of the book can be regarded as arguments for reaffirming the distinction between moral subjects and moral agents. However, in this chapter I shall restrict myself to doing two things. First, I want to develop the case for the tripartite distinction between patients, agents, and subjects—where these are understood in general, nonmoral terms. Second, I shall examine some apparently powerful arguments for thinking that, in the specifically moral case, the distinction between agents and subjects breaks down. That is, while the distinction between subjects and agents might, in general, be a legitimate one, there are reasons for supposing that the distinction between specifically *moral* subjects and *moral* agents is not. This chapter develops what I refer to as the *logical* case against the idea of a moral subject, understood as something distinct from a moral agent. The following chapter will develop what I call the *historical* case against this idea. The remaining chapters of the book will then try to show that these cases, while seemingly powerful and persuasive, in fact have little substance.

ANIMALS AS MORAL PATIENTS

When animals are discussed in the context of morality, the discussion almost always coalesces on the issue of whether animals should be thought of as moral *patients*, where

(1) X is a moral *patient* if and only if X is a legitimate object of moral concern: that is, roughly, X is an entity that has interests that should be taken into consideration when decisions are made concerning it or which otherwise impact on it.

In 1975, with the publication of his enormously influential book *Animal Liberation*, Peter Singer provided a case for the moral claims of animals based on a form of utilitarianism—preference-utilitarianism.[1] From the perspective of preference-utilitarianism, what matters is that, in our actions, we attempt to maximize the overall amount of satisfied preferences in the world. The way we currently treat animals—raising and slaughtering them for food in factory systems, subjecting them to painful experiments, and so on—results in a huge deficit of satisfied preferences in the world. Therefore, we should, on utilitarian grounds, radically alter the way we relate to and deal with animals. Tom Regan has provided an influential defense of the claim that animals possess moral rights, ones grounded in their status as what he calls subjects-of-a-life.[2] On the basis of this, Regan reached conclusions similar to Singer about the moral impermissibility of our current dealings with animals. While Singer and Regan disagree on theory—Singer is a utilitarian, Regan a deontologist—both are pursuing essentially the same kind of project: showing how major moral theories condemn the way we currently treat animals.

More recently, other major moral theories, including ones widely thought inimical to the moral claims of animals, have been argued to ground the claim animals have moral status—rights or some variant thereof. I have argued that a form of Rawlsian contractualism yields conclusions similar to those defended by Regan—that animals possess a broad array of moral rights, and that the way we currently treat them is, accordingly, morally wrong.[3] Attempts to apply the central

1. Peter Singer, *Animal Liberation* (New York: Thorsons, 1975).
2. Tom Regan, *The Case for Animal Rights* (Berkeley: University of California Press, 1983).
3. Mark Rowlands, "Contractualism and Animal Rights," *Journal of Applied Philosophy* 14.3 (1997), 235–34; Rowlands, *Animal Rights: A Philosophical Defence*; Rowlands, *Animal Rights: Moral Theory and Practice*; Rowlands, *Animal Like Us* (London: Verso, 2002). Mark Bernstein has also defended a contractualist account of the moral claims of animals in his *On Moral Considerability* (New York: Oxford University Press, 1998), as have Will Kymlicka and Paula Cavalieri, "Expanding the Social Contract," *Etica e Animali* 8 (1996), 5–33. An early version of this position was defended by Donald van de Veer, "Interspecific Justice," *Inquiry* 22 (1979), 22–50.

concepts of virtue ethics to our dealings with animals are also beginning to emerge.[4]

The theoretical commitments of these approaches are often quite different. Regan's account, for example, is based on the concept of moral rights. But Singer, as a good utilitarian of broadly Benthamite credentials, suspects that talk of rights is "nonsense." Regan's account is based on the idea that certain things have inherent value. The contractualist approach tends to eschew this in favor of acts of inherent valuing. Virtue ethical approaches are very different again—emphasizing that in our dealings with animals we must remain good, or morally virtuous, people. Nevertheless, the approaches do converge on a clear theme: Take a major moral theory—any major moral theory you like—then animals emerge as the possessors of moral status. They make moral claims on us. They have interests that we are morally obliged to take into account when we make decisions that impact on them. They emerge, in other words, as moral patients.

In one clear sense, these theoretically based accounts of the moral status of animals build on prominent elements of common sense. Few would argue that animals make absolutely no moral claims on us whatsoever. Taking a chainsaw to a living tree is one thing; taking it to a living dog is quite another. It may be true that the commitments of common sense are not entirely consistent. Nevertheless, the idea that animals make at least some moral claims on us—and therefore qualify as moral patients according to (1)—is evident in commonsense attitudes. If this is correct, the efforts of Singer, Regan, and others are best understood as concerned with the scope and extent of the moral claims of animals, arguing that these claims are far more extensive and substantial than common sense takes them to be.

4. Rosalind Hursthouse, *Ethics, Humans and Other Animals* (London: Routledge, 2000); Rowlands, *Animal Rights: Moral Theory and Practice*, chapter 5.

The claim that animals are moral patients is now widely accepted—both inside and outside the world of academic philosophy—although substantial disagreements remain concerning the scope and basis of the moral claims they make on us. However, most would agree that animals can be no more than moral patients. In particular, they are not, it is almost universally accepted, moral *agents*. It is to an examination of the concept of moral agency that we now turn.

ANIMALS AS MORAL AGENTS

The concept of moral agency is closely bound up with ideas of responsibility, evaluation, and praise or blame. That is:

(2) X is a moral *agent* if and only if X is (*a*) morally responsible for, and so can be (*b*) morally evaluated (praised or blamed, broadly understood) for, its motives and actions.

Here the notions of praise and blame need not be understood as, specifically, speech acts, but cover any sort of moral appraisal whether this is verbal or part of a silent, internal soliloquy.[5] Nothing in (1) and (2), of course, rules out one and the same individual being both a moral agent and a patient: most adult humans are both.

As far as both humans and animals are concerned, it is usually assumed that this is as far as the logical geography extends. Animals can be either moral agents or patients, or both. They are not, it is generally assumed, moral agents. Therefore, at most, they are moral patients. Nevertheless, there are dissenting voices. One of the earliest of these, at least in contemporary philosophical discourse, was Stephen Clark:

5. Thanks to Colin McGinn (in conversation) for encouraging me to make this clarification.

To be a "good dog" is to have those virtues of character that must be fairly widespread in a natural population of creatures if creatures of that kind are to survive and reproduce. A good dog is discriminating in her choice of mate, faithful to her cubs, prepared to spare her rivals and to accept her place in the social hierarchy of her group with good grace. Those animals that are of a kind that can be expected to identify others as individuals, and to reflect on their own actions towards those individuals, may show some signs of having preferred the paths of virtue to those of easy gratification. Human animals alone, so far as we can see, have taken the next step, that of trying to assess their own sentiments in the light of reason.... Good animals of any kind (including the human) have some grasp of the physical and social worlds in which they live and prefer the paths of friendship and fidelity to those of war.[6]

Here Clark does not use the language of agency. But he does wish to argue that animals can be virtuous (and, presumably, vicious) and are, therefore, legitimate subjects of moral evaluation. The epithet "good" dog is not metaphorical. To be ethically virtuous, on Clark's view, it is sufficient that one respond to a situation in the way in which a virtuous person (a "good man") would respond. Animals can satisfy this condition, and thereby qualify as "ethical." They do not, however, qualify as "moral":

Beasts are ethical: that is, they respond to aspects of a situation and to features of their kindred, that a good man also would respect. But they are not moral: for they do not, as far as we can see, have any occasion to moralize about themselves or to construct intellectual systems to accommodate their immediate responses.[7]

6. Stephen R. L. Clark, "Good Dogs and Other Animals," in P. Singer ed., *In Defence of Animals* (Oxford: Blackwell, 1985), pp. 50–51.
7. Stephen R. L. Clark, *The Nature of the Beast: Are Animals Moral?* (Oxford: Oxford University Press, 1984), p. 107.

Thus, in Clark's account, we find two elements: (1) a fairly minimal condition on the possession of the moral virtues—all that is required is that one respond to a given situation in the way a virtuous person would, and (2) a distinction between the way animals and humans are moral beings. Claim (2) is, in effect, an implication of (1). Given the minimal requirement for possession of a moral virtue, Clark is forced to accept that human morality often involves more than simply responding to a situation in the way a virtuous person would. Thus, Clark accepts that while animals can be morally—or, as he puts it, "ethically"—virtuous, they are not moral beings in the sense that humans are.

Similar claims can also be identified in the work of Steven Sapontzis, another early philosophical proponent of the claim that animals are capable of acting morally. According to Sapontzis, an action's being instinctual or conditioned is compatible with its also being moral. Thus:

> An action can be instinctual in the sense of being directed by something we have inherited, or conditioned, in the sense of being directed by something we have been taught, yet still be a response to [moral] goods and evils. For example, maternal instincts are responses to the needs of the young. A wolf's care for its young is not mechanical nor carried out inflexibly, without regards to the actual needs of the young in particular situations.[8]

To qualify as moral, it is sufficient that an action be an appropriate response to the presence, in a given situation, of moral goods or evils.

---

8. Steven Sapontzis, *Morals, Reasons, and Animals* (Philadelphia: Temple University Press, 1987), p. 32.

For better or worse, unswerving dedication, loyalty, and commitment to recognized values have been and still are commonly valued as highly as, or even more highly than, the mastery of "subtle" moral reasoning."[9]

Human capacities for abstract reasoning are required for the construction of moral theories. However, to suppose they are necessary for intentional, straightforward moral action is, Sapontzis argues, to confuse moral action with moral theory.[10] Thus, we find in Sapontzis's account, as in Clark's, a minimalist account of what is required for moral action combined with an acknowledgment that human moral action is not, in all cases, the same kind of thing as animal moral action.

Sapontzis also, in my view correctly, identifies the principal arguments employed against the idea that animals can act for moral reasons. First, he identifies the basic version of the argument:[11]

A1. Only rational animals can be moral agents.

A2. Animals are not rational.

A3. Therefore, animals cannot be moral agents.

As Sapontzis notes, in connection with this argument, three questions present themselves. First, what does "rational" mean in this context? Second, why is rationality, in the sense identified, necessary for acting morally? Third, do animals lack rationality in this sense? As Sapontzis correctly notes, the claim that animals are not rational is plainly false on at least some conceptions of rationality. Animals can identify causal relations and use their understanding of such relations to solve problems. Thus, A1 presupposes a quite specific sense of rationality. Sapontzis

9. Sapontzis, *Morals, Reasons, and Animals*, p. 23.
10. Sapontzis, *Morals, Reasons, and Animals*, p. 37.
11. Sapontzis, *Morals, Reasons, and Animals*, p. 28.

argues that the implicated sense of rationality is fixed by reference to the faculties of "normal, adult human beings."[12] Let us, following Sapontzis, designate this by putting quotes around the word "normal."

With the implicated concept of rationality fixed in this way, Sapontzis argues that this basic argument against the possibility of moral agency in animals fragments into two different (though compatible) alternative elaborations. First:

B1. An action is moral only if the agent recognizes that it is the moral thing to do and does it because it is the moral thing to do (i.e., "does it for the right reason").

B2. Only beings of "normal" intelligence are capable of such recognition and motivation.

B3. Therefore, only beings of "normal" intelligence can act morally.[13]

The second elaboration of the basic argument runs as follows:

C1. Only beings that are free to choose what they will do can act morally.

C2. Only beings of "normal" intelligence are free to choose what they will do.

C3. Therefore, only beings of "normal" intelligence can act morally.

Sapontzis has, in my view, correctly identified the two historically dominant versions of the case against moral agency in animals. Much

---

12. Sapontzis, *Morals, Reasons, and Animals*, p. 29.

13. Sapontzis, *Morals, Reasons, and Animals*, p. 31. Sapontzis distinguishes between agent-dependent and agent-independent conceptions of what is "the moral thing to do." As a result, his argument is, terminologically, slightly different from the one presented here. For our purposes nothing turns on this difference.

of this book will be concerned with these arguments or their variants. Nevertheless, there are important differences between the case I shall develop and the one prosecuted by Sapontzis.

First, Sapontzis argues that animals can be moral agents. I deny this. I shall distinguish (in the "Subjects and Agents" section of this chapter) between what I shall call *moral subjects*—the category of individuals that can act for moral reasons—and moral agents, understood as the category of individuals that are responsible for what they do. Animals, I shall argue, are moral subjects but not moral agents. Thus, while Sapontzis tries to show that the arguments fail to establish that animals are not moral agents, I try to show only that they fail to establish that animals are not moral subjects. Indeed, I suspect that the arguments may, to a considerable extent, support the claim that animals are not moral agents. Defense of this latter claim, however, must be postponed until after the reconstruction of moral agency carried out in chapter 9.

Second, Sapontzis's dialectical strategy differs from the one employed in this book. Sapontzis's focus is on premise 2 of each argument—that is, on B2 and C2. He accepts, at least for the purposes of discussion, the first premise of each argument.[14] My focus will be on the first premise in each argument. I shall argue that there is a deep, logical, and historical connection between the idea that moral action requires understanding of the nature and status of one's motivations and the idea that it requires the freedom to choose one's actions. I shall argue that the idea of control underwrites both these premises. Ultimately, it is in and around this idea that the case concerning the status of animal action will be fought and adjudicated.

---

14. "Thus, for the purposes of the following discussion, we will accept premises B1´ and C1 but will show both that there are counterexamples to premises B2 and C2 and that the reasons traditionally given to support these two premises are faulty." Sapontzis, *Morals, Reasons, and Animals*, p. 32.

Both Clark and Sapontzis end up endorsing a strikingly minimalist conception of virtue possession. The possession of a moral virtue, in the final analysis, amounts to possession of a disposition that is appropriately related to moral goods whose status as such is independent of the motivations of the virtuous agent. It is worth noting—for this is a point to which we shall return in the next chapter—that this minimalist account of virtue possession is not widely accepted. Most build far more into the idea of a moral virtue than simply responding, even if this response is reliable and correct, to the morally salient features of a situation.[15] The minimalist account of virtue possession, therefore, is not something that can be assumed. It must be defended. That is one of the principal tasks of this book.

Evelyn Pluhar also supports the limited attribution of moral agency to at least some animals. She writes:

> Is it really so clear, however, that the capacity for moral agency has no precedent in any other species? Certain other capacities are required for moral agency, including capacities for emotion, memory, and goal-directed behavior. As we have seen, there is ample evidence for the presence of these capacities, if to a limited degree, in some nonhumans. Not surprisingly, then, evidence has been gathered that indicates that nonhumans are capable of what we would call "moral" or "virtuous" behavior.[16]

David DeGrazia also supports the claim that some animals should be understood as moral agents:

15. An exception is Julia Driver, *Uneasy Virtue* (New York: Cambridge University Press, 2003). I shall discuss Driver's view in chapter 9.
16. Evelyn Pluhar, *Beyond Prejudice: The Moral Significance of Human and Nonhuman Animals* (Durham, NC: Duke University Press, 1995), p. 55.

These examples support the attribution of moral agency—specifically, actions manifesting virtues—in cases in which the actions are not plausibly interpreted as instinctive or conditioned. On any reasonable understanding of moral agency, some animals are moral agents.[17]

DeGrazia distinguishes different forms of moral agency. At one end of the spectrum is the idea that a moral agent is an individual capable of (1) deliberating on the basis of what it takes to be moral reasons, (2) acting on the basis of this deliberation, and (3) justifying its action by way of an explicit argument appealing to moral reasons. Few, if any, animals would qualify as moral agents in this sense. However, DeGrazia also claims that "there are different kinds and degrees of moral agency, and the crude statement that no non-human animals are moral agents cannot be sustained."[18] When an animal acts (morally) virtuously, and its action is independent of conditioning and instinct, this also qualifies as an instance of moral agency. However, this claim is qualified by the fact that DeGrazia distinguishes moral agency from moral autonomy.[19] The latter he understands in markedly traditional terms: "Autonomous beings can question their action-regarding preferences, note their influences, and decide whether they still prefer them."[20] Few animals qualify as autonomous beings, although some might.[21] I shall not distinguish the concepts of moral agency and moral autonomy. As I employ these concepts, they are interchangeable. And I shall not defend the claim that animals can be morally autonomous. Therefore it is unclear where DeGrazia's position fits into the scheme I shall defend.

17. DeGrazia, *Taking Animals Seriously*, p. 203.
18. DeGrazia, *Taking Animals Seriously*, p. 204.
19. I am unclear as to how DeGrazia understands these concepts to be related.
20. DeGrazia, *Taking Animals Seriously*, p. 207.
21. DeGrazia, *Taking Animals Seriously*, pp. 207–10.

Nevertheless, in the work of Clark, Sapontzis, Pluhar, and DeGrazia, we find an at least qualified support for the claim that some animals can be moral agents. Cognate claims, although in varying forms, can be found outside the ranks of professional philosophers in the work of Vicki Hearne, Jeffrey Moussaieff Masson, Susan McCarthy, Stephen Wise, and (as we saw in chapter 1) Frans de Waal and Marc Bekoff.[22] As we have seen, the claims ultimately have their roots in the work of Darwin, for whom animals can be motivated by the "moral sentiments," even if they fall short of being fully "moral beings."[23]

The claim that animals can be moral agents is, I shall argue, deeply problematic—and I suspect that proponents of this view have failed to appreciate just how problematic. First of all, the concept of agency is inseparable from that of responsibility, and hence from the concepts of praise and blame. If animals are moral agents, it follows they must be responsible for what they do. But if they are responsible for what they do, then, it seems, they can be held accountable for what they do. At one time, courts of law—both nonsecular and secular— set up to try (and subsequently execute) animals for perceived crimes were not uncommon.[24] I assume few would wish to recommend a return to this practice. At the core of this unwillingness is the thought

22. Vicki Hearne, *Adam's Task: Calling Animals by Name* (New York: Vintage Books, 1987); Jeffrey Moussaieff Masson, *Dogs Never Lie About Love: Reflections on the Emotional World of Dogs* (New York: Three Rivers Press, 1997); Jeffrey Moussaieff Masson and Susan McCarthy, *When Elephants Weep: The Emotional Lives of Animals* (New York: Delacorte, 1995); Stephen Wise, *Rattling the Cage: Toward Legal Rights for Animals* (Cambridge, MA: Perseus Books, 2000); Frans de Waal, *Good Natured: The Origins of Right and Wrong in Humans and Other Animals* (Cambridge, MA: Harvard University Press, 1996); Marc Bekoff, *The Smile of a Dolphin: Remarkable Accounts of Animal Emotions* (New York: Discovery Books, 2000); Marc Bekoff, *Minding Animals: Awareness, Emotion, and Heart* (Oxford: Oxford University Press, 2002).

23. Charles Darwin, *The Descent of Man* (London: John Murray, 1871).

24. See E. P. Evans, *The Criminal Prosecution and Capital Punishment of Animals* (London: Heinemann, 1906) for a wealth of examples. See also P. Dinzelbacher, "Animal Trials: A Multidisciplinary Approach," *Journal of Interdisciplinary History* 32 (2002), 405–21.

that animals are not responsible, and so cannot be held culpable, for what they do.[25] If this is correct, then their characterization in terms of moral agency of the sort we find in Clark, Sapontzis, Pluhar, DeGrazia, and others should be resisted.

One might object that the sort of punishment meted out by these courts is not warranted by the simple attribution of responsibility. After all, the animals will not understand why they are being punished, and the punishment will, therefore, play no role in amending their errant behavior.[26] Nor, it seems, will it play any role in deterring other animals from pursuing a "life of crime." This objection, I think, faces two problems. First, and less seriously, it only precludes punishment carried out for purposes of character reformation or deterrence. Punishment performed for retributive purposes would be permissible. Second, and more seriously, the objection merely succeeds in reinforcing the claim that animals are not moral agents. Why is it that the offending animals do not understand the connection between their actions and the subsequent punishment? This, it seems, can only be because they are incapable of grasping relations between cause and effect of the sort required to grasp the significance of their original offense. If so, they would fail to qualify as moral agents—if we assume that an understanding (the significance, likely impact, and so on) of what one is doing is a necessary condition of responsibility.

Bekoff and Pierce seem, to some extent, to be alive to the danger of attributing moral agency to animals. Their attitude toward the claim that animals can be moral agents is ambivalent.

By claiming that animals have morality, many people assume that we're also claiming that animals are moral agents.... [However,]

25. I shall explore, in a later chapter, the circumstances in which attribution of agency to non-humans might be justifiable, and the type of agency implicated in this attribution. This possibility is left open by the variegated conception of moral agency mentioned earlier.
26. My thanks to Colin McGinn (in conversation) for this objection.

agency, in general, needs to be rethought.... To claim that animals have moral agency is not, of course, to argue for sameness.... Moral agency is species-specific and context-specific. Furthermore, animals are moral agents within the limited context of their own communities.... Although we are willing to call animals moral agents, we believe the language of agent and patient is likely to promote philosophical confusion and should ultimately be avoided.[27]

There seem to be two distinct claims here—reflected in their distinction between moral agency as "species-specific" and "context-specific." According to the first claim—that of species-specificity—the *character* of moral agency varies from one species to another. In this regard, they quote approvingly from a paper by Paul Shapiro: "It would be naïve to assert that other animals are moral agents in the same sense in which most adult humans are."[28] This claim we have already identified in the work of Clark and Sapontzis: human moral agency, infused with abilities to engage in critical rational scrutiny and debate, is, in many cases, more complex than that of animals. We have also, in chapter 1, already encountered the potential danger inherent in a claim such as this. The danger is that it makes claims of animal moral agency vacuous. Animals qualify as moral agents only because we have defined moral agency in a peculiarly, and arguably inaccurately, inclusive way. At the core of the issue we find the minimal account of virtue possession endorsed by both Clark and Sapontzis. I shall return to this issue in the section "Normativity and Moral Agency" below.

The second is that of context-specificity. It is not entirely clear what this means, but the following passage seems to be indicative of what Bekoff and Pierce have in mind:

27. Bekoff and Pierce, *Wild Justice*, 144–45.
28. Paul Shapiro, "Moral Agency in Other Animals," *Theoretical Medicine* 27 (2006), 357–73. This sentence is quoted on p. 144 of Bekoff and Pierce, *Wild Justice*.

Wolf morality reflects a code of conduct that guides the behavior of wolves within a given community of wolves. Wolves are agents only within this context. The predatory behavior of a wolf toward an elk is *amoral*—it is not subject to condemnation or accolades.[29]

That is, while the species-specificity claim pertains to the character of moral agency, the context-specificity claim pertains to the appropriate objects of moral concern and action. These are restricted to groups ("contexts"). So the wolf can act morally only toward other wolves—indeed, toward members of its own pack. More generally, an animal that belongs to a given group cannot act morally (or immorally) toward individuals that do not belong to that group.

The function of Bekoff and Pierce's idea of context-specificity seems to be to allay one of the dangers inherent in the claim that animals can act morally. While expressing dissatisfaction with the idea of moral agency, Bekoff and Pierce endorse the claim that animals can act morally. However, moral action seems to entail the possibility of moral evaluation of that action. Few would want to claim, however, that when one animal eats another, it acts immorally. This is the danger, and the idea of context-specificity provides a response: the limits of moral action are limned by the limits of the group. However, this response is deeply problematic. In fact, I doubt that Bekoff, at least, will, on reflection, be willing to endorse it. First, there is a rather tricky problem of identifying the group. To see this, consider a rather touching story that Bekoff has told on more than occasion:

Marc's late dog Jethro once brought home a tiny bunny, whose mother had likely been killed by a mountain lion near Marc's home. Jethro dropped the bunny at the front door and when Marc came to the front door he looked up as if to say, "please

29. Bekoff and Pierce, *Wild Justice*, pp. 144–45.

help." Marc brought the bunny into his house, and put it into a cardboard box with water, carrots and lettuce. For the next two weeks, Jethro was pinned to the side the box, refusing to go out for walks, and often missing meals.[30]

It is reasonably clear that Bekoff thinks this is behavior for which Jethro should be commended: Jethro was acting morally. However, this does not seem compatible with their context-specificity claim. For it is difficult to see in what sense the bunny was a member of Jethro's group. Obviously, on pain of circularity, we cannot define Jethro's group in terms of the individuals toward which he does, in fact, act morally. So why is there any reason for thinking that the bunny belongs to Jethro's group? But if he does not, why is Jethro's behavior morally commendable? On Bekoff and Pierce's account, Jethro's behavior should be regarded as amoral. To take another example, is the toleration and patience that my rather un-Jethro-like German shepherd, Hugo, displays toward my children morally commendable, whereas the somewhat different behavior he displays toward the postman simply outside the scope of morality? Or if Hugo behaves well toward a neighbor's dog but not so well toward a stranger's dog, is it really plausible to suppose that there is such a gulf between the cases that Hugo's behavior can be assessed morally in the former case but not in the latter? In the case of social mammals living in the wild, it is often relatively easy to determine where the group begins and ends. But when we switch to domesticated animals, that clarity is lost.

Second, context-specificity—the idea that the limits of one's moral action coincide with the limits of one's group—seems to be incompatible with the idea that animals are moral patients. If the wolf's behavior toward the elk cannot be assessed morally, why suppose that our behavior toward, for example, intensively raised pigs is

30. Bekoff and Pierce, *Wild Justice*, p. 108.

a moral issue? The idea that we have moral obligations toward animals is, however, one that Bekoff enthusiastically advocates. The incompatibility of this claim with the moral standing—patienthood—of animals is not, of course, necessarily a strike against that position. Indeed, some might regard it as a strength. However, more generally, the idea that the limits of moral action are limned by the limits of one's group has underwritten some of the most pernicious social doctrines that humans have been capable of devising. And, I shall argue later, there is no need to go down that particular road.

The idea of the context-specificity is, I suspect, a deeply problematic one; and the case I shall develop for the possibility of moral action in animals makes no use of this idea. Instead, it employs a distinction not found in the work of the authors considered in this section. *Pace* Bekoff and Pierce, I suspect there is nothing wrong with the concept of a moral agent: that concept is clear, coherent, and relatively straightforward. But it would be a mistake to suppose that animals fall under this concept. Animals are not moral agents, but, nevertheless, I shall argue that they can act for moral reasons. They are not moral agents but they still can be moral *subjects*.

SUBJECTS AND AGENTS

I shall argue, although the argument proper takes much of this book to develop, that there is another available, as yet unoccupied, location in the logical geography of our discussions of the moral status of animals. While animals are indeed moral patients in the sense expressed in (1), and not moral agents in the sense expressed in (2),[31] they can also be moral subjects, where

31. In chapter 9, I shall place some qualifications on this blanket denial of moral agency to animals.

(3) X is a moral *subject* if and only if X is, at least sometimes, motivated to act by moral reasons.

The concept of a moral subject has almost invariably been conflated with that of a moral agent: to say that X is motivated to act by moral considerations is almost invariably thought to be equivalent to the claim that X is responsible for, and so can be praised or blamed for, what it does.[32] In some ways this conflation is odd: for as definitions (2) and (3) make clear, these claims are quite distinct. Claim (2) is one that concerns evaluation, but claim (3) concerns motivation. Moral agency and moral subjecthood should be as conceptually distinct as the concept of evaluation is distinct from the concept of motivation. And it is reasonably clear that, in general, these are quite different things: the motivation for an action is one thing, the evaluation of the action or the motivation quite another. Indeed, an evaluation is often of a motivation.

Nevertheless, there are powerful reasons—both logical and historical—for supposing that this general distinction between motivation and evaluation is not applicable in the *specifically* moral case—that is, in the case of specifically moral motivation and moral evaluation. This section explores the *general* distinction between motivation and evaluation—and argues that, in general, the concept of a subject of motivation does not collapse into that of an agent. That is, in general, a subject of motivation is not equivalent to an object of evaluation. The following section examines why this distinction is thought to break down in the specifically moral case.

Here is a way of making the general motivation/evaluation distinction—and hence the distinction between subjects of motivation and objects of evaluation—a little more graphic. Suppose that my

---

32. I use the term "almost" for the sake of safety. I know of nowhere in the literature where the concept of moral agency has been distinguished from the concept of moral subjecthood.

wife, worn down by the domestic squalor that goes with two young boys, a large dog, and a slovenly husband, has me (unknowingly) hypnotized. Now, whenever she utters the word "Rosebud," I experience an uncontrollable desire to mop the floor. This desire is, it seems, a motivational state, one that when combined with relevant cognitive states (the belief that this is a mop, the belief that this is a floor, and so on) will, ceteris paribus, result in a certain sort of behavior on my part. This floor mopping, however, is not something for which I can be praised or blamed. *Ex hypothesi*, it is the result of a motivational state that is outside my control. In other words, my behavior is motivated by a certain state, but this state is not the sort of thing for which I can be morally evaluated. The motivation for my behavior is one thing; the evaluation of that behavior is quite another. If hard determinism—in effect, a generalization of this case—were true, then no one could be morally evaluated for what she does, but it would not follow that she was not the subject of motivational states.

One objection is likely to proceed as follows: If someone has no control over the motivational state that provides the (whole or partial) cause of his behavior, then that state cannot be thought of as providing a reason for his behavior. Therefore, he is not, in fact, a subject of motivation in the relevant sense. This objection, however, is difficult to sustain. First, my uncontrollable desire to mop the floor does seem to be (part of) the reason why I am mopping the floor. If we want to deny this, we must be building much into the idea of a reason beyond that contained in common sense; and the burden of proof is, accordingly, going to be on those who want to aggrandize the notion in this way. If someone were to ask: "Why is Rowlands mopping the floor?" an appropriate answer would be: "He has an uncontrollable desire to do so." In response, one might comment: "That's most unlike him," and then the explanation might be continued: "His wife had him hypnotized." The latter explanation cites a cause of my uncontrollable desire. But the first explanation cites what certainly seems to be (a component of) a reason for my action. It is the content of my desire that I mop the floor that, when combined with the beliefs that what I have in my hand is a mop and that what lies beneath my feet is a floor, explains why I am acting in the way that I do. This deployment of content is commonly taken to be a hallmark of reason-giving explanations.

Nevertheless, one might object, while the uncontrollable desire to mop the floor is the sort of thing that can be a reason (or, rather, a component of a reason—I'll henceforth ignore this complication), it is not *my* reason. It is not my reason because I have no control over it. However, if we accept that the desire is (a component of) a reason, then the idea that it is not my reason seems difficult to sustain. Whose reason would it be if not mine? There are two possibilities:

(1) It is someone else's reason.
(2) It is nobody's reason.

The first option need not detain us. It is, after all, I and not anyone else that is mopping the floor. So the relevant alternative is (2). The problem with (2) is that it commits us to the possibility of ownerless reasons: that there can exist a reason that is a reason for no one. However, there are no ownerless reasons. All reasons are reasons for someone.

One temptation to suppose that there can be such things as owner-less reasons might stem from confusing the owned/ownerless distinction with a quite different one: the distinction between motivating and justifying reasons.[33] (The latter are sometimes also known as norma-tive reasons. However, the term "normative" will figure prominently in future discussion, and for reasons of clarity I shall reserve it for that purpose.) For example, given that I want to stay healthy, I have a reason

33. See, for example, Michael Smith, *The Moral Problem* (Oxford: Basil Blackwell, 1994).

to take regular exercise. If I understand the connection between exercise and health, then I have a motivating reason to exercise. If I know nothing of this connection, I have no such motivating reason. But it is still true that, given my desire for health, I have a reason to exercise—a justifying reason. A motivating reason is, roughly, one that drives or shapes an agent's behavior. A justifying reason need not do this—if, for example, the agent is unaware of it or its importance. Nevertheless, it is still a reason that the agent has—whether he knows it nor not. So we should resist any temptation to suppose that justifying reasons are ownerless. The reason I have to engage in regular exercise is, precisely, a reason that I have, and it is linked to a more basic desire of mine to stay healthy. Both motivating and justifying reasons track a person's interests—just in different ways. Therefore, both motivating and justifying reasons are owned: they belong to someone.

This conclusion might lead us to suspect that examples of ownerless reasons can be found by way of another distinction—that between internal and external reasons.[34] An internal reason for action is one that furthers a certain motive of the agent—whether the agent actually has this motive, or whether she would come to have this motive by following a "sound deliberative route."[35] Thus, internal reasons subsume both motivating and justifying reasons. An agent would have an external reason to φ if (1) she has reason to φ, and (2) there is no motive or interest of hers that is furthered by φ-ing. Whether there are such things as external reasons is controversial. Bernard Williams, who introduced them into philosophical discourse, went on to argue that there were no such things. We need not get involved. For our purposes, it is enough to note that even if there are such things as external reasons, they are not the same thing as owner-

34. Bernard Williams, "Internal and External Reasons," in his *Moral Luck* (Cambridge: Cambridge University Press, 1981), pp. 101–13.

35. Bernard Williams, *Making Sense of Humanity* (Cambridge: Cambridge University Press, 1995), p. 35.

less reasons. An external reason has its natural home in moral contexts. Those who believe in external reasons typically claim that one has a reason to do the right thing, even if there is no interest that one has that is furthered by doing so. This is sufficient to make it clear both that and why an external reason is not an ownerless one. An external reason to do the right thing is one that I have. It is also one that you would have, and that anyone else would have. External reasons are ones that everybody has—irrespective of their motives or interests. They are not reasons that nobody has.

Therefore: if there are no ownerless reasons, my desire to mop the floor is (1) a reason, and (2) my reason. It is a reason that motivates me to act, but not a reason for which I can be evaluated. The question of motivation is one thing; the question of evaluation is another. The general conceptual distinction between subjects and agents follows from this distinction between the motivation of an individual's action and the evaluation of that action.

Nevertheless, while the general distinction may be a legitimate one, there are persuasive reasons for supposing that it is not applicable in the specifically moral case. That is, when the type of motivation in question is moral motivation and the type of evaluation in question is moral evaluation, the general distinction between motivation and evaluation is no longer applicable. Thus, the standard view is that there is no distinction between a moral agent and a moral subject: the concept of the former collapses into that of the latter. The next section examines why this is commonly—indeed, almost invariably—thought to be the case.

NORMATIVITY AND MORAL AGENCY

As we saw earlier, evident in the work of people such as Clark and Sapontzis is a strikingly minimalist account of virtue possession.

According to Clark, to be morally virtuous it is sufficient that one respond to a situation in the way a virtuous person would. According to Sapontzis, to be morally virtuous requires only that one respond appropriately to the presence of morally salient features of a situation—moral "goods and evils." Few virtue theorists have been willing to follow Clark and Sapontzis in this regard: most build considerably more into the conditions required for possession of a moral virtue. And what is true of moral virtue is true of moral motivation more generally. Moral motivation, it is typically thought, requires far more than simply responding in appropriate ways to the morally salient features of situations. That this became the typical way of thinking about moral motivation is no accident, but stems precisely from the sorts of things moral motivations are supposed to be.

The example employed in the previous section required us to imagine a situation in which an individual—me—was motivated to act by a state that could plausibly be regarded as a reason (or component of a reason) for my action. However, in the imagined circumstance, I had no control over this motivation, and so could not be held responsible—broadly, praise or blamed—for its consequences. In the case of nonmoral motivation of this sort, the presence of a motivation in a subject is compatible with that subject having no control over this motivation or its presence. However, there are reasons for thinking that moral motivations are not like this. That is, there are reasons for thinking that a motivation can count as moral only if its subject has control over it.

To see this, imagine a person: let us call him, for reasons that I assume are relatively obvious, Sigmund. Sigmund is *motivation-blind*. That is, his motivations are always hidden from him. This is not to say that Sigmund has no self-knowledge at all—he is aware of his non-motivational states, to the extent he has them. It is only the motivational faculty of his mind that is closed to him. This part of his mind is something like a black box: replete with states that successfully guide Sigmund's behavior, but to which he has no first-person access. Sigmund is perhaps a little bemused to see that he is reacting appropriately to the slings and arrows of environmental circumstance. When buses hurtle toward him, he neatly steps out of the way. But he has no idea what motivates him to do so. He might be aware that he sees the bus, for example, and believe that there is a bus about to mow him down, but he is unaware that he wants to avoid it. Nonetheless, avoid it he does. The best he can do, in this regard, is engage in a little ex post facto hypothesizing. "I must have wanted to avoid that bus," muses Sigmund.

There is an obvious sense in which Sigmund is, as we might put it, "at the mercy" of his motivations. When engaged in action, he has no idea what motivates him to act in the way he does, and therefore has no control over those motivations (and, consequently, over what they do). He might respond appropriately to whatever the environment throws at him. But from his point of view, at least when he is engaged in thus responding, this seems like an improbable, if fortuitous, coincidence. In short, Sigmund has no control over his motivations, because he has no access to them.

Because he has no control over his motivations, it seems plausible to conclude that Sigmund is not an agent—certainly not in the sense that a normal adult human is usually taken to be an agent. Rather, Sigmund is pulled this and way that by motivations to which he is blind. To be an agent, it is usually thought, requires control over one's motivations, for without control there can be no responsibility. And if Sigmund is not an agent then, *a fortiori*, he is not a moral agent.

Nevertheless, even if Sigmund is not an agent, it is still true that he is motivated to act in various ways, even if he is blind to these motivations.[36] It is, therefore, still true that he is a subject of

36. Note I say that Sigmund might not be an agent. I do not say he is not an agent. The subject of agency will be discussed in chapter 8.

motivation. If so, then being an agent is not a necessary condition of being a subject of motivation. The question is: can he also be a subject of specifically moral motivation? Control over his motivations might be required for Sigmund to be a moral *agent*. But why should it be required for Smith to be a moral *subject*?

The answer is to be found in the Kantian dictum that *ought implies can*. Given that Sigmund has no access to his motivations, he has no control over them. Since he has no control over his motivations, they are not the sorts of thing that Sigmund can embrace or resist. But if Sigmund's motivations are not the sort of thing he *can* embrace or resist, then it makes no sense to say that he *should* embrace or resist them. Sigmund's motivations, in this sense, have no normative dimension. That is, they are not the sorts of things he *should* embrace or resist, endorse or reject. His motivations, therefore, make no *normative claim* on Sigmund. However, moral motivations are precisely things that make normative claims—exert a normative *grip*—on their subjects. Morally good motivations are ones that should be embraced by their subject; morally evil motivations are ones that should be resisted. Therefore, it seems we are committed to denying that Sigmund's motivations are moral ones.

The deep connection between normativity and control now becomes evident. Sigmund's having control over his motivations is a necessary condition of their possessing normative properties—of their making normative claims on him. Ought implies can: without a can there can be no ought. Therefore, without control there can be no normativity. Whatever else is true of Sigmund's motivations, they are not moral ones. Therefore, if an individual is not a moral agent, he cannot be a moral subject either. Being a moral agent is a necessary condition of being a moral subject.

It is also, fairly obviously, a sufficient condition. Holding someone responsible for his actions presupposes that what he has performed are actions. But whether or not something qualifies as an action depends on its connection to an antecedent motivation. What this motivation is, and the connection it bears to the resulting action, will vary according to one's preferred theory of action. But any theory of action will require that an action stand in some specified relation to a motivation. In short, one cannot be an agent without being a subject of motivation; and one cannot be a moral agent without being a subject of moral motivation.

Therefore, there are persuasive arguments in support of the claim that being a moral agent is both a necessary and a sufficient condition for being a moral subject. If so, then the general reluctance to distinguish moral subjects and moral agents is both natural and justified. If these arguments are correct, motivational states cannot make a normative claim on their subjects unless those subjects have control over those motivations. Accordingly, there are no moral subjects that are not also moral agents (and, in fact, vice versa). So the position I have said I want to defend—the possibility of there being moral subjects that are not moral agents, and animals being those subjects—seems dead in the water.

Nevertheless, this is the position I am going to defend. In the second half of this book, I am going to pick apart the largely unquestioned connection between normativity and control. I am going to pick apart this connection by showing that the requisite concept of control has no substance and cannot do the work it is supposed to do—namely, underwrite the normative status of motivations. But before I get to those arguments, I first want to broaden and deepen the case I am required to answer. This section has developed what we might think of as the *logical* case against the idea that moral subjects can be distinguished from moral agents. But this logical case has received important historical expression and elaboration in the moral theories of some of the most influential philosophers of all time. The precise form of this expression and elaboration varies with other commitments these philosophers hold. Nevertheless, the deep connection between normativity and control is evident in all of these theories. The following chapter examines two particularly important elaborations of the normativity-control connection: those contained in the moral theories of Aristotle and Kant.

4

The Reflection Condition:
Aristotle and Kant

ARISTOTLE AND THE VIRTUES

A virtue, as understood in the context of virtue ethics, is a *character trait* that is deeply entrenched in its possessor and also, crucially, multifactorial.[1] To say that it is *deeply entrenched* in its possessor is to say that it manifests itself on more than one occasion—indeed on many occasions—and as more than a single type of action. For example, if Smith possesses the virtue of honesty, this will manifest itself not just in the fact that she does not steal from others, but also in the fact that she will do her best to return what others have lost (rather than pocketing it for herself). And these sorts of behaviors are not ones she exhibits sporadically, but are relatively constant through time. All things being equal, she will return lost money not merely today, but on any day that she happens to find some. To say that a virtue is *multifactorial* is to say that it consists in more than behavioral tendencies or dispositions alone, even if these are stable through time. For Smith to have the virtue of honesty, for example, is not simply for her to have the tendency to do honest things. It is also for her to have the tendency to deplore dishonesty, both in others and, on those rare

---

1. This account is based on that defended by Rosalind Hursthouse, *On Virtue Ethics* (Oxford: Oxford University Press, 1999).

occasions she acts dishonestly, in herself also. It is for her to feel out-rage when she witnesses this dishonesty, and to make her outrage known, and so on. In order to be constitutive of a virtue, the stable behavioral dispositions must be located in an appropriate surround-ing context of beliefs, emotions, and attitudes of this sort. Implicated in the possession of a virtue, therefore, is not simply a disposition to behave in a certain way in given circumstances, but also the disposi-tion to have emotions, beliefs, feelings, and so on that are "appropriate" to these circumstances. The reason for this is pretty clear. A person can have the deeply entrenched tendency to do what is honest and refrain from doing what is dishonest because, and only because, she has the fear, equally deeply entrenched, of being caught. Since, in this case, the tendency to do what is honest and refrain from doing what is dis-honest is not situated in the appropriate surrounding milieu of emo-tions, beliefs, and other evaluative acts—it is not multifactorial—her tendency is not part of a virtue of honesty. She possesses no such virtue. Therefore, it would be unwise to attribute to a person a virtue on the basis of observing her actions—even if these actions are consis-tent through time—if one does not know the reasons for actions. In the possession of a virtue, actions, beliefs, and emotions are bound up in an indissoluble whole. Armed with these considerations, we can define the concept of a moral virtue as follows:

A moral virtue is a (1) a morally good, admirable, or otherwise praiseworthy *character trait*, where (2) this character trait consists in a relatively stable set of behavioral dispositions that are (3) embedded in an appropriate surrounding milieu of beliefs, emotions, and atti-tudes (broadly understood).[2]

The corresponding notion of a moral vice can then be defined as a bad, unworthy, or blameworthy character trait, where we understand

---

2. See, Rowlands, *Animal Rights: Moral Theory and Practice*, p. 99. I need take no stand, here, on the question of what makes a character trait a specifically moral one—good, admirable, or praiseworthy in a specifically moral, rather than an executive, sense.

the notion of a character trait and surrounding milieu in the same way. The concept of moral virtue is, of course, correlative to the concept of moral vice. To have a moral virtue is, at the same time, to abhor the corresponding vice. On the basis of this concept of a moral virtue, we can then define the morally virtuous person as one who has, and exercises, the various moral virtues—understood as defined above. Since having and exercising a given virtue precludes having and exercising the corresponding vice, a morally virtuous person is one who acts according to virtue (and so does not act according to vice).

As we saw in the previous chapter, Clark, DeGrazia, and Pluhar all framed their claims about the moral agency of animals in terms of the language of virtue.[3] The definition outlined above, however, introduces an element of psychological complexity to the possession of a virtue that, perhaps, they would not endorse. Nevertheless, it does not, on its own, preclude animals from possessing moral virtues—as long as we assume that animals can act, can believe, and can experience emotions. Nevertheless, the use of the concept of virtue to characterize the moral capabilities of an individual has its roots in the work of Aristotle; and Aristotle certainly would not have agreed that animals can be morally virtuous. The reason is that the Aristotelian account introduces one further element of psychological complexity into the possession of a moral virtue. His conditions on virtue possession are, accordingly, far more demanding than those adopted—implicitly or otherwise—by Clark, DeGrazia, and Pluhar.

In this passage from the *Nichomachean Ethics*, Aristotle emphasizes the psychological complexity of the virtues:

> But for actions in accord with the virtues to be done transparently or justly it does not suffice that they themselves have the right qualities. Rather, the agent must also be in the right state

3. Although Pluhar did employ what seem to be scare quotes when she used that language.

when he does them. First he must know that he is doing virtuous actions; second, he must decide on them, and decide on them for themselves; and, third, he must also do them from a firm and unchanging state.[4]

For an action to be an expression of a virtue, it must not simply be an example of what would commonly be regarded as a virtuous action (have the "right qualities"). In addition, the agent must (a) know that he is performing a virtuous action and (b) perform the action because it is a virtuous action ("decide on them for themselves"), and (c) this decision must be an expression of a stable disposition on the part of the agent.

It is the conjunction of conditions (a) and (b) that underlie Aristotle's hostility to the idea that animals could act virtuously. Together, they impose a minimal condition of reflection on the virtuous agent. To satisfy these conditions, the agent must understand what a virtue is, and be motivated by this understanding to perform a certain action because it would be virtuous—an expression of this virtue. I shall call this—the conjunction of (a) and (b)—the *reflection condition* on possession of a virtue:

For any action φ, performed by agent A, to be an expression of virtue, V, it is necessary that A (1) be able to understand that φ is an instance of V, and (2) perform φ because he wishes to be virtuous.

Condition (1) is not unambiguous. The notion of understanding that something is a virtue can be interpreted in two ways, one more cognitively demanding than the other. The cognitively demanding way interprets understanding φ to be a virtue as "understanding φ to fall

4. Aristotle, *Nichomachean Ethics*, trans. T. Irwin (Indianapolis: Hackett, 1999), 1105a27–35.

under the concept of virtue." This requirement seems unreasonably strong. If correct, someone could not know whether something was a virtue unless she were in possession of the correct concept of a virtue, and so must, among other things, be familiar with the debates surrounding the definition of this concept, and have (correctly) adjudicated between the competing positions. Few—animal or human— would understand that φ is a virtue in this sense.[5] According to a weaker—and, accordingly, more reasonable—interpretation, understanding that φ is an instance of a virtue only requires that agent A be able to distinguish, with a reasonable though not necessarily infallible level of success, those things that are virtuous from those things that are not.[6] I shall understand (1) in this weaker sense.

Why think that virtue possession must conform to the reflection condition? More precisely, why think that the reflection condition constitutes a necessary condition of the possession of a virtue? Aristotle closely ties the reflection condition to what, in the previous chapter, I labeled the *normative grip* of a virtue. Virtues and vices make normative claims on their subjects. Virtues are things individuals *should* aspire to possess and exercise. Vices are things individuals *should* aspire to excise from their personality.

Recall the death of Eleanor, matriarch of the First Ladies family of elephants, described in chapter 1. Grace, we might suppose, is motivated to attempt to help Eleanor by her sentiment of concern or compassion. However, a sentiment, in itself, will simply cause whatever it

5. In such circumstances, virtue, it seems, would be the preserve of a smallish number of professional moral philosophers. This may indeed have been something like Aristotle's view. But, in my view, it constitutes a *reductio*.

6. Consider an analogous case: the notion of understanding what water is. On the one hand, this might mean understanding something as falling under the concept of water—which, at least on one way of thinking about concepts, someone can do only if she is in possession of the concepts of hydrogen, oxygen, etc. On the other hand, it can mean being able to differentiate, with a reasonable though not necessarily infallible level of precision, which things count as water and which things do not. Children and the uneducated can understand what water is even if they do not possess the concept of water (in this stronger sense).

causes. Attempting to help Eleanor is something that Grace does, but can we give any sense to the claim that Grace was exhibiting a moral virtue when she acted in this way? This question actually divides into two: (1) Can we make sense of the idea that Grace is morally virtuous to feel compassion for Eleanor in these circumstances? (2) Can we make sense of the claim that Grace's behavior is a morally virtuous response to this sentiment? The sentiment, we are supposing, exerts *causal* pressure on Grace's behavior—in the sense of being the triggering cause of it. But can we make sense of the idea that it also exerts *normative* pressure? Is the sentiment one that Grace *should* have in these circumstances, and is her resulting behavior something that she *should* perform? An affirmative answer to (1) and (2) requires that there be normative standards of correctness governing both the having of the sentiment and the relation between the sentiment and the action.

For Aristotle, the second element of normativity is explained by the fact that, when they occur as constituents of a virtue, sentiment and action are internally, not externally, related. In other words, the normative character of the relation between sentiment and action is explained by way of the normative structure of virtue itself. To explain the first element of normativity, Aristotle needs to show that any given virtue is something that is appropriate to the circumstance in which it is exhibited. That is, he needs to show that the given context calls for or requires the exercise of this specific virtue: if the virtue is not exercised in this context, then something has gone wrong. If he can explain this first element of normativity, then the second comes for free—as a consequence of the normative structure of virtue.

Aristotle has two mutually reinforcing explanations of the first element of normativity. First, he emphasizes that the virtues are things that must be acquired:

> The virtues arise in us neither by nature nor against nature. Rather, we are by nature able to acquire them, and we are com-

pleted through habit. . . . Virtues, by contrast [to the senses], we acquire, just as we acquire crafts, by having first activated them. For we learn a craft by producing the same product that we must produce when we have learned it; we become builders, for example, by building, and we become harpists by playing the harp. Similarly, then, we become just by doing just actions, temperate by doing temperate actions, brave by doing brave actions.[7]

A virtue is something that must be acquired, and so can be acquired well or poorly, properly or improperly—and this possibility introduces at least an element of normativity into the possession of a virtue. This is why we can be praised or blamed for their possession or lack thereof. If virtues were like the senses, whose possession is a matter of nature and not our efforts, we could not be morally evaluated for their possession or lack—whether we have them or not is nature's "choice," not ours.

Second, and for our purposes more important, a virtue is something that can be exercised well or poorly. In a well-known passage from the *Nichomachean Ethics*, Aristotle remarks:

So also getting angry, or giving and spending money, is easy and everyone can do it; but doing it to the right person, in the right amount, at the right time, for the right end, and in the right way is no longer easy, nor can everyone do it. Hence, doing these things well is rare, praiseworthy, and fine.[8]

Whether or not an action counts as the expression of a virtue is a context-sensitive matter: only if the action is done to the right person,

7. Aristotle, *Nichomachean Ethics*, 1103a19–b2.
8. Aristotle, *Nichomachean Ethics*, 1109a27–30.

in the right amount, at the right time, and so on, does it count as the expression of a virtue. But whether the person is the right one, whether the amount is correct, whether the time is right—all these are difficult matters that call for judgment. This judgment is something that can be executed well or poorly: mistakes are always possible. And it is the possibility of mistake in the application of a virtue that underlies the normative grip of a virtue on the world.

In this passage, Aristotle is drawing attention to the importance of *practical wisdom*, or *phronesis*, in the possession of the moral virtues. While Grace's actual motivation in trying to help Eleanor is, of course, an empirical matter, let us suppose that she is, in fact, motivated by a sentiment such as sympathy or compassion.[9] If this sentiment were suitably entrenched in Grace's emotional profile—she is disposed to help other elephants in similar difficulties, and so on—then we might accept that Grace possesses the *natural* virtue of compassion. However, a natural virtue is not the same thing as a moral virtue. Moral virtues are what natural virtues become when they are supplemented by phronesis. As Hursthouse puts it:

> Both the virtuous adult and the nice child have good intentions, but the child is much more prone to mess things up because he is ignorant of what he needs to know in order to do what he intends....Adults are culpable if they mess things up by being thoughtless, insensitive, reckless, impulsive, shortsighted, and by assuming that what suits them will suit everyone instead of taking a more objective viewpoint. They are also, importantly, culpable if their understanding of what is beneficial and harmful is mistaken. It is part of practical wisdom to know how to secure

9. Or, if one prefers, a phenomenological facsimile of these emotions. One might, reasonably, maintain that such emotions are essentially moral ones, and the question of whether Grace is capable of moral emotions—as opposed to states that are merely phenomenologically akin to such emotions—has not yet been answered.

real benefits effectively.... Quite generally, given that good intentions are intentions to act well or "do the right thing," we may say
that practical wisdom is the knowledge or understanding that
enables its possessor, unlike the nice adolescents, to do just that,
in any given situation.[10]

The "nice" adolescent may possess natural virtues such as sympathy,
but in the absence of properly developed powers of phronesis, that is
all these virtues can be. Conversely, when an individual in possession
of natural virtues also possesses the requisite practical wisdom, those
merely natural virtues can now be transformed into properly moral
virtues. Let us call this the phronesis condition: an appropriate level
of phronesis is a necessary condition of the possession of the moral
virtues.

It would be a mistake to think that the reflection condition and
the phronesis condition are logically independent strands of
Aristotle's account of moral virtue. On the contrary, the connection
between the two conditions is intimate. According to the reflection
condition, to act virtuously, one must understand that the mooted
course of action is the virtuous thing to do in these circumstances,
and one must be motivated to do it precisely because it is the virtuous
thing to do in these circumstances. But how does one know this?
Aristotle's emphasis on phronesis is a reflection of the fact that one
does not attain this sort of understanding by turning one's attention
inwards and focusing on one's motivation—as if trying to glean its
virtuous status from intrinsic, introspectively accessible properties it
possesses. Rather, one understands that the course of action one is
inclined to follow is virtuous by understanding the morally salient
features of the situation—by understanding what the situation calls

10. Rosalind Hursthouse, "Virtue Ethics," *Stanford Encyclopedia of Philosophy*, http://plato.
stanford.edu/entries/ethics-virtue/.

for, or requires, morally speaking.[11] In other words, the phronesis condition is a way of understanding how an individual can come to satisfy the reflection condition. It may not be the whole story of how this condition comes to be satisfied. But if Aristotle is correct, it is an important part of this story.

The deep connection between normativity and control, identified in the previous chapter, is evident in Aristotle's account of moral virtue. Think of what Grace, from an Aristotelian perspective, lacks. Can Grace understand, as the reflection condition requires, that helping Eleanor would be a virtuous thing to do in these circumstances, and does she act because she wants to do what is virtuous? If Grace is unable to entertain these, and related, thoughts, then, from an Aristotelian perspective, no sense can be given to the idea that she is acting virtuously. Similarly, switching our focus from the reflection to the phronesis condition, we can ask: does Grace believe that pushing Eleanor to her feet is the wise thing to do in these circumstances, rather than merely compounding the suffering of an elephant that is done for anyway? Again, if we assume that Grace is unable to entertain questions of this form, we might conclude that she is lacking in the phronesis required for the possession of properly moral virtues, rather than their natural counterparts. From an Aristotelian perspective, lacking in the related abilities of reflection and phronesis, no sense can be given to the claim that Grace is doing what she *ought* to do. Grace is simply the subject of a feeling or sentiment on which she cannot reflect, and with respect to which she cannot bring to bear practical reasoning abilities. As a result, this sentiment simply pushes her this way and that. She has no control over whether she has this sentiment,

11. Compare: When someone asks me if I believe the problem of sovereign debt will precipitate a financial crisis as severe as the one caused by bank debt, I do not turn my attention inwards, shuffle through my beliefs, and then inwardly say to myself—"Yes, there it is. I do believe it!" I turn my attention outwards toward the worldly facts that would lead me to one conclusion or the other.

and no control over whether she acts on it or does not. She is, we might say, "at the mercy" of this sentiment (and others like it).

Therefore, the sentiment has no *normative grip* on Grace. That is, it is not the sort of thing that Grace should either embrace or resist. The sentiment simply does whatever it does to Grace, and she has no say in this matter. Given that Grace has no control over the sentiment and the various behaviors to which it disposes her, no sense can be given to the idea that she *should* endorse or reject the sentiment and resulting behaviors. But moral motivations are essentially things that have a normative grip on their subjects: morally good motivations are ones that should be embraced; morally bad ones should be resisted. Therefore neither Grace's motivation nor her resulting behavior can be regarded as moral. This is the guiding thought that Aristotle dresses in the language of virtue. The function of reflection and phronesis is ultimately to give subjects authority over their motivations: to make them the sort of thing one *should* embrace or resist by making them the sort of thing one *can* embrace or resist. Thus, in Aristotle, we find a historical iteration of the logical theme identified in the previous chapter: without control there can be no normativity.

THE KANTIAN TRADITION: NORMATIVE SELF-GOVERNMENT

Moral philosophers influenced by Kant or the Kantian moral tradition would have no hesitation in denying that, in attempting to help Eleanor, Grace is acting morally. For example, Christine Korsgaard, that most able contemporary representative of the Kantian approach to moral philosophy, writes:

> Kant believed that human beings have developed a specific form of self-consciousness, namely, the ability to perceive,

and therefore to think about, the grounds of our beliefs and actions as grounds. Here's what I mean: an animal who acts from instinct is conscious of the objects of its fear or desire, and conscious of it as fearful or desirable, and so as to-be-avoided or to-be-sought. That is the ground of its action. But a rational animal is, in addition, conscious that she fears or desires the object, and that she is inclined to act in a certain way as a result. That's what I mean by being conscious of the ground as a ground. So as rational beings we are conscious of the principles on which we are inclined to act. Because of this, we have the ability to ask ourselves whether we should act in the way we are instinctively inclined to. We can say to ourselves: "I am inclined to do act-A for the sake of end-E. But should I?"[12]

This ability—to understand the principles on which we are inclined to act—is, according to Korsgaard, part of the essence of morality in the Kantian image:

> [T]he capacity for normative self-government and the deeper level of intentional control that goes with it is probably unique to human beings. And it is in the proper use of this capacity—the ability to form and act on judgments of what we ought to do— that the essence of morality lies, not in altruism or the pursuit of the greater good.[13]

Bekoff and Pierce cite this latter passage from Korsgaard. However, their response seems curiously off-target:

12. Christine Korsgaard, "Fellow Creatures: Kantian Ethics and our Duties to Animals," in G. Peterson ed., *Tanner Lectures on Human Values* (Salt Lake City: University of Utah Press, 2004), pp. 148–49.

13. Korsgaard, "Fellow Creatures," p. 140.

Even if there are bona fide differences in kind, this does not mean that many aspects of morality aren't also shared, or that there aren't significant areas of continuity or overlap. We view each of these possibly unique capacities (language, judgment) as outer layers of the Russian Doll, relatively late evolutionary additions to the suite of moral behaviors. And although each of these capacities may make human morality unique, they are all grounded in a much deeper, broader, and evolutionarily more ancient layer of moral behaviors that we share with other animals.[14]

The Russian Doll analogy is due to de Waal, and in other contexts is very useful.[15] However, its invocation here misses Korsgaard's point, and the point of the Kantian moral tradition she represents: according to the Kant/Korsgaard view, there is one and only one layer of such a doll that qualifies as moral—the layer that involves normative self-government. Korsgaard claims that the ability to reflect on or form judgments about what we ought to do is the *essence* of morality. Any behavior that is not subject to this sort of normative self-reflection is not moral behavior. If a creature is unable to reflect on what it does, and ask itself whether this is, in the circumstances, a morally good thing to do, or ask itself whether what it feels in these circumstances is the morally right thing to feel, it is not a moral creature. Normative self-control is the essence of morality. Anything that is not subject to such control is not a moral phenomenon, appearances notwithstanding. Therefore, if we assume that Grace is unable to subject her emotions and actions to this sort of normative self-scrutiny, neither her actions nor the emotions that motivate them qualify as moral phenomena. In invoking the Russian Doll analogy, Bekoff and

14. Bekoff and Pierce, *Wild Justice*, pp. 140–41.
15. De Waal, *Primates and Philosophers*, pp. xiv, 21, and 39–40.

Pierce have, in effect, issued an invitation: Why don't you think of morality in this way? Korsgaard and Kant would likely respond with a firm "No thanks." To have any impact, the invitation needs to be strengthened into something more like an offer that cannot be refused. That is the task of later chapters.

Building on our discussion of Aristotle (in particular, on the idea that there are two elements of normativity involved in moral conduct), we might distinguish two logically distinct types of failure (presumably) exhibited by Grace. First, she is unable to critically scrutinize her emotion. That is, she is unable to engage in reflection of this sort: "I am motivated to help Eleanor. Is this a motivation I should endorse or reject?" That is, she is unable to ask if the concern she feels for Eleanor is something she should feel in these circumstances. Because of this inability, the emotion is not something over which she has control. She either has the emotion or she does not—and she has no say in this matter. Therefore, no sense can be given to the idea that she should or should not have this emotion. Ought implies can: since Grace has no say in the "can," no sense can be given to the "ought." Therefore, Grace's motivation does not have normative status: it exerts no normative grip on her. But if a state has moral content, then it is the sort of thing that one either ought or ought not to have depending on what that content is. Therefore, it seems we are forced to conclude that Grace's sentiment is, despite appearances, not a moral one. Presumably, this sentiment would then have to be regarded as a sort of nonmoral facsimile of compassion: perhaps a sentiment that resembled compassion in its phenomenological profile—in terms of what it is like to have it—but lacks the essential moral core that would convert this phenomenology into the properly moral emotion that compassion is taken to be.

The second failure exhibited by Grace concerns the way the sentiment motivates her behavior. Grace is not only unable to scrutinize her motivations; she is similarly unable to scrutinize the connection between her motivations and resulting actions. In particular, she is unable to scrutinize the suitability of the action vis-à-vis the motivation. Grace is, presumably, unable to ask herself if pushing Eleanor to her feet is a suitable way of implementing her motivation to help her. If this is correct, then, from the Kant/Korsgaard perspective, the connection between Grace's motivation and her resulting behavior is not a moral connection. Her inability to scrutinize the connection between her motivation and resulting action means that the former does not qualify as a moral reason for her action but only a cause of that action. Grace has no say in the way her motivation is expressed behaviorally—the motivation is simply expressed in whatever way it is expressed. Therefore, the relation between motivation and behavioral expression is not a normative one. That is, the motivation exerts only causal pressure on her resulting actions; it does not exert normative pressure. Equivalently: the motivation does not provide rational grounds for her behavior, and therefore does not qualify as a reason for this behavior. A fortiori, therefore, it fails to qualify as a moral reason.

One does not need to dig too deep to find that the idea of control is, once again, playing a prominent role in motivating the Kant/Korsgaard position. In her response to de Waal's Tanner Lectures, published as *Primates and Philosophers*, Korsgaard comments on the status of the lower animals—a spider crawling toward a moth that is caught in the middle of her web:

> Here we begin to be tempted to use the language of action, and it is clear enough why: when an animal's movements are guided by her perceptions, they are *under the control* of her mind, and when they are *under the control* of her mind, we are tempted to say they are under the animal's own control. And this, after all, is what makes the difference between an action and a mere

movement—that an action can be attributed to the agent, that it is done under the agent's own control.[16]

As the animal in question becomes more complex, the degree of control it is capable of exerting over its movements becomes correspondingly greater:

> Even if there is a gradual continuum, it seems right to say that an animal that can entertain his purposes before his mind, and perhaps even entertain thoughts about how to achieve those purposes, *is exerting a greater degree of conscious control* over his movements than, say, the spider, and is therefore in a deeper sense an agent.[17]

With humans, however, Korsgaard believes there is a qualitative leap. The reason is that we can choose our ends, and not merely choose how to achieve ends antecedently given to us by our nature and the demands of our environment: "For we exert a *deeper level of control* over our own movements when we choose our ends as well as the means to them than that exhibited by an animal that pursues ends that are given to her by her affective states."[18] As Korsgaard notes, this ability to choose ends—to assess and adopt them rather than merely have them—is what Kant called "autonomy." And is only when we have autonomy, Korsgaard claims, that morality emerges.[19] The reason this is a qualitative leap, Korsgaard claims, is because it requires a specific form of self-consciousness that only humans, in fact, have.

16. Christine Korsgaard, "Morality and the Distinctiveness of Human Action" in de Waal, *Primates and Philosophers*, p. 108. Emphasis is mine.
17. Korsgaard, "Morality and the Distinctiveness of Human Action," p. 109. Emphasis is mine.
18. Korsgaard, "Morality and the Distinctiveness of Human Action," p. 112. Emphasis is mine.
19. Korsgaard, "Morality and the Distinctiveness of Human Action," p. 112.

What I mean is this: a nonhuman agent may be conscious of the object of his fear or desire, and conscious of it as *fearful* or *desirable*, and so as something to be avoided or sought. That is the ground of his action. But a rational animal is, in addition, conscious *that* she fears or desires the object, and *that* she is inclined to act in a certain way as a result.... Once you are aware that you are being moved in a certain way, you have a certain reflective distance from the motive, and you are in a position to ask yourself, "but should I be moved in that way?" Wanting that end inclines me to do that act, but does it really give me a reason to do that act? You are now in a position to raise a normative question about what you *ought* to do.[20]

The centrality of the concept of control is, of course, very evident in this argument. The greater the degree of control an individual has over his actions, the greater the warrant there is for regarding that individual as an agent. In the case of humans, we have a type of control over our motivations ("ends") that no other creature has: we can choose our ends. This is grounded in a uniquely human form of self-consciousness that provides us with "reflective distance" between us and our motives that allows us to scrutinize those motives and ask ourselves whether they are ones we should endorse or reject. This is what makes moral action possible. In short, we have a form of control over our motives that no other creature has; and it is this control that allows us to act morally. Thus, Korsgaard's argument reiterates the tight connection between normativity and control that we identified in the previous chapter and also found to play a central role in the arguments of Aristotle.

20. Korsgaard, "Morality and the Distinctiveness of Human Action," p. 113.

THICK AND THIN: DIXON ON ANIMALS
AND MORAL EMOTIONS

Elements of both Aristotelian and Kantian arguments have been woven carefully together in B. A. Dixon's book *Animals, Emotion, and Morality*.[21] In this book, Dixon argues that animals do not possess what I have called morally laden emotions—emotions with moral content. The temptation to suppose otherwise, Dixon argues, is largely the result of a failure to appreciate the difference between what she calls *thick* and *thin* conceptions of emotions. The concept of emotion is fundamentally ambiguous. Only when emotions are understood in the thick sense can they be morally laden. However, the empirical evidence for emotions in animals establishes no more than that they possess emotions in a thin sense.

Consider, for example, the emotion of compassion: "A thin conception of the emotion of compassion identifies this as a feeling of kindness that motivates a person or animal to perform morally right action."[22] Animals might possess compassion in this sense. However, understood in this way, Dixon argues, compassion has no moral import—it is not a morally laden emotion. In arguing for this, Dixon treads a dialectical path familiar from our examination of the arguments of Aristotle and Kant.

Dixon comments: "But this narrow specification fails to capture the moral import of compassion since it fails to explain why we morally commend an agent for having this emotional state and what an agent must believe, judge or appraise in order for compassion to be appropriately directed."[23] For an emotion to possess moral content—to be a properly moral emotion—it must be situated in a surrounding

21. B. A. Dixon, *Animals, Emotion and Morality* (New York: Prometheus Books, 2008).
22. Dixon, *Animals, Emotion and Morality*, p. 78.
23. Dixon, *Animals, Emotion and Morality*, p. 78.

context of cognitive states: beliefs, judgments, appraisals, and the like. In this context, she borrows from Martha Nussbaum's account of the emotions, and lists three surrounding judgments that must be made if an emotion is to count as a moral one.[24] First, there must be a judgment that the suffering or misfortune of the object of compassion is serious or has "size" Second, there must be a judgment that the suffering is undeserved—either because sufferer does not deserve it at all, or because the suffering is out of proportion to what the sufferer does deserve. Third, there must be a judgment of "similar possibilities": we must judge that the suffering individual is relevantly like us to the extent that if we were in the individual's situation, we would be suffering too. Only when occurring in an individual context that involves these sorts of judgments can an emotion become a "thick" or morally laden one.[25]

This account, of course, by now looks rather familiar. These sorts of judgments, in part, make up what Aristotle called phronesis, or practical wisdom. Dixon's position then is that an emotion can qualify as moral only when it occurs in a surrounding context of phronesis, of the sort required to make sure that the emotion is directed, as Aristotle put it, "to the right person, in the right amount, at the right time, for the right end, and in the right way." Thus, Dixon writes:

> The cognitive-evaluative account of the emotions allows us to see exactly why a person should be praised for having the right emotional state. If the onlooker goes wrong about directing her compassion towards those who suffer only trivial annoyances or to those who bring their misfortune upon themselves through

---

24. Martha Nussbaum, *Upheavals of Thought: The Intelligence of the Emotions* (Cambridge: Cambridge University Press, 2001). I shall not address the issue of whether Dixon has understood Nussbaum correctly.

25. Dixon, *Animals, Emotion and Morality*, pp. 66–68.

their own fault, we say that compassion is not praiseworthy or, perhaps, we say that the emotion is not compassion.[26]

In this respect, Dixon is following the orthodox Aristotelian line. She follows this line also in her assessment of why phronesis is a necessary condition of an emotion qualifying as morally laden. Without phronesis we have only emotions in the thin sense, and these are not morally evaluable. Again, the idea of control is driving this argument, as it did in the arguments of Aristotle and Korsgaard. Thus, the requirement that a motivation be "voluntary" is a theme reiterated many times by Dixon:

> But importantly, feelings or emotions themselves do not constitute praiseworthy motivations to act because these do not have the quality of being entirely voluntary. Praise and blame are attributed to those features of a person's inner life that are voluntary.[27]

Again:

> Virtues are distinguished from natural capacities because the latter are not voluntary, and it is voluntary actions and character traits gradually acquired by habit and practice that are the appropriate objects of moral praise and blame.[28]

And again:

> What we should demand is a conception of compassion that specifies why it is a praiseworthy motivational state and why this

26. Dixon, *Animals, Emotion and Morality*, p. 68.
27. Dixon, *Animals, Emotion and Morality*, p. 76.
28. Dixon, *Animals, Emotion and Morality*, p. 78.

should count as displaying a virtue.... Bodily sensations are not voluntary acts, let alone praiseworthy ones, so it is not appropriate to commend a person or an animal for having such a sensation. In other words, when compassion is defined as a bodily state, it is not morally laden.[29]

In the absence of a surrounding context of phronesis or practical wisdom, feelings or emotions are simply things we have or do not have; and they are simply things that push this way or that way. We can be neither praised nor blamed for these sorts of things because we have no control over them and how they affect us. But if a state is a genuinely moral one, then it must be the sort of thing for which we can be morally evaluated, and this requires that we have control over that state. Therefore, these emotions in the thin sense cannot be regarded as moral states: they are not moral emotions. Or, to put the same point another way: we cannot be morally evaluated for our possession of emotions in the thin sense. But we can be evaluated for our exercise of our capacity for practical wisdom because we have control over that. Therefore, a surrounding context of phronesis is a necessary condition of our emotions being morally laden. Phronesis converts emotions from thin to thick because it injects the necessary element of control that is required for emotions to be morally evaluable.

Finally, let us recall the significance of phronesis in Aristotle's overall account of the moral virtues. Phronesis is, in part, what allows us to satisfy the reflection condition. To act virtuously—at least if that virtue is moral rather than natural—one must understand that what one proposes to do is virtuous and one must do it because one wants to be virtuous. We acquire this ability through the sort of phronesis that allows us to grasp which features of a given situation are morally salient. It is through understanding this that we are able to

29. Dixon, *Animals, Emotion and Morality*, p. 65.

understand, in this situation, which course of action would be virtuous and which would not. The importance of the reflection condition is also endorsed by Dixon:

> What is central to emotional motives like compassion is not merely that the agent is moved to perform morally right actions but that she understands that the action is virtuous and performs that action for the sake of virtue and not for some other reason. Being able to specify what the agent understands about what she does and why she does it is crucial to understanding the motivational state proper to virtue. That is why the conceptual analysis of the emotional state of compassion supplied by a cognitive-evaluative theory, like Nussbaum's, is essential to describing how compassion is morally-laden.[30]

The first two sentences express Dixon's commitment to the sort of reflection condition we have identified in both Kant and Aristotle. The final sentence, correctly in my view, associates the ability to satisfy this condition with the ability to engage in practical reasoning in the form of judgments, appraisals, and so on of the morally salient features of a situation—the sorts of judgments cited in the cognitive-evaluative theory. Thus, here again, we find a commitment to the general picture of what it is to act for moral reasons evident in the work of Aristotle and Kant.

THE CENTRALITY OF CONTROL

If the accounts described above are correct, then this, at least in broad outline, is what is required for a motivation to become a moral reason.

---

30. Dixon, *Animals, Emotion and Morality*, p. 76.

First, I am, let us suppose, the subject of an inner state—let us refer to it by the letter "M." Imagine M is like an itch. When I itch, I scratch. I can't help myself. M causes my behavior, but does not provide a reason for it. M cannot be a reason—it has no content. Nor can it have any moral status—I have no control over when it happens and what I do when it happens.

Now let us make M a little more like an emotion. We direct it toward the world. M occurs in the presence of a certain environmental situation, S. M is still not a reason—for that it needs content. To get that, we will need to strengthen the connection between M and S. Some philosophers believe this will do it: M has the *proper function* of occurring only in the presence of S. The tastes of others might run to the Fodorian rather than Millikanian: S is *asymmetrically dependent* on M. Others eschew naturalistic accounts of representation. Whatever story turns out to be true does not really matter for our purposes: just suppose we can find a way of specifying the connection between M and S such that M is about S and *that* S, therefore, can be regarded as the content of M. Then, M is now the sort of thing that might be a reason—at least, if it is suitably situated in a surrounding milieu of other cognitive and affective states.

However, M is not yet the sort of thing that can be a *moral* reason for my behavior. The reason, the tradition described in this chapter claims, is that it has no normative status. More precisely, while it has representational normativity—it should occur only when S occurs—it does not have moral normativity. To have moral normativity, I must have control over it. That is, I must have control over what I do with it. M cannot be like an itch that I unreflectively scratch whenever I feel it. Nor can it be like a perception of an external state of affairs: that perception would be about something, admittedly, but I have no choice in whether I have it. The perception simply forces itself upon me. For M to be a moral reason, I must be able to critically scrutinize M. That is, I must be able to reason as follows: I am experiencing

M and M is inclining me to φ. Should I act on this inclination, or should I resist it? This is one form that the reflection condition may take—a form preferred by Kant. If these ruminations can result in my controlling how I respond to M, then I now have control over my response.

How might I get this ability? One way—emphasized by Aristotle—is through coming to understand that φ-ing is an appropriate response to M in some situation but not others. Which situations are which depends on the morally salient features of the situation, and this is something that I know through practical wisdom or phronesis. The ability to critically scrutinize my motivations is, therefore, inextricably bound with my practical wisdom. Nevertheless, the end result is the same: because I am able to critically scrutinize my motivations, I now have control over them; and this injects the relevant element of moral normativity into my motivations. Control is what this extended historical narrative has always been about. A motivation can count as moral only when it is morally normative. And a motivation can be morally normative only when its subject has control over it. Control consists in the ability to critically reflect on or scrutinize one's motivations (a claim endorsed by both Kant and Aristotle), and this may be a function of the practical wisdom that allows one to grasp the morally salient features of a situation (a claim endorsed by Aristotle—or, at least, most obviously by Aristotle).

So: control—that is what it is all about. The extended historical investigation conducted in this chapter confirms the logical argument presented in the previous one. There can be no (moral) normativity without control. That is why animals cannot be moral subjects: they cannot control their motivations and so those motivations have no normative status.

The coming chapters will try to show that the implicated concept of control is empty. There is nothing in the world—the world of both animals and humans—that corresponds to it. We suppose that there is something that corresponds to it because we have fallen under the spell of a type of thinking that can only be described as *magical*. In the remainder of the book I shall argue that there is no such thing as magic. The first task, however, is to render the requisite concept of control a little more precise.

5

The Idiot

MYSHKIN M1

Let us suppose there is an individual whom we can call "Myshkin," after the prince in Dostoyevsky's *The Idiot*. There are certain minor differences between Dostoyevsky's Myshkin and my Myshkin—but none that need significantly affect the dialectical purposes to which I am going to put the latter. Prima facie, Myshkin has the soul of a prince. Throughout his life he performs many acts that seem, to the impartial bystander, to be kind or compassionate. Moreover, he performs these acts because he is the subject of sentiments or emotions that—again, at least prima facie—seem to be kind or compassionate ones. When he sees another suffering, he feels sad and compelled to act to end or ameliorate that suffering. When he sees another happy, he feels happy because of what he sees. If he can help an individual get what he or she wants without hurting anyone else, he will help because he finds that he enjoys doing it. In short, Myshkin deplores the suffering of others and rejoices in their happiness. His actions reflect, and are caused by, these sentiments. Thus, Myshkin is, or at least seems to be, motivated by sentiments, where these are understood as states individuated by their content.[1] When he is sad,

1. The qualification "at least seems to be" is not insignificant. There is a position in logical space that denies that Myshkin, given his lack of metacognitive abilities, could ever possess states with intentional content. This is because Myshkin is unable to belong to the *practice* of giving and accepting reasons as explanations of behavior. I shall discuss this objection in detail in chapter 8.

this sadness is about, or directed toward, the suffering of another. When he is happy, his happiness is about or directed toward the happiness of another. In short, Myshkin is *concerned* about others, and this concern is expressed in the form of various emotions that are directed toward, and have as their content, the welfare-related circumstances of other people.

What Myshkin does not do, however, is subject his sentiments and actions to critical moral scrutiny. Thus, he does not ever think to himself things like: "Is what I am feeling the right thing to feel in the current situation—that is, is what I *am* feeling the same thing as what I *should* be feeling?" Nor does he think to himself things like: "Is what I propose to do in this circumstance the (morally) correct thing to do (all things considered)?" He does not do this, let us suppose, because he is incapable of doing it. His dealings with others operate on a more visceral level. Give that this is so, what we might regard as Myshkin's moral profile looks something like this:

(M1) (1) Myshkin performs actions that seem to be morally good, and (2) Myshkin's motivation for performing these actions consists in sentiments or emotions that seem to be morally good, but (3) Myshkin is able to subject neither the actions nor the sentiments to critical moral scrutiny.

Are (1)–(3) sufficient for Myshkin to qualify as a moral subject—that is, for his motivations and resulting actions to count as moral ones? If we are convinced by the arguments of Aristotle, Kant/Korsgaard, or Dixon, we would answer in the negative. But how reasonable is this denial? Myshkin spends his life helping others, and does so because he delights in the happiness of others and abhors their suffering. We need to distinguish (*a*) whether someone qualifies as a moral subject, in the sense of being motivated by moral concerns, and (*b*) whether something qualifies as a moral subject in precisely the same way we do. Perhaps Aristotle and Kant only describe one way of being a moral subject? Perhaps there are others?

These questions, however, merely amount to an invitation to expand our conception of the moral subject. Unscientific surveys, conducted on the floors of philosophy conferences around the world, have indicated to me that there are many philosophers—some of them even moral philosophers—who would be happy to accept this invitation: willing to concede that Myshkin (M1) is a moral subject. However, as we have seen, Aristotle and Kant and other representatives of the tradition would politely decline this invitation. To inconvenience them, the invitation needs to be strengthened into something a little more insistent—a little more like an offer that can't be refused. But how do we do that?

MYSHKIN M2

As a beginning to this process of strengthening, we might work on the two, perhaps overly conciliatory, occurrences of "seem to be" in the above characterization. (M1) claims only that Myshkin performs actions that *seem to be* good, on the basis of emotions or sentiments that *seem to be* good. It does not claim that Myshkin's actions and sentiments actually *are* good. It is not too difficult to identify what this expression "seems to be" means in each case. Roughly:

Action A, performed by Myshkin in circumstances C, seems to be good in the sense that, ceteris paribus, if A were performed in C by a properly moral subject then we would have little hesitation in regarding A as a morally good action.

Sentiment S, entertained by Myshkin in circumstances C, seems to be good in the sense that, ceteris paribus, if S were entertained in C by a properly moral subject, we would have little hesitation in regarding S as the morally correct or appropriate sentiment to have.

No doubt there is some additional fiddly technical work to be performed on these definitions. Who is the "we" in question that judges this? Does "in the sense that" refer to a necessary, sufficient, or necessary and sufficient condition? And ceteris paribus clauses are, of course, notoriously elusive. Nevertheless, I think the above definitions are clear enough for present purposes.

The motivation for characterizing Myshkin's sentiments and actions as ones that "seem to be good" is fairly clear. Myshkin is motivated by emotions in what Dixon called the *thin* sense—kindly or compassionate feelings, and other cognate states. To describe these as feelings, in this sense, does not preclude their intentional character. If Myshkin feels sad because he witnesses the suffering of another, Myshkin's sadness is directed toward the other's suffering: he is sad *that* the other is suffering in this way. So Myshkin's sadness should not be equated with what, in chapter 2, I referred to as a *mood*. His sadness is an intentional state. However, if the Aristotelian-Kantian tradition is correct, these emotional states of Myshkin do not qualify as morally laden emotions—not without the surrounding milieu of cognitive abilities that allows us to make judgments of moral salience with respect to the circumstances and, on the basis of this assessment, critically scrutinize our motivations. But if these kindly and compassionate feelings—these emotions in the thin sense—are not moral phenomena, then neither, one might argue, are the actions they produce. So, to characterize either Myshkin's emotions or his actions as uncontroversially moral ones would be tendentious. In other words, those who reject the idea that Myshkin is a moral subject will also reject the idea that his emotions and actions count as good (for example, as genuinely—in the thick sense—kind or compassionate): such a description would be true only of a moral subject. The first stage in strengthening Myshkin's moral profile requires circumventing these arguments, and so converting the claim that Myshkin's sentiments and actions seem to be good into the claim that they actually are good.

To this end, let us introduce another figure into the dialectic. Marlow—christened after the skilled scrutinizer of motives who narrates some of Joseph Conrad's novels—is capable of the sort of critical moral reflection of which Myshkin is incapable. But our Marlow, it turns out, is more than just a gifted scrutinizer of his motivations and actions. When he asks himself questions such as, "Is this sentiment, S, the morally appropriate sentiment to feel in these circumstances?" and "Is this action, A, the morally right action to perform in these circumstances?" then Marlow gets the right answer—always (or, if one prefers, nearly so). Marlow is always right—or at least as always right as one can be in a domain as open to dispute as morality. When people want to know what is the right thing to do—they defer to Marlow. In matters moral Marlow is judged—as rightly as one can be in an area riddled with the possibility of dispute—an ideal *spectator* and *adjudicator* of matters moral.

Suppose, further, that on the basis of this reflection, Marlow comes to endorse the same sorts of sentiments and actions that Myshkin has and performs. That is, suppose for any given circumstance C, Myshkin has sentiment S and, as a result, performs action A. Marlow, an as infallible-as-it-is-possible-to-get-in-matters-moral scrutinizer of his sentiments and actions, independently comes to the conclusion that in circumstance C, it is morally correct to have sentiment S and perform action A. That is, Myshkin has stable dispositions to experience certain emotions and, consequently, perform certain actions in a range of identifiable circumstances, and Marlow— our ideal spectator—independently arrives at the conclusion that, for all identified circumstances, these are the morally correct sentiments to have and the morally correct actions to perform. If this were the case, we could strengthen (M1) as follows:

(M2) (1) Myshkin performs actions that are, in fact, good, and (2) Myshkin's motivation for performing these actions consists in emotions or sentiments that are, in fact, the morally correct ones to have in the circumstances, but (3) Myshkin is able to subject neither the actions nor the sentiments to critical moral scrutiny.

The appeal to the idea of an ideal moral spectator is, in some contexts at least, problematic. Here, however, it plays only a weak—nonessential—role as a way of making graphic the idea of moral objectivity. Purged of appeal to an ideal moral spectator, the idea would simply be this: it is an objective moral truth that in circumstances C, sentiment S is the morally right sentiment to have and action A is the morally right action to perform. I shall use the figure of Marlow for various expository and illustrative purposes as the arguments of this chapter unfold. However, for those hostile to the idea of an ideal moral spectator, it is worth remembering that Marlow plays only a nonessential role in these arguments.

The transition from (M1) to (M2) is a significant one: it effectively gives Myshkin *external reasons* for his actions, in the sense introduced by Bernard Williams.[2] An internal reason for action is one that furthers a certain motive of the agent—whether the agent actually has this motive, or whether she would come to have this motive by following a "sound deliberative route."[3] An agent would have an external reason to φ, on the other hand, if (1) she has reason to φ, and (2) none of her motives or interests is furthered by φ-ing.

In the case of (M1), it can be argued that Myshkin has no moral reasons for his actions: The Myshkin of (M1) is at the mercy of his motivations: he has no control over whether he embraces or resists

---

2. Williams, "Internal and External Reasons," pp. 101–13.
3. Williams, *Making Sense of Humanity*, p. 35.

them, and so they exert only causal, but not normative, pressure on his actions. But normativity is essential to an item's being a moral reason for action rather than a cause of behavior. Myshkin's motivations, therefore, while they might cause his behavior, are not moral reasons. However, (M2) introduces a new type of moral reason: the Myshkin of (M2) has *external* moral reasons for his actions. Myshkin cannot entertain those reasons, and therefore they are not internal. Nevertheless, they are moral reasons that exist for Myshkin to do what he does.

This would provide a way of strengthening (M1). If it works, then, in given circumstances, Myshkin has the morally correct sentiments and performs the morally correct actions. He also has moral reasons of a sort—external moral reasons for why he does what he does. However, I think we must considerably strengthen Myshkin's moral profile before we are in a position to claim, with any plausibility, that Myshkin is a moral subject. (M2) is only a beginning.

There are two problems. First, the idea of external moral reasons is a controversial one. Bernard Williams introduced them into philosophical discourse only to debunk them a few pages later. One who is skeptical of external moral reasons might regard the putative strengthening of Myshkin's moral profile as more apparent than real. Second, even if we understand (M2) as only a beginning, it is a beginning that many might be reluctant to accept, for it seems to have been purchased only by way of a question-begging assumption. The Myshkin of (M2) just "keeps getting things right"—experiencing emotions and so performing actions that are, morally speaking, perfectly appropriate to the circumstances. But how, one might wonder, does he do that? Myshkin, I have assumed, lacks the ability to critically scrutinize his motivations. I have also argued, in the previous chapter, that phronesis, or practical wisdom, is concomitant with this ability: one has the ability to critically scrutinize one's motivations to the extent that one has the ability to recognize the morally salient features of circumstances. One might expect therefore that Myshkin must also lack any substantial form of phronesis. But, if this is true, it becomes mysterious how Myshkin is able to "keep getting things right"—experiencing the right emotions and so performing the right actions in the appropriate circumstances.

This is an entirely reasonable objection. To avoid it—and I shall now argue that it can be avoided—I need to say a lot more about the sense in which Myshkin "keeps getting it right."

MYSHKIN AND PRACTICAL WISDOM

I have characterized Myshkin, in effect, as the subject of a certain type of moral *sensitivity*. Myshkin is sensitive to some of features of a situation that make it a good one (for example, the happiness of others), and to some of the features that make it a bad one (for example, the suffering of others). Myshkin has no more than this. Myshkin's moral sensitivity is, in other words, severely circumscribed. There are potentially many morally salient features of any given situation, and Myshkin is sensitive only to a small fraction of these. Therefore, the claim that Myshkin keeps "keeps getting it right" should certainly not be understood as a claim of any general moral infallibility on the part of Myshkin. Myshkin "keeps getting it right" only with respect to this narrowly circumscribed range of morally salient properties to which he is sensitive.

However, even with respect to this circumscribed range of properties—an individual's happiness, his sadness, and other relatively basic properties—Myshkin's lack of phronesis might be thought to make him vulnerable to several varieties of moral mistake—at least, as would be judged by someone with the expanded and cognitively enhanced moral sensibilities characteristic of normal, adult human beings. So in what possible sense can Myshkin be thought of as continuing to "get things right"? It cannot be in the sense that he fails to make moral mistakes.

To make progress on this problem, it is first necessary to identify the categories of mistake to which Myshkin is likely to be prone. The first two are, in fact, implicit in Dixon's cognitive-evaluative account of the emotions. Recall, according to Dixon, borrowing from Nussbaum, an emotion can count as thick or morally laden only when embedded in a surrounding milieu of judgments of *desert* and *size*. Myshkin is prone to errors of both sorts.

Myshkin, witnessing the suffering of someone else, feels sadness—and this, we are tempted to suppose, is evidence of his compassion. However, being incapable of understanding the idea of desert, Myshkin is unable to grasp that the individual brought this suffering upon himself. In other words, that he deserves his misfortune is a morally salient feature of the situation to which Myshkin is blind. And some might argue that it is a morally salient feature of the situation that overrides or negates the fact of the suffering, or at least it can be in certain circumstances.[4] If so, then Myshkin's feeling of compassion is *misguided* in the sense explained in chapter 2: it presupposes a claim of entitlement that the other, in fact, does not have.

Myshkin's sadness in the presence of the other's suffering may be misguided in another sense. Suppose Myshkin encounters an immensely successful novelist whose most recent book, unlike the others, was unfavorably received by the critics, and sold only a few hundred thousand copies instead of the customary millions. The author is wallowing in self-pity, and has not left his large oceanfront mansion in the Hamptons for several days. Myshkin is sensitive only to this suffering, and not any of the relevant background information. He is, therefore, prone to mistakes concerning the size or seriousness

---

4. Indeed, Dixon seems to be one of those people who thinks this way. See *Animals, Emotion and Morality*, p. 67.

of the suffering—for sometimes judgments of the size or seriousness of a misfortune can only be accurately made in the light of this sort of background knowledge. We can also imagine the converse case. A peculiarly spartan individual suffers the torments of the damned, but through it all manages to keep a proverbial stiff upper lip. Such an individual is unlikely to elicit much compassion from Myshkin even though he, in fact, deserves it. Myshkin's judgment concerning the extent of another's suffering is fatally dependent on how this suffering is presented, to Myshkin and others. This, to say the least, is hardly a reliable guide, and lacking in the phronesis that would allow him to see through this presentation, Myshkin is, accordingly, prone to make mistakes in this area.

There is a third, very important, category of mistake to which Myshkin is prone. It is difficult to supply a neat label for this category, but the idea is relatively clear. The mistake in question turns on Myshkin's failure to understand the difference between *local* and *global* interests of the other. The other may have a particular interest at a given time that is, unknown to him, incompatible with other interests he has. The local/global distinction can operate both synchronically and diachronically. Thus, one particularly obvious and important version of the local/global distinction is the distinction between short-term and long-term interests that a person has. Appreciating the difference between the two, and also appreciating that long-term interests can often be more important than their short-term counterparts, is an important component of phronesis, as this is usually understood. Consider the following example, supplied by Rosalind Hursthouse:

> We may say of someone that he is too generous or honest, generous or honest "to a fault." It is commonly asserted that someone's compassion might lead them to act wrongly, to tell a lie they should not have told, for example, in their desire to prevent

someone else's hurt feelings…those who have practical wisdom will not make the mistake of concealing the hurtful truth from the person who really needs to know it in the belief that they are benefiting him.[5]

The local/global distinction drives this case and many others like it. Filling in the details, we might imagine a scenario along the following lines: while the lie might temporarily alleviate the person's suffering, it deflects her from addressing the underlying causes of her unhappiness, and so, in the long run, creates more problems than it solves. It is not clear, of course, that this specific problem directly affects Myshkin—he would seem not sufficiently cognitively sophisticated to tell a lie to spare someone's feelings, although he would undoubtedly attempt to find other ways of alleviating the person's suffering. Hursthouse presents this example of lying as resulting from a lack of practical wisdom. But this obscures the fact that this form of lying can only occur in a subject who already possesses a substantial amount of practical wisdom. Lying to spare someone's feelings involves the ability to anticipate the difference between two possible futures—a future in which the lie is told and one in which it is not—and understand how a person will fare in each world. In the case described, the liar must have at least enough practical wisdom to understand that sometimes not all truths are ones that, as Hursthouse puts it, the person "really needs to know." The liar has simply misclassified the situation, taking it to be one in which the person did not need to know the truth when, in fact, it was one in which she did need to know it. That is a mistake, admittedly, but one that presupposes, and is only possible on the basis of, a substantial amount of practical wisdom. Still, the obverse failing might be applicable to Myshkin. If some lies should not be told, then perhaps also there are some

5. Hursthouse, "Virtue Ethics."

truths that should not be told. In certain circumstances, a lie might be something that someone really needs to hear. If Myshkin is lacking in practical wisdom, he might be incapable of this dissembling.

This example is, of course, merely a particular instance of a more general kind. Typically, in the case of human beings, there is a distinction between local and global interests, and the short-term/long-term distinction is one version of this. An intense desire to smoke—a local interest—is incompatible with the more global interest in remaining healthy. Myshkin, however, is only sensitive to local interests since, typically, it is only these that receive clear behavioral expression of the sort that underwrites Myshkin's sensitivity to suffering and happiness. Therefore, he would be unable to take the person's more global interests into account, and so might frequently end up adopting a course of action that is inimical to those interests.

In his dealings with others, therefore, Myshkin seems likely to make these three sorts of mistake pertaining to desert, seriousness, and the favoring of local over global interests. These mistakes concern not merely how Myshkin behaves toward others. The problem is not merely that Myshkin is likely to adopt the wrong course of action with respect to others. More than that, he is also likely to experience the wrong emotions—to experience sympathy or happiness where these are not warranted. If this is correct, how can we have any reason to believe (M2)? For this asserts that Myshkin's emotions and actions are always appropriate to the circumstances. Myshkin does not seem to possess the requisite degree of phronesis for (M2) to be true.

If this is the problem, the solution is reasonably obvious: we take phronesis out of the equation. More accurately: we make Myshkin's failure to possess the required level of phronesis irrelevant by, in effect, changing the required level of phronesis. This is not an arbitrary or unjustified move. On the contrary, it is crucial to bear in mind the role Myshkin plays in the arguments of this book. In comparing him to Dostoyevsky's hero, my suggestion is, of course, that Myshkin is a human individual—although I never explicitly said this. But even if we imagine him as human, his dialectical function is, of course, to go proxy for other animals—other social mammals in particular. So we might equally imagine Myshkin as an elephant, dog, wolf, coyote, chimpanzee, vervet monkey, or dolphin. In terms of his function in the arguments of this book, Myshkin is the quasi-human who goes proxy for other animals. The underlying idea is that our judgments about which individuals are and which are not capable of acting for moral reasons might be clouded by the species of the individual under consideration. Therefore, let us take an individual that is biologically human, but who differs from most other normal, adult humans in certain crucial respects. Thus, we imagine the Myshkin of (M2) as motivated by the sorts of things—emotions in the thin sense—that can motivate these other animals, but is lacking in the sort of practical wisdom that characterizes many (but certainly not all) adult human beings.

Given that this is Myshkin's dialectical function, we cannot uncritically insert him into a normal human context—that is, into a society made up of normal human adults and others. We cannot do this any more than we could insert a vervet monkey into a human context and then criticize it for perceived failures of practical wisdom. Rather, we must imagine that the other members of Myshkin's society are other "people" pretty much like him. Thus, if Myshkin, in a given dialectical context, is being used to make a point about the moral profile of elephants (e.g., Myshkin goes proxy for Grace), for example, then we have to imagine Myshkin living in a society composed of individuals whose cognitive powers are those of elephants. Myshkin is the dialectical inhabitant of simple societies: societies of relatively simple individuals whose cognitive powers are less than those of normal, adult human beings.

In societies such as these, mistakes of the sort we have identified simply will not be possible. Consider, first, the type of mistake that consists in an inability to make judgments of *desert*. Myshkin does not possess the level of phronesis required to judge whether someone's suffering is deserved or undeserved. So if Myshkin were inserted into a human context, he might frequently be found offering compassion to those who (arguably) do not deserve it because they have brought their misfortune upon themselves. But this would be the case only if Myshkin were inserted into an essentially human context—a society whose individuals do bring misfortune upon themselves through a variety of failures such as avarice, pride, arrogance, culpable thoughtlessness or myopia, and so on. However, the society in which Myshkin must be imagined to live is made up of simple individuals—like Myshkin in all essential respects. And their simplicity means that their suffering is never deserved. The members of Myshkin's society may make mistakes, errors of judgments, and their suffering may sometimes be the result of these errors. But these are not culpable errors and so this suffering is not deserved. Thus, the simplicity of the context in which we must imagine Myshkin to be placed renders him immune to errors of the first kind.

Consider, now, the second kind of error. The worry is that Myshkin is incapable of making reliable assessments of the size or severity of another's suffering, and thus the emotions he feels are not, in general, going to be appropriate to the situation. He might sympathize too much with the self-pitying millionaire author, and too little with the spartan of stiff upper lip. This problem arises because of a discrepancy between the way an individual presents or represents the severity of her suffering to Myshkin (and others) and the real severity of her suffering. However, the simplicity of Myshkin's presumed context will also make him immune to this sort of mistake. The misrepresentation of the severity of one's suffering, in whichever direction, is a human phenomenon, and not the sort of thing we find in wolves, coyotes, elephants, vervet monkeys, and other social mammals. In these sorts of animals, an individual's representation of its suffering is, in general, a reliable guide to the severity of that suffering. If this is correct, Myshkin will also be immune to mistakes of the second kind.

The third kind of mistake turns on the difference between the local and global interests of an individual (in both a synchronic and diachronic sense). The individual's behavioral expressions at any give time will tend to be more closely tied to short-term interests, and the extended behavioral profile that is revelatory of long-term interests will be far more difficult to identify. Therefore, it is perhaps inevitable that Myshkin will tend to privilege short-term interests over their long-term counterparts, and therefore find himself experiencing emotions that foster the short-term interests of an individual but are, at least sometimes, inimical to the individual's long-term interests. It is probably apparent by now why Myshkin is immune to mistakes of this third kind. The distinction between local and global interests is one that has its most natural expression in human contexts. In other social mammals, the distinction is far more attenuated. Consider, for example, the case of telling a lie, invoked by Hursthouse. Seeing someone suffering, I offer comfort in the form of a lie. But this only masks a deep-seated problem that inevitably reemerges later. To this extent, my attempt to comfort the sufferer only makes the situation worse. But even if Myshkin could tell lies, the context in which we must imagine precludes his committing this sort of mistake. The distinction between long-term and short-term, local and global, interests presupposes an at least minimal plan for how one's life is to go, a conception of the sort of life one would like to lead, and this, again is not the sort of thing Myshkin's peers are going to have. For them, life really is *just one thing after another*—and the distinction between short-term and long-term, particular and global, has little if any application. Thus, the simplicity of the other members of Myshkin's group once again renders Myshkin immune to mistakes of this sort.

To summarize: this is how Myshkin manages to keep "getting things right," even in the absence of the sort of practical wisdom that is required for a human to do so. First, Myshkin is the inhabitant of a context—a *society* broadly construed—where the suffering of individuals is never deserved. Second, in the context we must imagine Myshkin to occupy, there is no dissembling with regard to the size or severity of one's suffering. Third, Myshkin is the inhabitant of a context where there is little, if any, distinction between the local and global interests of an individual.

There is a more general point that emerges from these reflections on Myshkin's immunity to these kinds of error. The dialectic that has played out in the preceding pages can be expressed in the form of a distinction familiar from the work of Aristotle: that between *natural* virtue and *moral* virtue. According to Hursthouse, and this is indeed a typical view, natural virtue is "a proto version of full virtue awaiting perfection by phronesis or practical wisdom."[6] Moral virtue is the result of phronesis acting on the deliverances of natural virtue. Put in these terms, the worry that motivated the discussion of this section was that, because he is deficient in phronesis, Myshkin can possess only the natural virtues, not their moral counterparts. We might think of Myshkin as having the moral development of a child—at least in the way Hursthouse seems to think of children. Consider, again, the passage from Hursthouse distinguishing the "virtuous adult" from the "nice child," quoted in the previous chapter. While a nice child might have good intentions, he is prone to "mess things up" because of a deficiency of phronesis that renders him ignorant of what he needs to know in order to successfully prosecute his intentions. His lack of phronesis is likely to make him thoughtless, insensitive, reckless, impulsive, shortsighted, and so on. Practical wisdom tells one how to "secure real benefits effectively": it is the knowledge that

6. Hursthouse, "Virtue Ethics."

permits one to transform good intentions into effective actions.[7] The nice child possesses the natural virtues, but his lack of phronesis precludes possession of the moral virtues.

Perhaps this is true of children, perhaps not. But hopefully enough has been said to indicate that is a misconceived way of thinking about Myshkin. Children belong to a human society. But the dialectical function of Myshkin is, in effect, to be plugged into various nonhuman societies. Discussions of phronesis—and I think Hursthouse is guilty of this—typically overlook the deeply *contextual* or *situated* character of practical wisdom. What counts as practical wisdom varies from one context to another, from one social group to another. By this, I am not drawing attention to the obvious point that different people within a group can possess and exhibit different levels of practical wisdom. Everyone, presumably, knows that. This idea presupposes an understanding of what practical wisdom is, and a way of measuring or determining how much of it a given person possesses or exhibits. My point is that what practical wisdom actually is can vary across social groups, and is dependent on the cognitive complexity of the members of those groups. The case of Myshkin simply makes graphic this rather obvious point. If you plug Myshkin into a social group whose members never deserve their suffering, who never misrepresent the severity or extent of their suffering, members for whom there is little or no distinction between local and global interests, then what constitutes practical wisdom in that group will be different from what it is in groups such as ours. It is not that Myshkin is too cognitively unsophisticated to possess phronesis. Rather, it is that what counts as phronesis varies from one group to another, and is a function of, among other things, the cognitive abilities of members of each group. Myshkin does *not* lack phronesis, not at all. He possess all the phronesis that is required by and appropriate in whatever group

7. Hursthouse, "Virtue Ethics."

we choose to insert him—whether this is elephants, wolves, vervet monkeys, or any other species.

If we accept, as I have argued we should, that phronesis is group relative—where "group" here approximates to "species"—then it seems the Aristotle/Hursthouse account of the relation between natural virtue and moral virtue actually commits us to the claim that animals can be morally virtuous. The argument that would yield this claim runs, roughly, as follows:

(1) Moral virtues result from a combination of natural virtues and phronesis. That is, moral virtues are what you get when you apply phronesis to the deliverances of the natural virtues.

This is an assumption that is granted by Hursthouse and Aristotle.

(2) Myshkin possesses (some) natural virtues.

Myshkin delights in the happiness of others and is made sad by their sadness, and so on. These seem to be examples of natural virtues of the sort that, Hursthouse and Aristotle would accept, might be possessed by children and other individuals lacking in phronesis.

(3) Myshkin can be plugged into different (animal) groups.

This is the dialectical function of Myshkin as the quasi-human who goes proxy for other social mammals.

(4) Phronesis is group specific.

It seems this would have to be the case, given that the function of phronesis is, at least in part, to help its possessor negotiate and navigate her way through her particular social world. What constitutes phronesis will be a function of the complexity of the social group and its individual members.

(5) When Myshkin is plugged into group G, he possesses the sort of phronesis characteristic of, and appropriate to, members of group G.

This follows from the dialectical function of Myshkin in the overall argument, combined with premises (3) and (4).

(C) Therefore, Myshkin possesses (some of) the moral virtues appropriate to group G.

This follows from premises (1) and (5). Thus, if phronesis is group—that is, species—relative, and moral virtues result from the combination of natural virtues and phronesis, then the moral virtues must also be group relative. If there are genuine human moral virtues, there are also wolf moral virtues, coyote moral virtues, elephant moral virtues, and so on. This is a relatively obvious entailment of the claim that animals can possess natural virtues and the context-dependent nature of phronesis.

This section began with what seemed to be a serious objection to supposing that the Myshkin of (M2) is even logically coherent. It ends with reason for thinking that Myshkin (M2) can be morally virtuous. But Myshkin, I have emphasized, is just a dialectical place-holder for any social mammal. If Myshkin can be morally virtuous, so too can other animals. In the sections and, indeed, chapters to come, I shall not rely on this argument. I proceed thus for three reasons. First, the argument is perhaps too closely tied to the Aristotelian virtue-ethical apparatus to convince someone not wedded to that apparatus. Second, the notion of phronesis is sufficiently undetermined for someone to deny that it can be possessed by anything that is not human. I think such a denial would be unprincipled, but a general discussion of the concept of practical reason would, given the overall purposes of this book, take us too far afield. Third, and most important, the idea of moral virtues as species-relative would deliver us over to the sort of species-relative view of moral action favored by Bekoff and Pierce.[8] I want to defend a claim substantially stronger than this. While it is true that humans can act morally in ways that no animal can, there is also a type of moral action that humans and animals can share: moral action performed on the basis of morally laden emotions. When humans and animals act on the basis of such emotions, they are, I shall argue, both doing the same thing. This type of moral action is not species-relative. The species-relative character of moral virtue would not help me develop this case. Therefore, I am going to adopt a different dialectical tack in the arguments that follow. The function of this section has, therefore, simply been to show that the Myshkin of (M2) does make sense—that it is coherent to suppose that Myshkin (M2) keeps "getting it right" in his emotional responses to, and subsequent action in, at least some given circumstances. With this claim in place, let us now return to the main argument.

MYSHKIN (M3)

Would we want to say that Myshkin—as characterized by (M2)—is a moral subject? He does things that are, in fact, morally good, and he does them from motivations that are, in fact, morally commendable ones. There are reasons—moral reasons—that connect his sentiments and actions: it is just that these are external ones (if we assume there are such things). Should we really be so confident in the claim

8. See chapter 3.

that Myshkin does not qualify as a moral being? This is still an invitation to think of morality in a certain way; but is it still an invitation that can be reasonably declined?

I think it probably is. However, a skeptical moral philosopher who wishes to decline the invitation is committed to the idea that a necessary condition of being a moral subject is that one possesses *internal* reasons for one's actions. These internal reasons are, unlike their external counterparts, available to rational scrutiny; they are reasons that one not only can endorse but that one has, at some point, in fact endorsed. This idea is, of course, far from unreasonable. The existence of external reasons is controversial.

Indeed, even someone who accepts the existence of external moral reasons might be chary of the claim that Myshkin is a moral subject. There is, one might argue, a certain deficit that accompanies Myshkin's lack of internal reasons. There is a clear sense in which, although Myshkin gets things "right"—that is, in given circumstance C, he experiences the morally correct emotions and so performs the morally correct actions—he gets it right *by accident*. Myshkin acts on the basis of emotions he possesses, and he has scrutinized neither the emotions, nor the actions, nor the connection between the emotions and the actions. So, while there is a sense in which Myshkin gets things right, morally speaking, he does not get things right *for the right reasons*. And that is what is required for Myshkin to be a moral subject—a subject of properly moral motivation.

The picture of a reflective moral subject as someone who can get things right—that is, experience the right emotions, perform the right actions, and arrive at the right moral conclusions—*for the right reasons* is one that, I suspect, many will find compelling. Indeed, this is one way of developing the connection between normativity and control that, I argued, was central to the orthodox way of thinking about moral motivation. Nevertheless, there are two distinguishable ideas at work here. On one way of thinking about the failure of (M2) to capture the idea of moral agency, it is the element of *contingency* that is at fault. Myshkin may "get things right"—that is, in circumstances C, where C is a circumstance in which Myshkin can realistically expect to find himself—he experiences the morally proper emotions and performs the morally correct actions—but he does so *by accident*. The other way of developing the failure of (M2) is in terms of the idea that Myshkin fails to get things right *for the right reason*. However, these two ideas are not equivalent. It is possible to remove the contingency in Myshkin's moral profile without elevating him into a subject that gets things right for the right reasons. Indeed, it seems desirable to do this on independent grounds.

(M2) captures what we might call a certain kind of *normative sensitivity*. The Myshkin of (M2) is sensitive to (some of) the features of a situation that make it a good one or bad one—namely, the suffering or happiness of others. As a result of this sensitivity, Myshkin experiences emotions that are morally appropriate to these features of the situation. It is crucial that the emotions he experiences arise *as a result* of this sensitivity. We do not want to claim, for example, that on the one hand there is Myshkin's sensitivity to the good- and bad-making features of a situation, and that on the other there are the emotions he experiences, and the connection between them is merely accidental. We need a claim of dependence, and this was not, perhaps, made sufficiently explicit in (M2). In the case of Grace the elephant, for example, no one would want to claim that Grace was able to perceive Eleanor's distress and experience an emotion of a certain sort, but there was merely an accidental connection between the perception and the emotion. There is nothing accidental or contingent in the fact that Grace experiences certain emotions in given circumstances. Her emotional response is not something she merely exhibits: it is a part of her natural history to feel these sorts of things in these sorts of circumstances. To make sense of the empirical work that appears to demonstrate the existence of morally laden emotions in animals, we have to suppose that there are mechanisms that reliably connect sensitivity to morally salient features of the situation with emotional responses.

I am, for ease of exposition, going to refer to this mechanism as a *moral module*. I am using this locution simply as a means of referring to whatever mechanism plays the role of linking perceptions of situations with appropriate emotional responses. There is nothing else built into the idea of a moral module. It is not tied to any specific theories in cognitive science. Indeed, some of the uses to which I am shortly going to put this mechanism entail that the mechanism is not really a module in the sense typically employed in cognitive science. The invocation of a moral module is not intended to be, *in any way*, psychologically realistic. That is not its dialectical function at all. The expression "moral module" is simply an expression of convenience, and I shall, therefore, denote it using scare quotes.

The existence of a "moral module," in this sense, might be thought implicit in (M2), but it certainly was not made explicit. Let us do so now:

(M3) (1) Myshkin performs actions that are good, and (2) Myshkin's motivation for performing these actions consists in feelings or sentiments that are the morally appropriate ones to have in the circumstances, and (3) Myshkin has these sentiments and so performs these actions in these circumstances because of the operations of his "moral module," which connects perceptions of the morally salient features of a situation with appropriate emotional responses in a reliable way, and (4) Myshkin is unaware of the operations occurring in his "moral module" and so is (5) unable to critically scrutinize the *deliverances* of this module.

When the idiom of modularity is employed in cognitive science it is used in connection with a postulated mechanism that is *cognitively impenetrable*: its operations cannot be penetrated by, and so are not available to, subsequent belief- and concept-forming operations. This is true of the mechanism we are assuming that Myshkin possesses. Myshkin is, of course, aware of the results or, as I shall put it, *deliverances* of the mechanism: these are emotional states with ostensibly moral content and an identifiable, indeed usually rather urgent, phenomenal character. But he is unaware of the processes that produce these states—the processes that connect his perception of the situation with his emotional response. We could, perhaps, describe the hidden operations of Myshkin's "module" as *reasons* why he has a given emotional response to a given feature of the situation.[9] They are reasons for Myshkin's emotional response, merely reasons of which he is unaware. This, however, would involve a tendentious understanding of the concept of a reason; and it is open to someone to reject the idea that there can be reasons of which we not only are not aware but of which we can never be aware. Nothing turns on whether we characterize the operations of Myshkin's "moral module" as reasons for his emotions. I shall, therefore, avoid doing so.

So, once again, we have our question. Would we want to deny that the Myshkin of (M3) is a moral subject? Would it not be more reasonable to suppose that this Myshkin is a moral subject, merely one somewhat different from the critical moral appraisers of motivations and actions we take ourselves to be? My intuition is that, at this point, the denial of moral subjecthood to Myshkin has become unreasonable. Myshkin is indeed a moral subject; just a moral subject somewhat different from the ones we—or at least those of us in Kantian and Aristotelian traditions—take ourselves to be.

However, this is just an intuition. The primary opposition to it is likely to derive from the thought that while (M3) might have removed

9. Indeed, in a forerunner of this book I did just that. See my "Animals that Act for Moral Reasons," in T. Beauchamp and R. G. Frey eds., *Oxford Handbook of Ethics and Animals* (New York: Oxford University Press, 2011).

the offending element of contingency from Myshkin's moral profile—it is, now, no accident that he experiences the emotions he, in fact, experiences in given circumstances—it has not done so in the right way. (M3) might mitigate the contingency, but it does nothing to alleviate Myshkin's absence of control over what he feels and how he acts. Myshkin has no idea what is going on in his "moral module." He has no authority over its workings, and therefore no control over its outputs or deliverances. But control, tradition has determined, is a necessary condition of normativity. If Myshkin has no control over the workings of his "moral module," then the deliverances of this module have no normative status: they are not the sorts of things Myshkin should embrace or resist. Ultimately, the denial that Myshkin's motivations count as moral ones has its roots in the related ideas of authority and control. To have control over his motivations, we need more than their mere nonaccidental generation by a reliable mechanism. Myshkin must himself arrive at these motivations: he must adopt them *for the right reasons*, where these reasons are *available to his conscious scrutiny*.

MARLOW (M4)

It is relatively easy to see what must be added to the Myshkin of (M3) if he is to be able to arrive at the right motivation *for the right reasons*. We might capture the moral profile of *Marlow* as follows:

> (M4) (1) Marlow performs actions that are good, and (2) Marlow's motivation for performing these actions consists in feelings or sentiments that are the morally correct ones to have in the circumstances, and (3) Marlow has these sentiments and so performs these actions in these circumstances because of the operations of his "moral module," which connects perceptions of

the morally salient features of a situation with appropriate emotional responses in a reliable way, and (4) Marlow has access to the operations occurring in his "moral module" and, therefore, (5) is able to engage in effective critical scrutiny of the deliverances of this module.

The operations of Marlow's "moral module" can, at some suitably abstract level, be regarded as processes whereby connections between perceptions and subsequent emotions and actions are established, and these connections take the form of reasons, broadly construed. Perhaps Marlow's "moral module" is a utilitarian one. Marlow feels motivated to mitigate the suffering of another because, his "module" determines, this would increase the overall amount of happiness in the world. Or perhaps his "module" has been designed along more Kantian lines, and his motivation is the result of his "module" determining that this motivation is one that can be universalized. Perhaps his "module" is a Rawlsian contractualist "module" that endorses his motivation because it determines the motivation would be assented to by rational contractors under appropriate conditions of ignorance. For our purposes, this does not matter: the specific nature of Marlow's "module" is irrelevant.

None of this, I should reiterate, is intended to be psychologically realistic. My point is, rather, a conceptual one. Suppose (M3) is true of Myshkin, and (M4) is true of Marlow. Marlow, it is generally accepted, is a moral subject: an individual capable of acting for moral reasons. Myshkin, we are assuming—as mandated by Kantian and Aristotelian traditions—is not. If this is correct, then it is to conditions (4) and (5) that we must look to identify the *presumed* essence of what it is to act for moral reasons—for Myshkin and Marlow are identical with respect to conditions (1)–(3). It is easy to see the difference that conditions (4) and (5) make.

Myshkin's "moral module," we are supposing, is a reliable one, at least within certain markedly circumscribed boundaries. Thus, with respect to at least some situations, Myshkin's emotional responses and subsequent actions are—reliably—the morally appropriate or correct ones. So Myshkin has what we might call a *normative sensitivity* to some of the morally salient features of situations. He is sensitive to these features and this sensitivity can be normatively assessed—that is, evaluated as morally correct or incorrect. However, the operations of Myshkin's module are impenetrable to him. Thus, while his emotions and actions might be morally correct ones, he has no idea why they are so. His sensitivity may be normative but he has no understanding of the basis of this normativity.

The operations of Marlow's "moral module," on the other hand, are not impenetrable to him. This means that Marlow's "module" is not really a module in the sense employed in cognitive science: modules are, precisely, mechanisms that are cognitively impenetrable. However, as I mentioned earlier, I am using the idea of a "moral module" in a very loose, psychologically unrealistic, sense—as a way of designating the mechanisms that connect perceptions of morally salient features of situations with emotional responses to those features—and nothing of importance turns on this departure from common usage. Marlow has access to the operations of his "module." Therefore, he not only has the correct emotional responses and performs the correct actions, but he can understand *why* they are correct: he understands the reasons why they are the correct things to feel and do in these circumstances. Marlow can, therefore, "get things right"— respond emotionally and practically—*for the right reasons*. Because he has access to the operations of his "moral module," Marlow is *responsive to reasons* in a way that Myshkin is not. Like Myshkin, Marlow has a normative sensitivity to the morally salient features of circumstances in which he finds himself. Unlike Myshkin, he understands the basis of this normativity.

If Marlow is a moral subject and Myshkin is not, then, it seems, the essence of what it is to act for moral reasons will be found in the related idea of *access* to appropriate psychological processes—processes of moral reasoning, broadly construed—and the ability to engage in *effective critical scrutiny* of the deliverances of those processes. This is the orthodox view of moral action, and the view firmly embodied in traditions and positions we examined in the previous chapter. I do not, of course, endorse this orthodox view. In the next two chapters, I shall argue that it cannot be sustained. The related ideas of access and scrutiny, I shall argue, have little substance and cannot do the work required of them. That is, access and effective critical scrutiny are simply not the right sorts of things to give a subject control over her motivations.

6

The Phenomenology of
Moral Motivation

THE ASCNM SCHEMA

If the arguments of the previous chapter are correct, Marlow's eleva-tion to the status of moral subject—an individual capable of acting for moral reasons—proceeds by way of what we might think of as the ASCNM route. <u>A</u>ccess to processes of moral deliberation yields the ability to engage in critical moral <u>S</u>crutiny of the deliverances of these processes—morally laden emotions that motivate behavior. This ability is a necessary condition of a subject having <u>C</u>ontrol over these motivations. Control, in turn, is required for these motivations to have <u>N</u>ormative status—to exert a normative grip on their subjects. And normative status is a necessary condition of <u>M</u>oral status. A moral motivation is one that subject *should* endorse (if morally good) or reject (if morally evil).

Myshkin, as characterized by (M3), is not—if the Kantian and Aristotelian traditions are to be believed—a moral subject. Myshkin does possess many, arguably necessary, ingredients of a moral subject.[1] He possesses a normative sensitivity—a sensitivity that can be evalu-ated as morally correct or incorrect—to (some of) the morally salient features (the good- and bad-making features) of the situations in

---

1. I say "arguably" necessary. I take no stand on whether they are, in fact, necessary.

which he finds himself. This normative sensitivity has not come about by accident but is, rather, grounded in the operations of a reliable mechanism or "moral module" that links perception, emotion, and action. The outputs, or *deliverances*, of his "moral module" take the form of emotions or sentiments, and these motivate him to think and act in ways that are (morally) appropriate to the exigencies of the situation. However, having no access to the operations of his "moral module," Myshkin is unable to subject these deliverances of the module to critical scrutiny. These motivations can, therefore, consist only in emotions in Dixon's "thin" sense that carries no moral import. And Myshkin's inability to engage in critical moral scrutiny of the deliverances of his "moral module" entails that, from both a Kantian and Aristotelian perspective, he does not qualify as a moral subject.

The Marlow of (M4), however, is a moral subject—a subject capable of acting for moral reasons. Myshkin simply acts on the deliverances of his moral module; but Marlow can question them, scrutinize them, and so endorse or reject them. Of course, much work is still required: in particular, the content of the concept of critical moral scrutiny needs to be identified. However, assuming we can do this (in ways that are acceptable to Kantian and/or Aristotelian traditions), Myshkin's ability to subject the deliverances of his "moral module" to critical moral scrutiny means that he will qualify as a moral subject. It means also that these deliverances can consist in emotions in Dixon's "thick" sense that does carry moral significance.

In this, and the following two chapters, I am going to attack the ASCNM schema. First, however, there is a little pruning to be done. I have presented Marlow's ability to engage in critical moral scrutiny of his motivations as deriving from his access to the processes by which these motivations are generated. This is, of course, a common way of thinking about scrutiny: I can scrutinize my motivations to the extent I have access to—and so can evaluate—the reasons that led me to have them. This sort of access is, however, tangential to the arguments I shall develop. This is for three reasons. First, while this is a natural way of thinking about the basis of the ability to scrutinize one's motivations, nothing in the arguments I shall develop commits me to the assumption that it is the only basis of this ability. Given that it is better to dispense with unnecessary assumptions whenever possible, that is what I shall do. Second, it is not clear that this sort of access is really an additional step in the ASCNM schema. The distinction between access and scrutiny is, in this case at least, somewhat tenuous. The importance of Marlow's access to the reasons that generate his motivations is precisely that it allows him to evaluate— that is, scrutinize—those reasons. It is Marlow's scrutiny of his reasons that grounds the possibility of his scrutinizing his motivations. Third, and most important, I shall attack the connection between S and C in this schema. If this attack is successful, it does not matter what comes before S: there is still no way to get from control to normativity and morality. Therefore, for these reasons, the notion of access will play no further role in the arguments of this book. The ASCNM schema has, effectively, been pruned to the SCNM schema.

In this chapter and the next, I shall focus on S-C link in the schema—on the connection between the ability to engage in critical moral scrutiny of one's motivations and having control over those motivations. I shall argue that we have no viable understanding of the way in which a subject's ability to engage in critical moral scrutiny of its motivations could give that subject control over those motivations. This is what we might think of as the negative part of the argument to follow. Chapter 9 examines the C-N link—the connection between control over one's motivations and the normativity of those emotions. If the arguments of this chapter and chapter 7 are correct, we have no workable concept of control as it is thought to apply to motivations, hence no understanding of the way in which control can underwrite the normativity of motivations. If we do not wish to abandon the idea that at least some motivations are normative ones—in a moral sense—then we need an account of the normativity of motivations that does not derive from the control we have over them. Providing such an account is the goal of chapter 9. This is what we might think of as the positive part of the argument to follow. In between chapters 7 and 9 is chapter 8, which examines, and contests, another way of accounting for the normativity of motivations—a way that is also inimical to the idea that animals can be moral subjects.

THE CONCEPT OF CRITICAL MORAL SCRUTINY

Marlow shares Myshkin's normative sensitivity to morally salient features of situations. The crucial additional ingredient that converts Marlow into a moral subject is, it is generally thought, his *ability to engage in critical scrutiny of the deliverances of his "moral module."* These deliverances take the form of emotions that concern, in one way of another, the well-being of others, and motivate behavior on the basis of this concern. There are three elements of this claim that require further comment.

First, we need to observe a distinction between *generic* and *specific* conceptions of critical moral scrutiny. There is a *generic* sense of critical scrutiny that amounts, roughly, to this: to scrutinize one's motivations is to examine their compatibility with moral principles that one antecedently endorses. Here, I am using the term "principles" in a very broad sense: I am not committed to any specific stance on the debate between *generalist* and *particularist* accounts of moral reasoning and justification. One might think of these "principles" simply as moral contents or propositions, and it is open to regard these propositions as deeply contextual items whose validity can vary from case to case. I shall continue to employ the term "principles," but that is merely for ease of exposition and contains no broader commitments.

However, there are also more specific—theory-laden—conceptions of critical moral scrutiny. Thus, we might imagine the following counterpart Marlows. There is a Kantian Marlow—Marlow K—for whom critical scrutiny amounts to answering the question: is my motivation universalizable? That is, can I consistently will that it be adopted by all members of the kingdom of ends? There is a utilitarian Marlow—Marlow U—for whom critical moral scrutiny amounts to answering the question of whether acting on this motivation would increase utility (in whatever way Marlow U thinks of it). There is a contractualist Marlow—Marlow C—for whom critical moral scrutiny amounts to answering the question of whether the course of action to which his motivation inclines him would be assented to by rational contractors under appropriate conditions of ignorance. There is a virtue ethical Marlow—Marlow V—for whom critical moral scrutiny amounts to answering the question of whether his motivation is one that would be endorsed by a virtuous person. These, of course, by no means exhaust the options. There are many possible Marlows, each one armed with a different conception of what it is to critically morally scrutinize one's motivations. Indeed, each counterpart Marlow is itself open to a variety of interpretations—each counterpart has subcounterparts.

There is an obvious problem engendered by adopting a specific conception of critical moral scrutiny—at least for the purposes of the arguments I shall develop. If we do so, and also accept that such scrutiny is required for a motivation to qualify as moral (via the SCNM route), it follows that most of our possible Marlows are not subjects of moral reasons. That is, they are not moral subjects (and so not moral agents either). This is, of course, very implausible. The question of which, if any, moral theory turns out to be correct is obviously important in determining which motivations/actions are morally correct and which are not. However, it is not plausible to suppose that the correctness or otherwise of a given moral theory plays a role in determining whether a motivation qualifies as moral *tout court*. If it did, then moral action—action performed on the basis of moral reasons—would be restricted to a vanishingly small subset of the human population. This, in my view, is a *reductio* of the attempt to employ a specific—theory-laden—conception of critical moral scrutiny in an account of what makes a motivation a moral one. Moreover, even if one were to embrace the *reductio*—and perhaps few *reductios* are ever sufficiently *ad absurdum* to attract absolutely no adherents—it does mean that animals would lack nothing that all but a very few humans have. And if only vanishingly few humans ever act morally, then the answer to the question of whether animals can do so suddenly becomes rather obvious. At the same time the question loses much of its interest. Therefore, it seems necessary—both on grounds of plausibility and given the dialectical purposes of this book—to work with the generic concept of critical moral scrutiny. The ability to engage in critical moral scrutiny is the ability to compare one's motivations with antecedently accepted principles—broadly understood as moral propositions or contents—and to ascertain their mutual compatibility or incompatibility.

Second, whatever the specific form critical moral scrutiny takes, we should distinguish *mere* critical scrutiny from *effective* critical scrutiny. It is assumed not only that Marlow has the ability to critically scrutinize his motivations but also that he is not absolutely hopeless when he does so. Suppose, for example, we are dealing with Marlow K—the Marlow of Kantian persuasion. Marlow K scrutinizes his motivations by attempting to ascertain whether they are universalizable—whether he can consistently will that they be adopted by all ends-in-themselves. Suppose, however, that Marlow is hopeless at this task—perhaps because he has not properly understood what it is to be universalizable, or perhaps because some defect in his reasoning processes causes him to consistently misidentify which maxims are and which are not universalizable. Whatever the reasons, Marlow typically arrives at the wrong answer with respect to his motivations. We might say that Marlow is engaged in critical scrutiny of his motivations, but this scrutiny is ineffective. Alternatively, we might opt to use "scrutiny" as a success term, and deny that Marlow is engaging in critical scrutiny. Which option we take is, for the purposes of this book, unimportant. The salient point is that once the effectiveness of the scrutiny falls below a certain level (irrespective of whether this means we are no longer dealing with scrutiny) many will be tempted to deny that we are dealing with a moral subject. I do not endorse this claim—simply note it. To sidestep this (irrelevant) complication, I shall regard Marlow as an effective scrutinizer of his motivations— whatever the specific content of "scrutiny" and whatever level of success is required to make this scrutiny "effective."

Third, we should distinguish Marlow's *ability* to engage in effective critical scrutiny of his motivations from his *exercise* of that ability in various cases. It is almost certainly too much to require of Marlow that he exercise his ability to effectively scrutinize his motivations on every occasion on which he is (morally) motivated to act. We—moral subjects all of us—often act unreflectively, sometimes thoughtlessly. To make the actual exercise of this ability on every occasion we respond to morally salient features of a situation a necessary condition of being a moral subject would almost certainly entail that there are no moral subjects. To be a moral subject, Marlow must simply have the ability to effectively critically scrutinize his motivations. It seems plausible to suppose that he must exercise this ability on at least some occasions. This plausible assumption is, however, not one to which I am committed, and I shall not presuppose it in the arguments to follow. I shall sometimes, for the sake of brevity, talk simply of "effective critical scrutiny"— sometimes even just "scrutiny"—of motivations. These should *always* be understood as elliptical forms of the ability-construction.

With these preliminary remarks completed, it is now possible to identify at least the general contours of the process of (effective) critical moral scrutiny of motivations. Such scrutiny is best thought of as a multilayered phenomenon. To begin with:

(1) Marlow recognizes that he has certain motivations—states that incline him to act in one way or another. This recognition can be expressed in thoughts of the form: I am inclined to φ because of motivation M.

On the basis of this recognition, he can ask himself certain questions such as:

(2) Is M a motivation I should endorse or reject?

This recognition and interrogation is, of course, only the beginning of Marlow's critical moral scrutiny. Marlow also understands how he should to proceed to answer (2). Thus:

(3) Marlow brings to bear moral principles or propositions that he antecedently holds. He assesses M in the light of these principles. Is M compatible with these principles? Is it incompatible with them? Is it entailed by these principles?

In answering these questions, Marlow can come to decide whether M is permissible, impermissible, or perhaps obligatory. However, there is no reason to suppose that the ability to engage in critical moral scrutiny is restricted to questions of this sort. If Marlow is an appropriately critical subject, he will realize that further questions need to be asked concerning his antecedent adoption of these moral principles or propositions. Thus:

(4) Marlow asks if there is any reason to suppose that his antecedent acceptance of the moral principles he brings to bear in

this case has been shaped by extrarational factors (features of his upbringing, education, and so on).

Not only does he ask this question, he can also make a decent attempt at answering it—by engaging in (what seem to him) processes of impartial and honest reflection on the type of upbringing and education he has had, and the likely consequences of these factors on his processes of moral deliberation.[2] Furthermore:

(5) Marlow asks if there is any reason to suppose that his ability to properly assess compatibilities and incompatibilities between motivations and principles might be compromised by certain nonrational biases that he has acquired.

Such biases might lead him to conclude that a motivation and a principle are compatible when they are in fact not, or incompatible when they in fact are. Once again, Marlow does not simply ask this question but attempts to answer it—perhaps through a similar examination of his history, making (what see to him) reasonable inferences concerning what sort of biases this history might have produced, and then engaging in the sort of self-scrutiny that, he hopes, might determine whether these biases are affecting his abilities in these cases.

An individual who engages in critical moral scrutiny of this sort is sometimes referred to as a *morally autonomous* subject. The concept of moral autonomy applies both to individuals and to their motivations and actions. Marlow would qualify as a morally autonomous *subject* if he has the ability to engage in critical scrutiny of his motivations that conforms to the sort of profile outlined in (1)–(5). His motivations would qualify as autonomous if they meet the following

---

2. Of course, that a process of reflection seems to Marlow to be honest and impartial is no guarantee that it actually is. This point will be developed in chapter 7.

conditions: *if* Marlow were to subject his motivations to the sorts of scrutiny outlined in (1)–(5), he would endorse them, or continue to endorse them.[3] And Marlow's actions are morally autonomous if they are performed on the basis of morally autonomous motivations.

The concept of moral autonomy implicated in (1)–(5) is a familiar one. Nothing I shall say in the arguments that follow should be interpreted as an attack on this concept of autonomy. On the contrary, I believe that principles (1)–(5) collectively delineate, with an acceptable level of precision, a useful concept. Marlow is capable of engaging in the sort of scrutiny implicated in (1)–(5), and Myshkin is not. This is a clear and important difference between Marlow and Myshkin. I am quite happy to capture this difference by way of the claim that Marlow is a morally autonomous subject and Myshkin is not. Moreover, in chapter 9, I shall defend a certain conception of autonomy: a conception that broadly conforms to the principles (1)–(5), but with an additional interpretation of their significance. Thus, I should not be interpreted as attacking the idea of moral autonomy.

What I am going to attack is a certain conception of what moral autonomy—critical scrutiny that conforms to (1)–(5)—does. That is, I am going to attack a certain conception of the *significance* of this autonomy. According to this conception, the significance of the moral autonomy of a subject is that it confers normativity on the motivations of that subject, and does so via the medium of control. To the extent that Marlow has the ability to engage in processes (1)–(5), he is an autonomous subject, and his motivations and actions can also qualify as autonomous. These are claims with which I agree. The significance of Marlow's moral autonomy is that it imbues him with

---

3. David DeGrazia has defended an account of autonomy along broadly these lines. See his *Taking Animals Seriously*, pp. 204–7. See also his "Autonomous Action and Autonomy-Subverting Psychiatric Conditions," *Journal of Medicine and Philosophy* 19 (1994), 283–88.

control over his motivations. This is a claim that I shall vigorously contest.

MORAL PHENOMENOLOGY: THE CASE OF MORAL SUPER-BLINDSIGHT

If the ability to engage in effective critical scrutiny of one's motivations—the sort of ability embodied in principles (1)–(5)—yields control over those motivations, some account is required of why this is so. There appear to be two broad options. The first is that the scrutiny-control connection is basic or primitive. This is tantamount to the claim that there is no explanation of how the ability to engage in critical scrutiny of one's motivations yields control over those motivations. It just does. But if there is no explanation of how effective critical scrutiny yields control, then there is, similarly, no explanation of why such scrutiny is required for control. It just is. However, in these circumstances, it seems one might be justifiably skeptical of the role scrutiny plays in grounding the moral status of motivations. According to the SCNM schema the normativity of a subject's motivation arises as a result of a subject's control over them. The normative status of a subject's motivations is a necessary condition of those motivations being moral ones. However, if there is no explanation of how scrutiny yields control, then the whole schema seems based on an unexplained and unjustified assumption. It is difficult to see any reason for thinking of this assumption as anything more than a prejudice. If the case against the possibility of animals being moral subjects rests ultimately on an unexplained and unjustified assumption, then that case, presumably, has little substance. To give it substance, more needs to be said about the relation between scrutiny and control.

If the S-C connection is not primitive, there must be some properties of S—of the ability to engage in critical moral scrutiny of one's motivations—in virtue of which S is a necessary condition of, or underwrites, C. The question, then, is: what properties might these be? What are the features or qualities of effective critical scrutiny of one's motivations that underwrite a subject's control over those motivations?

One possibility is that we look for these features in the phenomenological differences that effective critical scrutiny brings to the table. There are important differences between the phenomenological character of the experiences undergone by Myshkin and Marlow when they find themselves in situation that call for a moral response or otherwise raise moral questions. It is true, of course, that Myshkin's motivational states are conscious ones, and so they possess associated phenomenology. Indeed, this was built into our preliminary description of Myshkin: when he witnesses suffering, he *feels* both sad and compelled to act to mitigate this suffering; when he witnesses happiness, he *feels* happy, and so on. When Myshkin acts to mitigate an individual's suffering, one phenomenological manifestation of this act might be, for example, a feeling of relief. When Myshkin acts on another's suffering, or rejoices in her happiness, there is, in these moments, certainly something that it is like to be Myshkin. However, Marlow brings something else to the phenomenological table. Fundamentally, Marlow engages in moral deliberation in a way that Myshkin never could. Myshkin simply acts on his motivations. Marlow acts on his motivations too—but before he does so, he scrutinizes at least some of them. Marlow can agonize over his motivations. Marlow can feel the pull of conflicting motivations in a way that Myshkin cannot. We might use a Sartrean idea to provide a general characterization of this difference. Marlow's motivations are *troubled* in a way Myshkin's can never be. Myshkin *lives* his motivations: he has them and acts on them and there is a phenomenology associated with this. But Marlow's motivations often come with nagging questions. I am inclined to do this—but should I? Is this an inclination I should embrace or one that I should resist? These questions have their own phenomenology. With Marlow also, there is the phenomenology associated with bringing, or attempting to bring, moral principles or considerations to bear on this question. Is this motivation really compatible with my antecedent moral principle, P? Perhaps it is difficult to tell, and Marlow's evidence-based judgments pull him in different directions. If all goes well, Marlow may encounter the phenomenological sense of a satisfactory resolution achieved. Failing that, Marlow will encounter the phenomenology associated with the suspicion that one's deliberations have not yet reached a successful resolution, or perhaps the phenomenology of the suspicion that a successful resolution will never be reached, and so on. There are clear phenomenological differences between Myshkin and Marlow. The question is: are they the sorts of differences that could confer the status of moral subject on Marlow while denying that status to Myshkin?

The initial prospects of an affirmative answer appear bleak. If these phenomenological differences confer moral subject status on Marlow, they do so through the medium of control—according to the SCNM schema. However, it is unlikely that, in general, any meaningful sense of control can be engineered from reflections on phenomenology. A clear and distinctive phenomenology associated with Marlow's moral deliberations does not show that he has control over those deliberations or the motivations that form their basis. Thus, the hard determinist is, typically, at pains to not deny the phenomenology of freedom. He simply denies that our sense of being free adds up to our actually being free. Similarly, that we seem to have control over our motivations, a seeming that is bound up with the phenomenology of moral deliberation, does not entail that we actually do. If it is control over motivations that separates Marlow from Myshkin—as the SCNM schema mandates—then we will not find this in moral phenomenology.

This point can be pushed further—and, if correct, shows quite independently of the SCNM schema that the phenomenology of moral deliberation is a poor indicator of who is and who is not a moral subject. Here is a useful way of thinking about the Myshkin characterized in (M3). Myshkin is characterized by ("suffering from" would be tendentious) a form of what we might call *moral super-blindsight*. In its ordinary sense, "blindsight" refers to a deficit of phenomenal consciousness.[4] Due to lesions of the visual cortex, a blindsighted subject will claim to have no awareness of an object in a certain portion of her visual field. Yet, when asked to guess what the object is, or where the object is, she succeeds in guessing accurately at rates significantly above chance. It would be mistaken to think of blindsighted subjects as functionally equivalent to those with normal vision. They are not, and will often have great difficulty navigating their way around the environment, at least under normal conditions. Nevertheless, the phenomenon of blindsight is typically taken to be indicative of the possibility that phenomenal consciousness and the sort of functional abilities that constitute access-consciousness can come apart. The subject can identify an object in front of her, even though she professes to have no awareness of that object.

Based on this possibility, we can imagine a case of what we can call *super-blindsight*. A person with super-blindsight has no visual phenomenal consciousness. If you were to ask her what she sees, she will tell you: nothing. Nevertheless, she easily navigates her way around, avoiding objects in her path, and so on. If you ask the subject: how did you know that object—the one she just avoided—was there? She would respond: I just had a feeling there was something there. You toss a baseball in her direction, and she easily catches it. You ask:

---

4. Lawrence Weiskrantz, *Blindsight: A Case Study and Implications* (Oxford: Oxford University Press, 1986).

How did you do that? She responds in the same way. That is how the super-blindsighted person manages to get around her environment: on the basis of what we would think of as gut feelings. But these feelings are utterly reliable—or at least as reliable as the visual impressions had by sighted people. As a result, the super-blindsighted subject is able to navigate around her environment with a level of success that is roughly the same as the sighted person.

Can the super-blindsighted subject see? This question is ambiguous. On the one hand, it could mean: does the super-blindsighted subject have visual consciousness? A negative answer to this question is plausible. However, the question could also mean: is someone with super-blindsight a visual subject? A negative answer to this question is far less plausible. Thus, if we asked the subject what is the object in front of her, she would point her eyes in the appropriate direction. Light would strike her eyes, and a message would be sent via the optic nerve to the visual cortex. Various information-processing operations would occur there, and the result would be a feeling with, for example, the content: "It's a cabbage!" Note also that the processes in question are sensitive only to the visually salient properties of objects. It is not as if, for example, the processes give her access to the innards of the cabbage, but only to the properties that could be seen by someone of normal sight.

It would be implausible to say that, in this case, the super-blindsighted subject is not seeing. It is not simply that she detects objects, but the way in which she detects them that is decisive. Thus, for example, she is not locating objects by echolocation. She is using her eyes, and the deliverances of her eyes are processed in the visual cortex of her brain. It is just that these processes that usually result in a perception possessing visual phenomenology now result in a feeling of, let us suppose, a more visceral character. Rather than denying that she is seeing, I think it is far more plausible to claim that this is what seeing consists in for a super-blindsighted subject.

(M3), in effect, provides a characterization of someone suffering from what we might call *moral super-blindsight*. Myshkin performs the right (i.e., morally correct) actions, experiences the right emotions or sentiments, and his actions, emotions, and the morally salient features of the situations in which he finds himself are all connected by way of the reliable operations of his "moral module." However, the operations of his "moral module" yield only sentiments. These are the equivalent, in the moral domain, of the feeling: "It's a cabbage!" Just like our super-blindsighted visual subject, Myshkin has no idea why he feels the way he does, or why he should do the things he does. But, also just like our super-blindsighted visual subject, Myshkin keeps getting things right, morally speaking.

The case for Myshkin being counted as a moral subject seems to parallel, and thus be as sound as, the case for our imagined super-blindsighted subject being a visual subject. The capacity to see is compatible with differing visual phenomenologies. And so too, I think we should accept that the capacity to be moral—to be motivated by moral considerations—is compatible with differing moral phenomenologies. Rather than denying that the morally super-blindsighted person is a moral subject, it is far more plausible to claim that, this is precisely her way of being a moral subject. This is what, for her, being a moral subject consists in. Being a moral subject is not so closely tied to phenomenology that we can deny someone the status of moral subject simply because her associated moral phenomenology differs from ours. In other words, moral phenomenology is not a decisive determinant of moral subjecthood.

CONCLUSION

According to the SCNM schema, the ability to engage in effective critical moral scrutiny of one's motivations confers on a subject control over those motivations. However, if the connection between scrutiny and control is to amount to anything more than an unsubstantiated assumption, we need some account of which properties of scrutiny yield control. What is it, precisely, about the ability to engage in critical moral scrutiny of one's motivations that gives one control over those motivations? I have argued that phenomenological properties—properties constitutive of the phenomenology of moral deliberation—are unlikely to be able to play this role. This conclusion is, I think, hardly unexpected. However, there is a more plausible account of what these relevant properties might be. It is to this that we now turn.

7

Moral Motivation and Metacognition

MORAL SUBJECTS AND METACOGNITION

Marlow can engage in critical scrutiny of his motivations of the sort outlined in principles (1)–(5). Myshkin cannot do this. This difference between Marlow and Myshkin will have various phenomenological accompaniments—of the sort identified in the previous chapter. Marlow's motivations are *troubled* ones in a way Myshkin's can never be. I have argued that the phenomenological properties of Marlow's moral deliberation are unlikely to imbue Marlow with control over his motivations. However, the most glaring differences between Marlow and Myshkin are not phenomenological but *metacognitive*. Marlow is capable of metacognition, but Myshkin is not. Could this be the decisive difference that separates Marlow from Myshkin?

It is easy to feel the intuitive pull of the idea that Marlow's ability to metacognize could imbue him with control over his motivations. Myshkin is the subject of motivations of various sorts. However, because he cannot reflect on those motivations, but simply act on them, he is, in one fairly clear sense, at their "mercy." These motivations push him this way and that—causing him to act one way or another. But Myshkin has no control over where—and how far—these motivations push him. These motivations are, one might suspect, always merely causes: they are states that belong, as Sellars

CAN ANIMALS BE MORAL?

once put it, to the *space of causes*. They have no normative dimension: they exert no normative grip on Myshkin.

Marlow, on the other hand, has metacognitive abilities, and these allow him to survey and critically evaluate his motivations. Because of these abilities, he can think things like: "I am motivated to perform act A. Is this a motivation I should embrace or resist?" Not only is Marlow able to ask these questions, he knows how to proceed in trying to answer them. He brings antecedently accepted moral principles or propositions to bear on these motivations, assessing their mutual compatibility or incompatibility. He can, in turn, question these antecedently accepted moral principles, perhaps attempt to seek a reflective equilibrium between motivations and principles, and so on.

These intuitive abilities support a picture of Marlow as an individual quite different from Myshkin. Myshkin is "at the mercy" of his motivations. He has them, and he acts on them—and that is all he can do. He is tossed this way and that—a bobbing cork on a sea of motivations. Marlow's metacognitive abilities, on the other hand, allow him to float above this sea. He is able to observe his motivations and, by following certain evaluative procedures, adjudicate between them. Because of this, Marlow has control over his motivations in a way that Myshkin does not. In virtue of his metacognitive abilities, Marlow can decide which motivation he is to act on and which he is to reject. And, in virtue of this, Marlow's motivations have a normative dimension that Myshkin's lack. Marlow's motivations belong to the *space of moral reasons*, not the space of causes.

I find this picture intuitively compelling—and so, I suspect, do many others. Nevertheless, I shall argue that the picture is misguided. Metacognition of the sort implicated in principles (1)–(5) is, I shall argue, simply not the sort of thing that can imbue a subject with control over its motivations. That this picture of Marlow's control over his motivations is intuitively compelling is a symptom of a certain kind of magical thinking that often underpins an appeal to the meta-level—at least when this appeal is made in the cause of explanation. Marlow's metacognitive abilities cannot confer control over motivations. To suppose that they can is to fall victim to a common but illicit picture—a type of fallacy that I shall label the *miracle-of-the-meta*.

CONSCIOUSNESS AND HIGHER-ORDER THOUGHTS

I am going to introduce the error of reasoning I shall label the *miracle-of-the-meta* by way of what I think is a particularly obvious example of this fallacy. This example is supplied by what has become known as the higher-order thought (HOT) model of consciousness.[1] The idea underlying the HOT model of consciousness is that metacognition, in the form of higher-order thoughts, confers consciousness on mental states. The idea under examination in the remainder of this chapter is that metacognition can confer control (and, via control, normativity) on motivations. In the latter case, of course, the implicated metacognition involves more than merely higher-order thoughts, but also higher-order processes of scrutiny, assessment, evaluation, and so on—of the sort embodied in principles (1)–(5). Nevertheless, I shall argue that the same problem arises in both cases. The idea that metacognition can confer consciousness on first-order states and the idea that metacognition can confer control over (first-order) motivations are both expressions of the idea that something magical happens when we move from the first order to a higher order. They are both forms that the miracle-of-the-meta can take.

---

1. See, for example, David Rosenthal, "Two Concepts of Consciousness," *Philosophical Studies* 49 (1986), 329–59.

I want to exploit the parallels between the higher-order account of consciousness and the higher-order account of control because I think the problem with the former is relatively clear.[2] I shall use this problem to throw some light on the problems with the idea that metacognition can confer control on motivations. I say that the HOT model provides a "particularly obvious" example of the miracle-of-the-meta fallacy. But, in fact, I have had a not inconsiderable amount of trouble convincing people that the HOT account is guilty of a fallacy of any sort. I shall try to do better here. It is, perhaps, worth remembering that the HOT model, in this context, plays merely an illustrative role. The case against metacognition conferring control over motivations is logically independent of the HOT example, and so can stand or fall independently of this example. Thus, even if one does not agree that the HOT model falls victim to the miracle-of-the-meta error, it is still an open possibility that the metacognitive explanation of control does.

In order to properly understand HOT models of consciousness, we need two distinctions: First, there is the distinction between *creature* and *state* consciousness. We can ascribe consciousness both to creatures or individuals (for example, Jones is conscious as opposed to asleep) and to mental states (for example, Jones's belief that Ouagadougou is the capital of Burkina Faso is, at certain times, a conscious belief). The HOT model is an attempt to explain state consciousness, not creature consciousness. Second, there is the distinction between *transitive* and *intransitive* consciousness. We sometimes speak of our being conscious of something (for example, Jones is conscious of the fact that Ouagadougou is the capital of Burkina Faso). This is transitive consciousness. Transitive consciousness is a

---

2. For extended discussion, see Mark Rowlands, "Consciousness and Higher-Order Thoughts," *Mind and Language* 16 (2001), 290–310, and *The Nature of Consciousness* (Cambridge: Cambridge University Press, 2001), chapter 5.

form of creature consciousness. Creatures—individual subjects of mental states—are conscious of things in virtue of the mental states they possess. But those mental states themselves are not conscious of anything. That is, only creatures are transitively conscious; mental states are not. Intransitive consciousness, on the other hand, can be ascribed both to creatures and to states. Our representative creature, Jones, is intransitively conscious when he is conscious, as opposed to asleep, knocked out, or otherwise unconscious. A state—Jones's belief that Ouagadougou is the capital of Burkina Faso—is intransitively conscious when (and only when) he is consciously entertaining it.

The core idea of HOT models is that intransitive state consciousness can be explained in terms of transitive creature consciousness. This idea can be divided into two claims. First, and roughly, a mental state M, possessed by creature C, is intransitively conscious if and only if C is transitively conscious of M. Second, a creature, C, is transitively conscious of mental state M if and only if C has a thought to the effect that it has M. Jones's belief that Ouagadougou is the capital of Burkina Faso is intransitively conscious when, and only when, Jones is transitively conscious of this belief. And Jones is transitively conscious of this belief when, and only when, he has a higher-order thought about the belief—a higher-order thought to the effect that he has this belief. Thus, intransitive state consciousness is to be explained in terms of transitive creature consciousness, and transitive creature consciousness, according to HOT, is to be explained in terms of a higher-order thought—a thought about a mental state.

The HOT account of intransitive state consciousness faces a reasonably obvious dilemma, best introduced by an example. Suppose Jones is in pain. According to the HOT model, this pain is intransitively conscious if and only Jones has a higher-order thought about this pain—a thought to the effect that he is in pain. However, either the higher-order thought to the effect that he is in pain is itself intransitively conscious or it is not. If the higher-order thought about the pain is itself intransitively conscious, then the HOT account has done nothing to explain intransitive state consciousness. The attempted explanation has cited a state that possesses the very property that the explanation is supposed to explain. The nature of intransitive state consciousness has not been explained; this explanation has merely been deferred. If intransitive consciousness of a mental state requires a higher-order thought about states, and if the higher-order thought is intransitively conscious, then we would need to postulate another thought—a third-order or "higher-higher-order thought" in order to explain the intransitive consciousness of the higher-order thought. But then, once again, the question arises of whether this third-order thought is or is not intransitively conscious. In other words, supposing that the higher-order thought is intransitively conscious yields an infinite regress.

The way to stop this regress before it starts is to deny that the higher-order thought must be intransitively conscious. Jones's thought to the effect that he is in pain need not be intransitively conscious in order to ground the intransitive consciousness of his pain. And this, therefore, is the typical view adopted by HOT theorists. However, it is, I shall try to show, a position that has crippling difficulties of its own. These difficulties make up the second horn of the advertised dilemma.

Suppose that the higher-order thought that (allegedly) confers intransitive consciousness on Jones's pain is not itself intransitively conscious. Then, among other things, Jones will not be aware of thinking that he is in pain. He will, in effect have no idea that he is thinking this. But how can thinking that he is in pain make him aware of his pain if he has no idea that he is thinking he is in pain? The problem is that the HOT account understands intransitive state consciousness via transitive creature consciousness. Jones's pain is intransitively consciousness to the extent that he—the creature, Jones—is transitively conscious of it. But an intransitively unconscious thought—a thought that he has that he has no idea he is having—is not the sort of thing that can make him transitively conscious of anything. In general, intransitively unconscious thoughts do not make us aware of anything—that is *precisely what it is for them to be intransitively unconscious*. That is, intransitively unconscious thoughts are not the sort of thing that can underwrite transitive creature consciousness.

I, like the mythical Jones, believe that Ouagadougou is the capital of Burkina Faso. When I consciously entertain this belief it makes me aware of a fact—the fact that Ouagadougou is the capital of Burkina Faso. However, it is only rarely that I consciously entertain the belief. Most of the time this belief is one of my unconscious beliefs—which, of course, at any given time the vast majority of my beliefs are.[3] What makes a belief unconscious? Well, the unconsciousness—nonconsciousness—of a belief consists in the fact that it does not make me aware of what it would make me aware of if it were conscious. My unconscious belief that Ouagadougou is the capital of Burkina Faso is unconscious because, and to the extent, it does not make me aware that Ouagadougou is the capital of Burkina Faso. When it is in unconscious form, as it is most of the time, I still possess this belief because I am disposed to deploy this belief in the control of action under certain eliciting conditions. For example, someone asks me what is the capital of Burkina Faso, and I reply without hesitation. However, this is the crucial point: when it is in unconscious form, it does not make me aware of the fact that Ouagadougou is the capital of Burkina Faso—and this is precisely what it is for the belief to be unconscious. This is an instance of a more general point: intransitively unconscious

---

3. The idea of an unconscious belief, in this context, should be denuded of any Freudian connotations—when I talk of unconscious beliefs, I mean simply beliefs that are not conscious. That is, "unconscious" as I use the term here is equivalent to "nonconscious."

states do not make the creature that has them transitively conscious of anything at all—that is precisely what makes them intransitively unconscious. Conversely, if they do make the creature that has them transitively conscious of their objects, that is because they are, in fact, intransitively conscious rather than unconscious. But the explanatory strategy of HOT models is to explain intransitive state consciousness in terms of transitive creature consciousness. And this means that they cannot allow the relevant higher-order thoughts to be intransitively unconscious.

The HOT theorist can object that the higher-order thought that confers intransitive consciousness on my pain is an *occurrent* thought—something actively occurring in us shaping our psychological profile and resulting actions—and this makes it crucially different from my belief that Ouagadougou is the capital of Burkina Faso, which does not make me aware of the relevant fact because it exists in dispositional form. In other words, it might be objected that my argument has traded on the dispositional/occurrent distinction rather than, as I claimed, the conscious/unconscious distinction. But if this response is to work, we must be able to understand two things: (1) how one can occurrently entertain a thought in a nonconscious manner, and (2) where doing so makes one aware of what the thought is about. How can a nonconscious thought that I am, let us suppose, occurrently entertaining make me aware of what that thought is about?

We can, I think, make sense of the idea of occurrently entertaining an intransitively unconscious thought. Suppose I think unconsciously—perhaps due to various mechanisms of repression—the thought that someone very close to me is seriously ill. What would this mean? We might explain it in terms of various unexplained feelings of melancholy that assail me when I am talking to the person, or a vague sense of foreboding that I can't quite pin down or render precise. The thought, it might be argued, is occurrent because it is playing an active role in shaping my psychological life and, through that, my behavior. The truth of this account can be contested, but it does at least make sense. However, what we can make no sense of is the idea that this unconscious but occurrent thought makes me aware of what it is about. If it were to do this, then I would have to be aware of the fact that my friend is seriously ill. But as soon as I am aware of this fact, then I am consciously thinking that my friend is seriously ill. That is, the thought has become intransitively conscious. To undergo the dawning realization that my friend is seriously ill is precisely to slowly come to think—to consciously think—that my friend is seriously ill.

Therefore, while we might be able to make sense of the idea of occurrently entertaining an unconscious thought, what we cannot make sense of is the idea that this thought should make us aware of what it is about. That it does not make us aware of what it is about is precisely what it is for the thought to be intransitively unconscious. Conversely, as soon as it does make us aware of what it is about, it is an intransitively conscious thought—because making us aware of what it is about is precisely what it is for the thought to be intransitively conscious.

The moral is clear. Whether dispositional or occurrent, intransitively unconscious thoughts do not make us transitively conscious of what they are about. That is precisely what it means for them to be intransitively unconscious. This means that the dilemma facing the HOT model is serious—indeed, in my view, crippling. The defining explanatory strategy of HOT models is to explain intransitive state consciousness in terms of transitive creature consciousness. And transitive creature consciousness is explained in terms of higher-order thoughts. However, if these higher-order thoughts are intransitively unconscious, then they cannot underwrite transitive creature consciousness, and the HOT model fails. If, on the other hand, the higher-order thoughts are intransitively conscious, the HOT model faces an infinite regress. Either way, I suspect, the prospects for a successful HOT explanation of consciousness are grim.

METACOGNITION AND CONTROL: THE MIRACLE-OF-THE-META REITERATED

The idea that a higher-order thought about a mental state could explain the intransitive consciousness of that state is one example of the fallacy I have called the *miracle-of-the-meta*. In essence, the fallacy involves the attribution of miraculous powers to metacognition or metacognitive abilities. The idea that metacognition could explain the normative status of a motivation, via explaining a subject's control over that motivation, is, I shall now argue, another example of this sort of miraculous thinking.

Consider, first, the general form this "miracle" takes. There is a set of first-order states that are taken to be intrinsically lacking in some regard. That is, taken in themselves they seem to lack a property that we routinely accept that they have. This property is then supplied through extrinsic means. These extrinsic means consist in a set of second-order states that take these first-order states as their objects. These second-order states supply the first-order states with the feature they were taken to be lacking. However, upon examination, this strategy turns out to be fatally flawed. In particular, the issue that arose with regard to the first-order states—their apparent lack of possession of a given property—is simply reiterated at the second-order level. With regard to HOT models of consciousness, the delinquent property of first-order mental states was consciousness. Second-order states—higher-order thoughts—were invoked to supply this delinquent property to the first-order states. However, the same issue of delinquency that arose at the first-order level is reiterated at the second-order level. Specifically the second-order states could supply the delinquent property of intransitive consciousness to the first-order states only if they already possessed this property. This undermines the pretensions of the HOT model to provide an explanatory account of what intransitive state consciousness is. The appeal to higher-order states ultimately presupposes the feature it is supposed to explain.

The idea that we can explain a subject's control over her motivations by appeal to metacognitive abilities is, I shall now argue, a version of the same fallacy. To see this, let us first return to the predicament of Myshkin. We are tempted to suppose that in the absence of the relevant metacognitive abilities—the ability to form higher-order thoughts about his motivations—Myshkin is at the "mercy" of his motivations. They push him this way and that. Unable to critically scrutinize these motivations, he has no control over what they cause him to do. Metacognitive abilities, however, supposedly transform Marlow. Armed with these abilities, he can sit above the motivational fray, thinking about his motivations—observing, judging, and evaluating them, coolly deciding the extent to which he will allow them to determine his decisions and actions. Marlow can ask himself whether he should follow the dictates of a given motivation, whether he should embrace it or resist it. More than merely asking himself the questions, Marlow knows how to proceed with the business of answering them. He compares his motivations and their likely consequences with moral principles that he antecedently holds, assessing the compatibility or lack of compatibility between motivations and principles. Myshkin is unable to do any of this—both the questions and the procedures for answering them are beyond him. Therefore, no sense can be given to the idea that he *should* do it. Ought implies can. Marlow's ability to subject his motivations to this sort of scrutiny, therefore, gives him control over his motivations and, as a result, lends those motivations a normative status that Myshkin's lack. This is the general picture that underlies the assignation of Marlow to the category of subject capable of acting for moral reasons and the failure to assign Myshkin to this category. I shall argue that this entire picture is misguided. Metacognition, in its various forms, is not the sort of thing that could imbue a subject with control over its motivations.

AUTONOMY AS AN IDEAL

The sort of metacognitive abilities implicated in principles (1)–(5)—identified in the previous chapter—are of various kinds. First, there is *recognition*: the ability to recognize a motivation. Then there is *interrogation*: the ability to ask oneself whether this motivation is one that should be embraced or one that should be resisted. Third, there is *judgment*: the ability to assess the compatibility between motivation and an antecedently adopted moral principle or proposition. Then there are further acts of interrogation and judgment involved pertaining to the status of one's antecedently adopted moral principles or propositions and also to one's ability to reliably make judgments of compatibility and incompatibility, and so on. Recognition, interrogation, and judgment are the general categories of metacognition involved in the ability to effectively scrutinize one's motivations.

Someone who can engage in these sorts of metacognitive processes is often said to be a morally autonomous subject. As mentioned earlier, nothing I shall argue should be taken to count against the possibility of there being morally autonomous subjects—understood as subjects whose metacognitive abilities conform to principles (1)–(5). My argument concerns what conforming to these principles should be understood to give to a subject. I shall try to show that conforming to these principles, and so possessing metacognitive abilities such as recognition, interrogation, and judgment, does not imbue a subject with control over its motivations. While there is nothing, necessarily, wrong with the concept of moral autonomy understood in this sense, it would be a mistake to suppose that moral autonomy is the sort of thing that can confer control over motivations.

Broadly speaking, there are two different ways of understanding the idea of moral autonomy.[4] One of these ways can, for our purposes, quickly be dispensed with. This way understands moral autonomy as an *ideal* to which one can aspire, but which is never fully realized in actual cases. The status of moral autonomy as an ideal would seem to stem from the suspicion that the sorts of processes outlined in (1)–(5) are, in principle, not completable: with respect to motivations, antecedently accepted principles or propositions, abilities to judge, and so on, there are always further questions that can be asked, further avenues for interrogation that must be explored. This suspicion would be allied to skepticism concerning the picture of a subject all of whose motivations are transparent to her.

It is reasonably clear that if we understand autonomy as an ideal, then autonomy is not the sort of thing that can imbue a subject with control over its motivations. Something to which one can merely aspire—something whose actualization would require one to meet conditions that one cannot meet—is not the sort of thing that can confer control over one's actual motivations. For example, suppose Jones is an emotionally incontinent individual, in a roughly Aristotelian sense. Jones rarely opts for the mean between two extremes. However, he knows enough about Aristotle's Doctrine of the Mean to wish that he were different. He regards the doctrine as specifying an ideal that he aspires to meet, and genuinely struggles to

---

4. Here I am indebted to Joel Feinberg, "Autonomy," in John Christman ed., *The Inner Citadel: Essays on Personal Autonomy* (New York: Oxford University Press, 1989), pp. 27–53. Feinberg also identifies a fourth sense of moral autonomy—a set of rights expressive of one's authority over oneself—that are not relevant to the purposes of this chapter.

meet—though unfortunately seldom does. It is clear that Jones's ideal confers no control over his motivations. Indeed, that is the very problem Jones faces. This is true more generally. Nothing has, so far, ruled out the claim that living up to a moral ideal might imbue a subject with control over its motivations—that is, in effect, the topic of the following section. But the ideal, in itself, is impotent in this regard.

Therefore, any prospect of finding a connection between moral autonomy—the convenient designator I am using for the ability to engage in the sorts of scrutiny implicated in principles (1)–(5)—and control over motivations must rest on understanding autonomy as something an individual might actually possess rather than merely an ideal to which that individual might aspire. It is to this *actualist* understanding of moral autonomy that we now turn.

AUTONOMY AND CONTROL

According to what I shall call the *actualist* interpretation of moral autonomy, one possesses autonomy to the extent one is capable of engaging in processes of recognition, interrogation, and judgment of the sort outlined in principles (1)–(5). A morally autonomous subject is one with the ability to engage in these sorts of processes, even if they are open-ended, and can never be brought to an ultimate resolution. A stronger view might claim that one possesses moral autonomy only when one is actually engaged in these processes. That is, moral autonomy turns on the exercise of the ability and not simply possession of the ability. This view entails that humans are morally autonomous individuals only on relatively infrequent occasions— and that some humans are, perhaps, never morally autonomous. The arguments I shall develop apply to both positions equally. However, since the dispositional or ability-based version of the actualist thesis is both more plausible, and entailed by the stronger view that requires exercise of the ability, my focus will be on that. If the dispositional view falls, so too does the stronger version *modus tollens*.

I shall argue that if we understand moral autonomy in terms of the ability to engage in processes of the sort outlined in (1)–(5), then it is not the sort of thing that can confer control over motivations. To suppose that it is would be to fall victim to a version of the fallacy I have labeled the *miracle-of-the-meta*: the mistake of thinking that something magical happens in the transition from first order to meta-level, a magic that renders the metalevel immune to the tribulations of the first order. To see why, let us return to the case of Marlow.

Marlow's engaging in the sorts of processes of critical scrutiny outlined in (1)–(5) allows him to stand outside—or above—the motivational fray in a way that Myshkin can never replicate. While Myshkin is simply pushed in this way and that by his motivations, Marlow scrutinizes his: assessing the compatibility between his motivations and his antecedently held moral principles, interrogating those principles and examining his judgments of compatibility or incompatibility, and so on. Marlow's engaging in these sorts of critical processes is supposed to give him a control over his motivations that Myshkin lacks, and so lends Marlow's motivations a normative status that Myshkin's motivations do not possess.

However, what if Marlow's metacognitive abilities were not at all like their portrayal in this account? What if they were, in certain crucial respects, like the motivations that they take as their objects? Marlow can undoubtedly think to himself thoughts such as, "What is it that is motivating me to do this?" and "Is this motivation something that I should act upon, or something that I should reject?" In answering questions such as this, he can bring to bear antecedently accepted moral principles or propositions, and assess the compatibility or lack thereof, between principle and motivation. He can, in turn, question his antecedent commitments, and his ability to accurately and impartially makes judgments of compatibility, and so on. However, suppose the answers he gives to all these questions are ones over which he has little control: being, for example, crucially sensitive to features of the situation in which he finds himself—features of which he has only a dim awareness and whose influence on him largely escapes his conscious grasp. In other words, while Marlow could still observe and evaluate his motivations, this observation and evaluation would be both clouded and shaped by contextual factors of which he has little awareness and over which he has little control. In such a circumstance, it would seem that Marlow is at the "mercy" of his metacognitive, higher-order, assessments of his motivations. These assessments pull him in this way or that—make him evaluate his motivations one way or another—but they work in subterranean ways. He has little grasp, and just as little control, over their workings.

This problem arises at every stage in the sequence of processes outlined in (1)–(5). The appeal to Marlow's antecedently held moral principles will be of little help—for the same sorts of worries obviously arise with them. Perhaps his commitment to these principles is the result of contextual factors of which he has little awareness. But that, it is thought, is the function of claims (4) and (5) in the process of scrutiny. Marlow can also scrutinize his commitment to these principles, and examine his judgments of compatibility and incompatibility between these principles and his motivations. However, exactly the same worries are reiterated at this juncture. Perhaps his scrutiny of his principles is clouded. Perhaps his assessment of his ability to accurately and impartially make judgments of compatibility is skewed.

In raising these worries, I am, of course, alluding to recent influential work in moral psychology of a broadly *situationist* orientation.[5]

---

5. See, for example, Philip Zimbardo, *The Lucifer Effect: How Good People Turn Evil* (New York: Random House, 2007).

Situationist accounts of the moral subject can be contrasted with *dispositionalist* accounts. According to the latter, very roughly, the moral subject is constituted, in part, by a set of dispositions that are internal to the subject, and the subject is responsible for their formation and preservation. These dispositions make up what we might call the *character* of the person. Included in these dispositions will be ones that pertain to the evaluation of motivations. Thus, the character of the moral subject is, in part, made up of dispositions to classify given motivations as ones that should be acted upon or ones that should be resisted.

Situationist accounts, however, see things very differently. According to a (probably unrealistically) strong version of situationism, a person's character is as malleable as the situations in which she finds herself. Change the situation, and the subject's dispositions to morally evaluate motivations in one way rather than another will also change. Thus we might imagine Marlow as a participant in a Stanford Prison Experiment,[6] or as a guard at Abu Ghraib. If the situationist account is correct, we should expect Marlow's evaluation of his motivations to vary with these variations in circumstances. However, the relevant contextual factors operate at all levels of the process of scrutiny. They apply not simply to Marlow's evaluations of his motivations but also to all the resources he brings to bear on these evaluations: his antecedent adoption of certain moral principles, his judgments of compatibility and lack thereof, and so on.

Therefore, the idea that Marlow's metacognitive abilities confer control and, via control, normativity on his motivations—a normativity that Myshkin's motivations therefore lack—seems, at the very least, a hostage to empirical fortune. If Marlow is, as the situationist argues, at the mercy of his metacognitive assessments of his

---

6. Craig Haney, Curtis Banks, and Philip Zimbardo, "Interpersonal Dynamics in a Simulated Prison," *International Journal of Criminology and Penology* 1 (1973), 69–97.

motivations in the way that Myshkin has been portrayed as being at the mercy of his motivations, then it is unclear how possession of metacognitive abilities can imbue Marlow with control over his motivations; and therefore it is equally unclear how they can imbue these motivations with normativity. If this is correct, then the attempt to deny animals the status of moral subjects based on their perceived lack of metacognitive abilities is, similarly, hostage to empirical fortune. At the very least, it requires a resolution of the dispositionalist-situationist dispute.

However, any resolution of this debate is, for our purposes, relatively unimportant. Underlying these empirical concerns is a deeper, and for our purposes more significant, conceptual point. The appeal to metacognition attempts to explain the normativity of our emotions by way of our control over them. This overlooks the fact that the very issue of control that arises at the level of motivations is also going to be replicated at the (second, third, fourth, and so on order) level of our evaluation of those motivations. This failure to see what is, ultimately, a fairly obvious point is a symptom of the pull exerted on us by the miracle-of-the-meta. Metacognition, of the sort embodied in principles (1)–(5), was supposed to allow Marlow to sit above the motivational fray, and calmly pass judgment on his motivations, thus providing him with control over those motivations and so transforming them into normative items as the SCNM schema specifies. However, there is no reason to suppose that metacognition is above this motivational fray. If first-order motivations can pull Myshkin this way and that, then second-order evaluations of those motivations can do exactly the same to Marlow. If Myshkin is indeed at the "mercy" of his first-order motivations, as the traditional picture would have us believe, then, logically, Marlow is similarly at the "mercy" of his second-order evaluations of these motivations. In short, second-order evaluation of our first-order motivations cannot lift us above the motivational fray that we think endemic to the first-order motivations, for the simple reason that we can be motivated to evaluate our motivations in one way rather than another.

It does not matter how many orders we ascend, the issue of control arises at each of them. It arises at the level of Marlow's third-order evaluation of his acquisition of the moral principles on which his second-order evaluations are based. The miracle-of-the-meta would have us believe that something miraculous happens in the jump from first- to second-order cognition. When second-order states take first-order states as their object, that is when something wonderful happens. Or, if it does not happen there, we can find it in the move from second- to third-order cognition, and so on. Somewhere, the miracle tells us, we will find a level that is immune to the tribulations of the lower order. But there are no miracles, and there is no such level. Our second-order states—evaluations, assessments, effective critical scrutinizings—allow us to control our first-order motivations. But this overlooks the fact that they will do so only if we, in turn, control our second-order evaluations. Precisely the same issue that arose at the first order will be reiterated at the second order. It will be reiterated at whatever level to which we ascend. The fallacy of the miracle-of-the-meta arises from overlooking this point. It is clear that the same fallacy arises whether we are talking about higher-order abilities or the exercise of those higher-order abilities.

The suspicion that, in connection with the idea of moral autonomy, the appeal to the second order will merely reiterate whatever problems, issues, and deficiencies arise at the first order has been raised, in different ways, by Thalberg,[7] Friedman,[8] Meyers,[9]

7. Irving Thalberg, "Hierarchical Analyses of Unfree Action," in Christman, *The Inner Citadel*, pp. 123–36.
8. Marilyn Friedman, "Autonomy and the Split-Level Self," *Southern Journal of Philosophy* 24 (1986), 19–35.
9. Diana Meyers, *Self, Society and Personal Choice* (New York: Columbia University Press, 1989), pp. 25–41.

and Noggle.[10] This objection has typically been countered by the addition of further factors pertaining to the conditions under which such reflection must take place. For example, a common response is to insist that the reflection must take place under conditions free of distorting factors, or must reflect an adequate causal history, and so on.[11] When advanced as part of an analysis of the concept of moral autonomy, there is nothing wrong with these additional conditions. However, in the present context, they are clearly irrelevant. The idea I am disputing is that moral autonomy—in the form of the sort of scrutiny implied in principles (1)–(5)—functions by imbuing a subject with control over its motivations. The invocation of conditions free of distorting factors or ones reflecting an adequate causal history will help in this role only if they are the sort of things over which the autonomous subject has control. In other words, invocation of these factors with the goal of explaining a subject's control over its motivations would be just another expression of the miracle-of-the-meta.

CONCLUSION

According to the SCNM explanatory schema, the ability to engage in effective critical scrutiny of one's motivations provides one with control over those motivations, thus transforming them into normative states. However, we have failed to identify any satisfactory account of the connection between effective critical scrutiny and control. The

10. R. Noggle, "Autonomy and the Paradox of Self-Creation: Infinite Regresses, Finite Selves, and the Limits of Authenticity," in J. S. Taylor ed., *Personal Autonomy: New Essays on Personal Autonomy and Its Role in Contemporary Moral Philosophy* (Cambridge: Cambridge University Press, 2005), pp. 87–108.

11. See, for example, John Christman, "Autonomy and Personal History," *Canadian Journal of Philosophy* 21.1 (1991), 1–24. Also Alfred Mele, *Autonomous Agents: From Self-Control to Autonomy* (New York: Oxford University Press, 1995).

SCNM explanatory schema, therefore, breaks down at the S-C stage. The phenomenological features associated with effective critical scrutiny are, I have argued, implausible candidates for conferrers of control. It is also implausible, on independent grounds, to suppose that the category of moral subject can be identified or explained through an appeal to moral phenomenology. The appeal to metacognitive abilities overlooks the fact that the same issue of control that arises at the first order will simply be reiterated at the second order (and third, and fourth, and so on).

If the arguments of this chapter are correct, then the case against Myshkin qualifying as a moral subject rests on a conception of control that is unsupported. It is Marlow's control over his motivations, we were tempted to assert, that decisively distinguishes him from Myshkin. This control gives his motivations a normative grip that Myshkin's lack, and so makes his motivations the sorts of things that could qualify as moral. However, the requisite idea of control has, on examination, proved elusive. Phenomenology will not supply it. And the attractiveness of the thought that it can be found in metacognitive abilities—the ability to engage in higher-order thoughts about one's motivations—rests on the fallacy of the miracle-of-the-meta. But the dialectical function of Myshkin is, of course, to go proxy for other animals. To the extent that the case against Myshkin qualifying as a moral subject rests on an unsubstantiated, seemingly mysterious, conception of control, so too does the case against (at least some) animals.

The next chapter examines an alternative strategy for understanding normativity, but one that is also inimical to the idea that animals can act for moral reasons. The account of normativity built in to the SCNM explanatory is an individualistic one. It is the individual's ability to engage in effective critical scrutiny of her motivations that provides her with control over those motivations. This means that it is her motivational states that can have normative status and so her states that might qualify as moral motivations. Thus, according to the SCNM scheme, the normativity of an individual's motivations derives from features of that individual.

There is, however, a distinctive and influential strand of twentieth-century philosophy of mind and language that suggests it is a mistake to think of normativity as a feature of individuals or individual behavior. Normativity is *essentially* a property of communities—in particular of community *practices*. This suggests another way of thinking about the normative status of motivations and also, by extension, an alternative means of trying to exclude Myshkin from the category of moral subject. Here, the focus is not on normativity through the lens of individual control, but normativity through the lens of community practice.

According to this alternative account of normativity, the reason animals do not qualify as moral subjects—cannot act for moral reasons—is not to be found in features of their individual psychology. Rather, they cannot act for moral reasons because their possession of such reasons is essentially dependent on their belonging to a certain kind of *practice*. To be a moral subject it is necessary that one belong a *moral practice*. Humans belong to such practices. Animals do not. That is why we are moral subjects and they are not. This *moral practice hypothesis* is the subject of the next chapter.

8

Moral Reasons and Practice

TWO FUNCTIONS OF MORAL PRACTICE

The SCNM explanatory schema is based on the individualistic assumption that the source of the normativity of a subject's motivations is to be found in features internal to that subject: specifically the subject's ability to engage in effective critical scrutiny of her motivations and the resulting control over her motivations that this ability engenders. That normativity has this sort of individualistic grounding is an assumption clearly endorsed by both Aristotle and Kant. Kant sees this ability as grounded in a specific form of self-consciousness, unique to humans, that allows them to see the grounds of their actions *as* grounds. Aristotle associates the ability to scrutinize one's motivations as a function of phronesis, and the resulting ability to understand the moral salience of a situation. In the previous two chapters, I argued that we have no workable account of the relation between effective critical scrutiny and control. If this is correct, the SCNM schema breaks down at the S-C stage.

The sort of individualism implicit in the SCNM schema is incompatible with a prominent, and still influential, theme of twentieth-century philosophy of mind and language. According to this theme, associated with Wittgenstein and Sellars among others, if we want to understand normativity, the individual subject is the wrong place to look. Normativity is essentially embedded in social practices. If we want to understand the normativity of a subject's motivations, we need to look not at that subject in isolation, and not at any features or abilities intrinsic to that subject, but at the relation between the subject and the social environment in which he or she is embedded. The implications of this idea for the central thesis of this book— that animals can act for moral reasons—can take two different forms. The first questions whether these alleged moral reasons are really reasons; the second questions whether these alleged moral reasons are really moral.

I have argued that animals can be the subjects of moral emotions—emotions that have moral content. In virtue of their content, these emotions provide reasons—moral reasons—for what animals do. I am committed to the claim that these motivating emotions are reasons. They are not merely causes that push animals this way and that. Rather, they are reasons that are individuated by their content, and, in virtue of this content, can provide appropriate, normatively evaluable, responses to environmental circumstance. That is, and this is a theme to be substantially elaborated in the next chapter, animals possess a normative sensitivity to (some) morally salient features of their situations, where this is grounded in the operations of a reliable mechanism or module. What makes this sensitivity normative is precisely the fact that their sensitivity consists in their possessing emotions that have content.

Given that this is the position I am defending, the appeal to practice might prove relevant in two logically distinct ways. First, one might argue that an individual's belonging to a practice is a necessary condition of that individual's possessing *reasons*—of any sort. Animals, in virtue of their (presumed) failure to belong to a practice, cannot possess reasons for action because they cannot possess states that have content. Second, one might argue that while belonging to a practice is not required for the possession of reasons as such, it is a necessary condition of the possession of specifically *moral* reasons. Thus animals, in virtue of their (presumed) failure to belong to a practice, cannot be motivated to act by moral reasons—although they may be motivated by nonmoral counterparts. Implicit in each claim is, I shall try to show, a correspondingly different conception of the sort of thing a practice must be. I shall consider each of these claims in turn.

REASONS AND PRACTICE

Reasons, whether moral or not, have content. It is common, for example, to think of reasons as belief-desire couplings. Both beliefs and desires are individuated by their content. Emotions, I have argued, possess both factual and evaluative content, and in this they can provide reasons for action that mirrors the factual-affective motivating profile of belief-desire couplings. What distinguishes two tokens of anger, for example, is that one has the content that Jones snubbed me while the other has the content that Jones carelessly trod on my toe. But both also involve additional evaluative content: he was wrong to do so (or variations on this evaluative theme: he should have been more careful, and so on).

According to the first version of what I shall refer to as the *practice hypothesis*, content is possible only in the context of a practice. An individual's possession of reasons, therefore, requires that the individual be appropriately embedded in a practice. Given that reasons are content-bearing states, then to the extent animals are not thus embedded, they cannot possess reasons for what they do.

The locus classicus of this position is the later work of Wittgenstein. Wittgenstein's argument for the practice hypothesis begins with the notion of a "sign." Words are the most obvious examples of signs. Signs have meaning, but this is not intrinsic to them. A word-token can, in itself, mean anything—and therefore, in itself, means nothing. To have meaning it must be interpreted. However, the category of sign is not restricted to linguistic items. Anything that "comes before the mind" has the logical status of a sign. Let us suppose I mentally picture a dog. This mental image can, in itself, mean an indefinite number of things. It might represent a particular dog, or dogs in general—or mammals, or things with fur, or things with four legs, or things with tails, and so on. In order to mean anything at all, it must be interpreted. Interpretation fixes meaning. The significance of practice, according to Wittgenstein, is that it alone can supply an interpretation to signs.

The meaning of a sign is normative: there is a correct and incorrect way of using the sign. The fundamental problem of understanding meaning is accounting for this normativity: accounting for the difference between the correct and incorrect use of a sign. A natural thought is that we might circumscribe the use of a sign by way of a *rule*—one that specifies how the sign is to be used. Wittgenstein undermined this idea by showing that it leads to a certain kind of paradox: the *rule-following paradox*.

Suppose an individual begins a mathematical sequence as follows: 2, 4, 6, 8, 10, 12 . . . 996, 998, 1,000. However, when he reaches 1,000, he continues as follows: 1,004, 1,008, 1,012, 1,016 . . . It is natural to suppose that, upon reaching 1,000 he made a mistake. He was following a certain rule—the "$x + n$" rule. His behavior after reaching 1,000 departed from this rule and was, to that extent, a mistake. However, there is another possibility. Perhaps, he was not following the "$x + n$" rule at all. Perhaps all along he was following the more complex rule: "$x + n$ iff $x \leq 1,000$, if not $x + 2n$." Thus, the question is: What constitutes the person following the "$x + n$" rule (and subsequently making a mistake) and not the "$x + n$ iff $x \leq 1,000$, if not $x + 2n$" rule (and subsequently carrying on correctly)? To capture the normative character of signs we need to be able to distinguish between what a person *should* do with a sign and what he *in fact* does with it. The success of the appeal to rules, therefore, requires that we be able to identify what constitutes following one rule rather than another. And to this, we need to be able to distinguish between following one rule incorrectly and following a distinct rule correctly.

We cannot simply say that after reaching 1,000 the individual made a mistake because he was supposed to go on doing "the same thing." What counts as "the same thing" is a matter of which rule he was following: if he was, all along, following the "$x + n$ iff x ≤ 1,000, if not $x + 2n$" rule, then when he reached 1,000 he did, in fact, keep doing "the same thing."

Nor is it plausible to suppose that when a person follows a mathematical rule, this rule must somehow "pass before their mind." How would that occur? If the picture of the rule "$x + n$" appears before his conscious gaze, the problem is that this rule is, logically, just another sign. To mean anything, it must be interpreted, and this means interpreting its constituent signs. Perhaps, for example, "+" is used in such a way that it means "+ add iff $x ≤ 1,000$, add $2n$ otherwise." If so, when the person reaches 1,000 he, in fact, continues to follow the rule correctly. Perhaps one might think that following the rule consists in the person consciously thinking to himself: "When I reach 1,000 I shall continue adding 2 and no other number." But this faces the same problem: we now need to interpret the signs "adding," "number," and so on. And, of course, any appeal to the idea that the rule followed is "When I reach 1,000 I will continue adding 2 and not 1, 3, 4, 5,...n" would entail that whenever a person correctly follows a rule he must simultaneously be thinking an infinite number of thoughts. The upshot is, Wittgenstein argued, that no item of which one is consciously aware, no item that comes "before one's conscious gaze" can provide an interpretation of what one is supposed to do because the item is itself subject to a variety of interpretations. The problem persists if we switch our focus from mental to behavioral facts. A person's behavior at any given time is compatible with his following an indefinite number of rules. Indeed, since numbers are infinite, a person's continuing the series 2, 4, 6, 8, 10, 12...is compatible with his following an infinite number of algebraic formulas.

My purpose here is not to assess Wittgenstein's arguments, but simply to note his conclusions. The first of these is that there is no fact about the individual person at any given time that determines that he or she is following one rule rather than another. Thus, if we focus on the individual at a time, we arrive at a paradox:

> This was our paradox: no course of action could be determined by a rule, because every course of action can be made out to accord with the rule. The answer was: if everything can be made out to accord with the rule, then it can also be made out to conflict with it. And so there would be neither accord nor conflict here.[1]

Wittgenstein's second conclusion concerns how to avoid this paradox. This requires appeal to the concept of a *custom* or *practice*:

> And hence also "obeying a rule" is a practice. And to think one is obeying a rule is not to obey a rule. Hence it is not possible to obey a rule "privately": otherwise thinking one was obeying a rule would be the same thing as obeying it.[2]

If there is no distinction between obeying a rule and merely thinking that one is obeying it, then there are no normative standards governing the application of that rule. Only practice can supply the required distinction. Therefore, Wittgenstein's position amounts to this: meaning is not possible in the absence of a practice because normativity is not possible in the absence of a practice.

If this is correct, the implications for the claim that animals can possess reasons are clear. Reasons, or the components of reasons, are individuated by their content. But content is simply meaning. The

1. Ludwig Wittgenstein, *Philosophical Investigations*, trans. G. E. M. Anscombe (Oxford: Blackwell, 1953), sec. 201.
2. Wittgenstein, *Philosophical Investigations*, sec. 202.

content of the belief that animals can act morally is identical with the meaning of the sentence, "Animals can act morally." The content of Smith's indignation that Jones has snubbed him is the meaning of the sentence (as uttered by Smith), "Jones has snubbed me—and was wrong to do so." As reasons for action, emotions have content. And content is the same thing as meaning. Therefore, if meaning is not possible in the absence of a practice, neither is content. And if reasons are individuated by their content, then in the absence of a practice there can be no reasons. If animals do not belong to a practice, they cannot have reasons for what they do. Therefore, without belonging to a practice, animals cannot be moral subjects in the sense defended in this book.

EVALUATION OF THE PRACTICE HYPOTHESIS

There are two ways in which one might respond to this appeal to practice in the constitution of reasons. The first is to reject the appeal. The second is to accept it but argue that animals can, in fact, belong to practices in the relevant sense.

Let us begin with the first approach. There is a serious—perhaps crippling—problem with the appeal to practice. At least, this problem is evident when the appeal is understood as a way of grounding the possibility of meaning or content—and that is the way it is understood when it is employed to deny that animals can possess reasons.[3]

---

3. It is possible to understand the appeal to practice in a nonconstructivist way. Understood in this way, the appeal does not serve to give an account of how meaning or content is possible but, rather, is a way of unmasking and so challenging the assumptions that led to the paradox in the first place. As an example of this interpretation, see John McDowell, "Meaning and Intentionality in Wittgenstein's Later Philosophy," *Midwest Studies in Philosophy* 17 (1992), 30–42. The nonconstructivist version has no implications for the question of whether animals can possess reasons, and I shall therefore focus on the decidedly orthodox constructivist alternative.

The problem is that the appeal is circular: it presupposes content rather than explains it.[4] Practice is what we do. What we do are actions. But actions are individuated by intentions (or volitions, tryings, or belief-desire complexes—depending on one's view of action). For example, I am patting my head while rubbing my stomach. How many actions are present here depends on how many intentions there are. If there is one—the intention to pat my head and rub my stomach at the same time, then there is one action. But if there are two intentions, which just happen to be contemporaneously instantiated, then there are two actions. Actions are individuated by intentions (or volitions, tryings, and so one). However, intentions are individuated by their content. One intention is type-distinct from another if and only if a different proposition is embedded in the that-clause used to ascribe them. The appeal to practice, therefore, cannot explain how content is possible for the simple reason that it presupposes content. But if the appeal to practice cannot explain content, we have no reason for supposing that content is impossible in the absence of a practice. And if we have no reason for supposing that content is impossible in the absence of a practice, we have no reason for supposing that animals are precluded from possession of reasons by their supposed failure to belong to the relevant practice.

It might be thought that we can avoid this problem by appealing to a more basic, nonintentional conception of practice. As such, practice would, effectively, consist in series of bodily movements. The problem, however, is that this conception of practice seems useless for the purposes of escaping the rule-following paradox. In the case of following the mathematical "$n + 2$" progression, for example, we

4. The late Susan Hurley puts this by saying that the appeal to practice falls victim to what she calls the "myth of the giving"—as opposed to Sellars's more famous "myth of the given." The myth of the given takes the content of perception as an unproblematic given: as pure input from the world, unadulterated by the conceptual abilities or activities of the subject. The myth of the giving takes the content of action as similarly unproblematic, as consisting in pure output to the world.

would have to imagine that the behavior in question consists in non-interpreted sounds of certain pitch and duration or marks on paper of certain shape. But then the question of which rule the subject is following cannot even be raised. There is no reason for supposing that there is anything like rule-following going on—as opposed to merely random squeaks or squiggles. To even set up the paradox in the first place, it is necessary to suppose that the subject's behavior is interpreted—and therefore intentional—behavior. And this means that the appeal to content ultimately presupposes content.[5]

The second response to the appeal to practice is to accept it, but argue that animals can belong to a practice in the relevant sense. The "relevant sense" is the one endorsed by Wittgenstein: "To understand a sentence means to understand a language. To understand a language is to be master of a technique."[6] There are two distinct ideas at work here: *mastery* and *technique*. To have mastery of a technique is to have the ability to employ it as the occasion warrants. The technique in question is that of adjusting one's use of a sign to bring it into line with customary or practiced norms. To belong to a practice, therefore, is to have the ability to adjust one's use of a sign in accordance with the norms of that practice. It is far from clear that animals cannot belong to practices in this sense. Indeed, it is rather implausible to suppose that they do not belong to practices in this sense.

Consider a well-known example. Vervet monkeys give predator-specific alarm calls.[7] In fact, this phenomenon is by no means unique to vervet monkeys, having also been observed in ring-tailed lemurs,[8]

5. For a far more developed account of this problem, see Mark Rowlands, *Body Language: Representation in Action* (Cambridge, MA: MIT Press, 2006), pp. 61–63.
6. Wittgenstein, *Philosophical Investigations*, sec. 199.
7. R. M. Seyfarth, D. L. Cheney, and P. Marler, "Monkey Responses to Three Different Alarm Calls: Evidence of Predator Classification and Semantic Communication," *Science* 210 (1980), 801–3.
8. K. Zuberbühler, D. Jenny, and R. Bshary, "The Predator Deterrence Function of Primate Alarm Calls," *Ethology* 105 (1999), 477–90.

white-faced capuchin monkeys,[9] Diana monkeys,[10] and Campbell's monkeys.[11] In the case of vervet monkeys, three alarm calls, in particular, have been documented: calls for leopard, python, and martial eagle. Leopard alarm calls are short, tonal calls produced in a series of inhalations and exhalations. Python calls are high-pitched "chutters." Eagle alarm calls are low-pitched grunts.[12] The different calls elicit different responses. The first response is the same to all the calls: the monkeys look at the individual who made the call. The direction in which this individual is looking provides information about the location of the predator. Following this, behaviors diverge depending on the call. Leopard alarm calls cause the monkeys to run up trees, out to the exterior branches that will not support the weight of the leopard. Python alarm calls make the monkeys stand erect on their hind legs looking at the ground. Eagle alarm calls make the monkeys take cover in nearby vegetation.

Juvenile vervet monkeys exhibit less discrimination and greater frequency of errors in their alarm calls. Leopard calls are made in the presence of many terrestrial animals. Many types of bird elicit eagle calls, and python calls are sometimes made in the presence of sticks lying on the ground. As the monkeys mature, however, their discrimination improves and the frequency of their mistakes diminishes. To a significant extent, this is the result of their being "corrected"—sometimes quite painfully—by older monkeys.

When these alarm calls are the subject of discussion by philosophers, it is typically in the context of what they reveal—or fail to

---

9. C. Fichtel, S. Perry, and J. Gros-Louis, "Alarm Calls of White-faced Capuchin Monkeys: An Acoustic Analysis," *Animal Behaviour* 70.1 (2005), 165–76.

10. K. Zuberbühler, "Referential Labelling in Diana Monkeys," *Animal Behaviour* 59.5 (2000), 917–27.

11. K. Ouattara, A. Lemasson, and K. Zuberbühler, "Campbell's Monkeys Use Affixation to Alter Call Meaning," *PLoS ONE* 4.11 (2009), e7808.

12. You can listen to these calls at this website: http://www.wjh.harvard.edu/~mnkylab/media/vervetcalls.html.

reveal—about the mental capacities of vervet monkeys. I am employing these examples in a different way: as a straightforward example of a communicatory *practice*—irrespective of what that reveals about underlying psychological abilities. As they grow up, the juvenile monkeys slowly learn to adjust their use of signs to bring them into accordance with customary norms. They become masters of a technique of employing signs in accordance with the norms of a practice. Given the Wittgensteinian conception of a practice, there is no basis for denying that the vervet monkeys are engaged in a practice.

Consider, as a second example of a communicatory practice, the play behavior of dogs and other canids documented by Marc Bekoff. In connection with the play behavior of dogs, Bekoff and Pierce write:

> Because there is a chance that various behavior patterns that are performed during ongoing social play can be misinterpreted as being real aggression or mating, individuals have to tell others, "I want to play."...Play frequently begins with a bow, and repeated bowing during play sequences remains the name of the game. A dog asks another to play by crouching on her forelimbs, raising her hind end in the air, and often barking and wagging her tail as she bows. After each individual agrees to play and not to fight, prey on, or mate with the other, there are ongoing rapid and subtle exchanges of information so that their cooperative agreement can be fine tuned and negotiated on the run so that the actors remain playful.[13]

These behaviors are part of a conventional system whose function is to communicate that what is going on should not be construed as

13. Bekoff and Pierce, *Wild Justice*, pp. 122–23.

aggressive, sexual, or predatory. Any successfully socialized dog will know both how to understand and how to produce these signs. These signs are normative: they should be employed in certain circumstances but not others. And the standards of correctness for their deployment are upheld by the threat of sanction: "cheaters" who use a play bow as a precursor to an attack are unlikely to be chosen as play partners on subsequent occasions. If adequately socialized, as a dog matures it learns the conventions of play behavior, adjusting its behavioral signs to bring them into line with community norms.

The more general point that these examples make is a fairly obvious one. Any social animal will form part of a group. The coherence and stability of the group requires communication between its members. This communication can take oral form—as in the alarm calls of various types of monkey—or the form of bodily gestures, as employed by dogs and other canids. But whatever specific form this system of communication takes, there are standards of correctness governing its use. That is, the employment of a given sign on a given occasion can be normatively assessed. Thus, on any given occasion, individual animals can employ a sign correctly or incorrectly, and this is determined by the norms of the practice. Therefore, if a practice is understood as the ability to adjust one's use of a sign to bring it into accordance with customary norms, there is little doubt, I think, that animals engage in practices.

To summarize: *either* the appeal to practice should be rejected on the grounds of circularity—in which case it poses no threat to the claim that animals can possess reasons—*or* the appeal should be accepted, but there is every reason to suppose that animals can satisfy it as well as humans. In which case, once again, the appeal does not jeopardize the claim that animals can have reasons for what they do. Either way, the appeal to practice does little to jeopardize the first component of the central claim of this book: that animals can be the subjects of *reasons*.

MORAL REASONS AND PRACTICE

The thesis defended in this book is that animals can act for moral reasons. As I mentioned earlier, the appeal to practice can be thought to jeopardize this thesis in two logically distinct ways. First, it can be thought of as calling into question the claim that animals act for reasons. Second, while not questioning the claim that animals can act for reasons, it can call into question the claim that these reasons can be specifically moral ones. I have argued that the first claim is, understood in either one of two possible ways, without merit. I shall now switch focus to the second claim.

The conception of practice implicated in the second charge—that whatever reasons animals possess are not moral ones—is quite different from that implicated in the first charge (that animals cannot possess reasons *tout court*). Underwriting the first charge—that animals cannot act for reasons *tout court*—was what I called the *practice hypothesis*. Underwriting the second—that animals cannot act for specifically moral reasons—is what I shall refer to as the *moral practice hypothesis*. The two hypotheses should be distinguished not only because they are employed to establish different conclusions, but also because embodied in each of them is a quite distinct conception of what a practice is. In particular, the conception of practice implicated in the moral practice hypothesis is, in a sense to be made clear, far richer than that implicated in the simple practice hypothesis. The reasons for this are clear. The moral practice hypothesis is not in the business of explaining meaning or content. Rather, it assumes that content is possible, and then provides an account of the conditions that must be met if this content is to attach to genuinely moral reasons—in this case, to moral emotions.

This conception of practice is exemplified in practice-based arguments developed by Dixon. She writes:

The *practice of morality* opens out into myriad social settings where our emotions are judged to be sometimes appropriate or sometimes not because they are directed at the wrong person or informed by reasons that are not relevant. Learning to compose the scene in the right way is learning to make these evaluations so that our emotional responsiveness fits the situation.[14]

As an example, she discusses how a child might be taught the importance of giving or sharing. This would be facilitated through a series of related questions such as: Is giving always the right thing to do? Can you give away something that does not belong to you? If you give someone a gift, should you expect to get something back? If you have a cold should you try to give it to other people? If you give someone a hug and you get a hug back, what does that mean?[15] It is through questions such as these that the child learns both the concept (or rather the concepts) of giving and, equally important, the significance of giving in our lives. These questions, and ones like them, are part of the practice of morality, as Dixon understands it. Animals, she claims, cannot belong to the practice of morality in this sense:

So while I agree that a trained police dog probably is sufficiently cognizant of "human social skills" to refrain from biting the children it visits in the hospital, the dog does not possess an understanding of even very simple moral concerns that prohibit such an action. One way of putting this is to say that trained domestic animals do not participate in the *practice of morality*.[16]

There are two distinguishable components in Dixon's argument. First, there is her understanding of "the practice of morality." Second,

14. Dixon, *Animals, Emotion and Morality*, p. 189. Emphasis is mine.
15. Dixon, *Animals, Emotion and Morality*, p. 190. Emphasis is mine.
16. Dixon, *Animals, Emotion and Morality*, p. 197.

there is her denial that animals can belong to this practice. I shall consider each of these in turn.

THE PRACTICE OF MORALITY

Let us suppose we are dealing with a two-year-old child—Ruthie. Ruthie has what we see as a problem: on occasion, when the excitement gets too much for her, she tends to bite people.[17] To convince her that this is not a good thing, we might ask her a series of questions of the following sort: How would you feel if Johnny bit you? Would you feel happy or sad? Which is it better to feel—happy or sad? And so on. The function of these questions is to induct Ruthie into the practice of morality. In asking them, we are teaching Ruthie to see her behavior in a new light—Dixon describes this as "learning to compose the situation."[18] Thus, in learning to answer and ask these questions, Ruthie, in effect, acquires a form of ethical perception: an ability to see what is morally salient in a situation.

The practice underlying this ability may be characterized, in general terms, as *the practice of giving reasons, both to oneself and others, for what one does.* Ruthie learns to think of her behavior not simply as something she does or not do, but in terms of consequences for others and, as a result, justification. I am inclined to bite Johnny, but if I do he will feel sad. Should I do it? In virtue of her induction into the practice of morality, the idea goes, Ruthie has become the sort of creature that is capable of thinking about a situation in terms of its morally salient features. And, in virtue of this, she is becoming the sort of creature that is capable of acting on the basis of moral reasons. Prior to this training, biting was something she merely did. But her

---

17. My thanks to Dr. Seuss for informing me that all Ruths are toothy. See his *The Tooth Book.*
18. Dixon, *Animals, Emotion and Morality,* p. 180.

induction into the practice of morality means that her behavior is now something she can assess in terms of moral reasons—and these reasons are the sorts of things she can supply to herself and others for the purposes of explaining and justifying her actions.

It is clear that in Dixon's idea of a moral practice the concept of a practice is very different from that implicated in Wittgenstein's solution to the rule-following paradox. For Wittgenstein, belonging to a practice is equivalent to having the ability to adjust one's use of a sign to make it conform to customary norms. There is no mention of reasons or other mental states because one of the goals of the appeal to practice is to show the possibility of such states by accounting for the possibility of content. The contrast with Dixon's richly psychological conception of moral practice is, therefore, glaring. This does not, of course, count against Dixon's conception, given the differing purposes to which the two conceptions of practice are being put. However, there is another difference between them that is more germane to our concerns.

When Wittgenstein appeals to practice it is a means of accounting for normativity in a way that does not appeal to intrinsic states—and especially not mental states—of a subject. Put in terms of the SCNM schema identified earlier, Wittgenstein's appeal to practice is intended as a way of sidestepping the S-C component of the explanatory chain. The Wittgensteinian proposal, in effect is to ignore scrutiny and control and instead explain normativity in terms of the ability to adjust one's use of a sign to bring it into line with what is customary or practiced.[19] However, Dixon's appeal to moral practice appears to function in a very different way: far from sidestepping the S-C component of the chain, Dixon's appeal to practice reiterates the SCNM chain, but

19. It is, of course, possible to think of this ability as a form of control—control over one's use of signs. However, that is not important for our purposes. What is crucial is that the S-C connection—the connection between scrutiny and control—has been broken. If ability is a form of control, then this is socially, rather than individualistically, interpreted.

merely adds a stage prior to S. The significance of moral practice, in Dixon's sense, is that it provides one with a kind of ethical perception that consists in learning to "compose the scene in the right way":

> Learning to compose the scene in the right way is learning to make these evaluations so that our emotional responsiveness fits the situation. Ethical perception is directed to these particulars that matter morally in a wide range of activities and settings.[20]

And again:

> One way of putting this is to say that trained domestic animals do not participate in the practice of morality. This includes emotional responsiveness and ethical perception where these capabilities are informed by recognizing, judging, and evaluating the morally salient features of a situation. For this reason, trained animals are not morally responsible for their actions.[21]

The claims are, of course, by now very familiar. Indeed, they are a restatement of what I earlier called the *reflection condition*, in particular as this condition was developed in the work of Aristotle. To act virtuously, Aristotle argued, one must understand that what one proposes to do is virtuous and one must be motivated to do it precisely because one wants to be virtuous. Implicated in this understanding is the sort of phronesis that allows one to identify the morally salient features of a situation. Dixon's argument is thus a reiteration of the familiar claim that animals cannot be moral because they do not understand what they do. Or, as Dixon puts it, they do not "possess an understanding of even very simple moral concerns."

---

20. Dixon, *Animals, Emotion and Morality*, p. 189.
21. Dixon, *Animals, Emotion and Responsibility*, p. 197.

Therefore, the significance of Dixon's appeal to practice is that it allows one to satisfy the reflection condition, in more or less the form defended by Aristotle. The significance of induction into a moral practice is that it imbues the inducted with ethical perception—the ability to "compose the situation" ethically.[22]

But if this is so, Dixon's appeal to practice does not attempt, as the analogous appeal attempts in Wittgenstein, to sidestep the SCNM schema. On the contrary, it reinforces that schema. The significance of induction into a moral practice is that it makes one the sort of individual who is capable of engaging in effective critical scrutiny of his motivations: for the ability to engage in this scrutiny is coextensive with the ability to perceive the morally salient features of situations. That is, induction into a moral practice is a necessary condition of engaging in S—effective critical scrutiny of one's motivations. In effect, Dixon has not jettisoned the SCNM schema, but merely expanded it. Instead of SCNM, we now have the PSCNM chain of explanation.

If the arguments of the previous chapter are correct, this is a problem for Dixon's account. The SCNM explanatory chain, I argued, breaks down at the S-C stage. We have no workable account of how the ability to engage in effective critical scrutiny of one's motivations gives one control over those motivations. If this argument is correct, then it does not matter how many explanatory stages one adds prior to S, the schema will still break down at the S-C stage. Dixon's appeal to the "practice of morality," therefore, simply elaborates an idea that is fundamentally misguided.

---

22. Here I am, of course, drawing on the interdependence of Aristotle's phronesis condition and his reflection condition. "Composing the situation ethically" amounts to satisfying the phronesis condition. The significance of this, among other things, is that it allows one to satisfy the reflection condition. In Dixon's terms: composing the situation ethically is what allows one to understand whether one's inclinations are right or wrong ones.

ANIMALS AND MORAL PRACTICE

Dixon's conception of the significance of moral practice reiterates a theme associated with Freud: the internalization of the external. Freud understood this as the internalization of the father's voice, and Dixon's understanding of practice does not, of course, involve that. Instead, it involves the idea of the internalization of the external questioner and of verbal responses initially given to that questioner. Thus, questions are asked of Ruthie with respect to her oral proclivities, and the responses she gives help her to see the morally salient features of situations. Eventually Ruthie learns to ask, and respond to, these questions herself, and so becomes someone capable of morally scrutinizing her motivations and inclinations. The result is, of course, a strikingly intellectualized conception of what a moral practice must be. Animals, on this view, cannot be inducted into such a practice because they cannot understand, and so cannot respond to, these sorts of questions. In what is left of this chapter, I shall argue that this intellectualized version is not the only available conception of a moral practice. If the "practice of morality" is the practice of giving reasons to oneself and others for what one does, it is undoubtedly true that animals cannot belong to this practice. However, I shall argue that there is little reason for supposing that this is the only way of understanding the idea of a moral practice.

First, however, there is a necessary qualification. Dixon frames the exclusion of animals from moral practice in terms of the idea of moral responsibility: "For this reason [their failure to belong to the practice of morality] trained animals are not morally responsible for their actions."[23] I agree that animals, trained or otherwise, are not morally responsible for their actions. My claim is that they can be moral subjects, but not moral agents. Therefore, if Dixon thinks their

23. Dixon, *Animals, Emotion and Morality*, p. 197.

failure to count as moral agents is the extent of the implications of the (alleged) failure of animals to belong to the practice of morality, there would be little point in pursuing Dixon's argument further. However, given that Dixon does not draw the distinction between moral subjects and moral agents—between acting for moral reasons and being morally accountable for ones actions—it is likely that Dixon thinks that the perceived failure of animals to belong to the practice of morality also precludes their acting for moral reasons. Whether or not this is, in fact, the case, it is this claim that is the target of the present section.

Dixon accepts that the trained police dog "probably is sufficiently cognizant of 'human social skills' to refrain from biting the children it visits in the hospital." I am not sure if Dixon intends this remark sarcastically, but there is, of course, a lot more to a trained German shepherd's being a moral subject than refraining from biting people. Let us take the example of Hugo, a German shepherd trained in protection but also a family dog. Hugo loves working with the bite sleeve, approaching his training with an enthusiasm that borders on the manic. Although he weighs no more than ninety pounds, he will regularly knock his one hundred and eighty pound owner (me) off his feet when working with the sleeve—as he has been trained to do. However, if my four-year-old son puts on the sleeve, Hugo will merely walk up to him, and gently chew on it.

I use this case simply as an example of three key features of the moral profile of trained animals. First, Hugo is sufficiently intelligent to understand the differing consequences of the same behavior when it is directed toward two different individuals. He understands that if he behaves toward my son in the way he behaves toward me, my son will be hurt. This is a form of canine practical wisdom targeted at a morally salient feature of the situation in which Hugo finds himself. Hugo does not wish my son to be hurt. This is a manifestation of his *concern* for my son's welfare. Second, anyone who has seen Hugo work with the sleeve will understand his intense desire to bite it. It is a Kevlar sleeve, but when he gets a good grip, I can feel my bones begin to crunch beneath. In being presented with a sleeve that is attached to the arm of a four-year-old child, Hugo has to inhibit this strong desire. *Practical wisdom, concern,* and *inhibition of desire* are the three advertised key features of the moral profile of this particular trained, domestic dog.

Let us look in a little more detail at Hugo's induction into the practice of morality—at least as I would present it. This induction is not, of course, primarily a matter of teaching Hugo not to bite people. Not biting people is, admittedly, an important feature of Hugo's moral profile: but it is what we might think of as a surface feature, rather than a deep feature of that profile. One might think of it as possessing a status similar to that of ostensive definition in the overall use of language. As Wittgenstein put it: "an ostensive definition explains the use—the meaning—of a word only when the overall role of the word in language is clear."[24] Refraining from biting people, as Dixon thinks of it, is a behavior that makes sense only in the overall context of what, and continuing with the Wittgensteinian theme, we might call Hugo's *form of life.* Hugo's induction into the practice of morality consists, fundamentally, in providing him with a form of life. Specific behaviors, including the inhibition of desires, are expressions of this form of life.

Consider, for example, the sorts of processes involved in Hugo having concern for the bodily welfare of my four-year-old son. In part, and like all forms of life, this is a matter of Hugo's *natural history.* Having concern for his pack comes naturally to Hugo, as part of his biological endowment. If I had a pet rattlesnake, for example, no amount of training would induce the requisite concern. But in the case of Hugo training does augment what is already biologically there.

24. Wittgenstein, *Philosophical Investigations,* sec. 30.

Building on his natural history is, to a significant extent, a process of teaching Hugo through example. The concern that Hugo exhibits for my son is a function of the concern that I exhibit for my son. For Hugo, it is through my actions, rather than through mere words, that I demonstrate that my son is of value to me—and therefore, that he should be valued. For Hugo, induction into a moral practice is done through example rather than a process of questioning. When he sees the tears of my son being met with hugs and soothing words, this behavior will impress itself on Hugo. If his tears were instead met with callousness or indifference, then Hugo would be inducted into a very different type of moral practice, and so become a very different dog.

The example set is not merely my example. Hugo learns not merely from the way I act but the way others act—and, crucially, the way I see to it that others act—toward him. If my son becomes a little too rough with Hugo, or he becomes a little too rough with my son, I must step in and defuse the situation. This is not done by separating the parties, but by realigning their behavior. "Gentle," I say soothingly, at the same time arranging for the offending boy to gently stroke Hugo's back. The message in this is one that my son and his dog quickly absorb: this is how we behave. If Hugo is the one that is too rough, I will tell him to sit, quietly stroke his head, and say, quietly, soporifically, "Calm down." The example is being set not just be me, but also, through me, by other members of our moral practice. Sometimes carelessness, by either party, must be marked by harsh words. But this is the rare exception rather than the rule.

Induction into a moral practice is not achieved through a process of questioning and responses in the way that Dixon imagines. This sort of process does, of course, play a role in the case of humans. But the process is a superstructure that is erected on a foundation of example. It is a process that makes sense only if there has been a lot of prior, as Wittgenstein would put it, "stage setting." Wittgenstein once remarked that he considered taking as the motto for his work the dictum that Goethe put in the mouth of Faust, "In the beginning was the deed." Induction into a moral practice is fundamentally done through example—through deed rather than word. This is the way we behave. This is the way we act. Word—the process of question and answer envisaged by Dixon—plays a significant role in the induction of humans into moral practices. But there is no reason for thinking that this is the only way an individual can be inducted into the practice of morality. With trained dogs, concern is bequeathed them as a matter of their biological heritage but is perfected by the examples they are set and so the forms of life with which they are provided. Does Hugo understand that hurting my son is wrong? Possibly not: and, if not, this deficit may exclude him from the category of moral agents. Nevertheless, he exhibits concern for my son, and as a result inhibits his desires when doing so is necessary. This is enough for him to qualify as a moral subject: one motivated to act by moral reasons. The concern he exhibits is bequeathed him both by natural history and by form of life. And the latter comes by way of the deed.

9

Reconstructing Normativity
and Agency

TWO PUZZLES

Moral subjects are individuals capable of acting for moral reasons. I have argued that the case against the possibility of animals qualifying as moral subjects ultimately turns on the idea that animals lack control over their motivations. If a subject, S, lacks control over its motivations, then those motivations are not the sort of thing that S *can* endorse or reject. Therefore, since ought implies can, they are not the sort of thing S *should* endorse or reject. They, as I put it, exert no *normative grip* on S. However, it is part of the essence of moral motivations that they exert a normative grip on their subjects: moral motivations are essentially the sorts of things that should be endorsed (if they are morally good) or rejected (if they are morally bad). Therefore, if S lacks control over its motivations, those motivations cannot be moral ones.

Nevertheless, I have argued that the requisite concept of control has proved elusive. Historically speaking, the strategy has been to locate a subject's control over its motivations in its ability to engage in *effective critical scrutiny* of those motivations. We have seen this strategy at work in Aristotle and Kant, and seen it reiterated in the work of contemporary figures such as Dixon. However, I have argued that this strategy rests on a connection between critical scrutiny and control that has, more than a little ironically, not been subjected to critical scrutiny. We have, in fact, no idea how effective critical scrutiny is supposed to yield control. Indeed, a subject's scrutiny of its motivations seems to be simply the wrong sort of thing to yield control over those motivations because the very issue of control that arises for the motivations also arises with respect to their scrutiny. To suppose otherwise is to fall victim to an illicit picture that I labeled the *miracle-of-the-meta*.

This conclusion, however, might seem curiously misdirected— establishing what is, for my purposes at least, the wrong conclusion. This book defends the claim that animals can be moral subjects in the sense that they can act for moral reasons. The target of my dialectical ire should, accordingly, be the denial of this claim. However, if the arguments developed so far, and outlined above, are correct, then what they would appear to establish is a rather different claim: humans are not capable of acting for moral reasons. Humans are not moral subjects. If, as is generally thought, the possibility of moral motivation presupposes that a subject, Jones, have control over her motivations, and if Jones has no control over these motiva- tions—because the requisite notion of control is empty—then it seems there is no possibility of Jones acting morally. But the lack of control over motivations is one exhibited by humans as well as ani- mals. My advertised goal was to establish the possibility of moral action in animals. Instead, if the arguments developed so far are correct, they would seem to establish the impossibility of moral action in humans.

This, to say the least, is a little worrying. There are, however, two distinct ways this worry can manifest itself. One is as a puzzle concerning *normativity*. The other is as a puzzle about *agency*. If humans have no control over their motivations, then it would seem they are not moral agents. And, given that control is required for normativity, if humans have no control over their motivations, those motivations have no normative status. I, however, find little attraction in the claim that humans—adult, unimpaired humans at the very least—are not moral subjects. And I find almost as little attraction in the claim that humans are not moral agents. This means that I need to understand the ideas of both normativity and agency in ways that do not rely on the problematic concept of control. That is, I need to reconstruct the ideas of normativity and agency in a way that divorces these concepts from that of control. That is the task of this chapter.

While I find little attraction in the claims that humans are not moral subjects and that they are not moral agents, there are those who find these claims substantially more attractive than I do. And, to a considerable extent, good reasons can be mustered in defense of this opposing view. It goes without saying that this book is not a suitable forum for adjudicating this dispute. Thus, the claims I shall defend in this chapter are best stated in conditional form. *If* one is convinced, or at least inclined, to the view that some humans are moral subjects or moral agents or both—that they can act for moral reasons or be held responsible for their actions or both—*then* there is nothing in the argument of this book that requires questioning these convictions or inclinations. I shall argue that it is, in fact, possible to reconstruct the concepts of normativity and agency in a way that divorces them from the elusive idea of control that I have done my best to undermine. This reconstruction can make sense of the claim that both humans and animals can be motivated to act by considerations that are normative (in a moral sense). And it can make sense of the idea that whereas many humans can plausibly be thought of as moral agents, responsible for what they do, the same is not true of any animals. This task of conceptual reconstruction begins with normativity.

RECONSTRUCTING NORMATIVITY I: THE MORAL "OUGHT" AND THE PRUDENTIAL "OUGHT"

Earlier, I argued that Myshkin is a moral subject—a subject of moral motivation. More precisely, I argued there are no persuasive reasons for supposing that he is not a moral subject. The reasons for denying him this status turned on the role that control—in the form of effective critical scrutiny—was thought to play in constituting a motive as normative (and so, at least potentially, moral).[1] Nevertheless, this was a negative argument. There are no reasons for denying Myshkin the status of moral subject. But if we are to be persuaded of the status of Myshkin as a subject of moral motivation, something more positive needs to be said. That is what the reconstruction of normativity tries to do.

To qualify as moral, Myshkin's motivations must exert a normative grip on him. That is, they must be the sorts of things that Myshkin *should* endorse or reject. Traditionally, the concept expressed by "should" is explicated in terms of Myshkin's control over his motivations. So, in the absence of this control, how do we explain the meaning of this "should"? Given that Myshkin has no say in whether he endorses or rejects his motivating emotions, what sense can we make of the claim that he *should* endorse or reject them? The answer, of course, is going to be a broadly *consequentialist* and *externalist* one.

To understand this consequentialist and externalist alternative, let us first look at another sense of "should" or "ought": the *prudential* rather than moral "ought."[2] Let us consider the case of

---

1. Or, on the role of practice, discussed and hopefully dispensed with, in the previous chapter.
2. Colin McGinn (in conversation) suggested this comparison. The comparison of the moral with the prudential "ought" is a dialectical strategy he associates with Thomas Nagel.

someone we shall call Prudence. Most of the actions Prudence performs in her life are prudent ones. Her motivations for these actions consist in cognitive and affective states that also seem to be prudent ones. That is, Prudence typically acts prudently, and her prudent behavior is the result of motivations that, most prudential observers would accept, are prudent ones. Prudence is, however, unable to subject her motivations to critical prudential scrutiny. That is she is unable to ask herself questions such as: I am inclined to act on the basis of motivation M. Is this an inclination I should embrace or one that I should resist? While often acting on the basis of what certainly appear, to the prudential bystander, to be prudential motives, Prudence is unaware that this is what she is doing. That is, she is unaware that her motives are prudential, and lacks the metacognitive abilities required to categorize her motives in this way. Is Prudence a prudential agent? That is, does she do more than merely *seem* to act in prudential ways and on the basis of prudential motives? Does she, in fact, act prudentially and on the basis of motives that are, in fact, prudential?

There is, I think, little temptation to be found in a negative answer to this question. And whatever temptation there is, I also suspect, dwindles to approximately zero when we add one more claim. Suppose Jude (short for "Judicious"), an ideal prudential spectator—an ideal judge of what is and what is not, in any given situation, the prudent way to behave—agrees that Prudence is both acting in prudent ways and is motivated to act by prudent motivations. That is, Jude agrees that Prudence is the subject of prudent desires, that her beliefs provide effective ways of implementing or realizing these desires, and that her resulting actions are, thereby, demonstrably prudent ones. Jude is never wrong—or hardly ever wrong, depending on how one likes to think of one's ideal prudential spectator—about these things.

What we might think of as Prudence's prudential profile corresponds to the (M2) version of Myshkin's moral profile. Prudence performs actions that are, in fact, the prudent ones to perform in the circumstances, and she performs them because of motivations that are, in fact, prudent ones to have in these circumstances. If we add a reliability clause—Prudence's motivations are the result of the operations of a reliable "prudential module," understood as a mechanism that translates perceptions of circumstances in prudent plans for dealing with those circumstances—then Prudence's prudential profile will correspond to the (M3) version of Myshkin's moral profile. However she is incapable of subjecting her motivations to critical prudential scrutiny. That is, she is incapable of considering whether her motives are ones that, prudentially speaking, she should embrace or resist. Jude, on the other hand, has this critical ability and unquestionably qualifies as a prudential subject—an individual who acts for prudential reasons. Does Prudence's lack of this critical ability disqualify her from the category of prudential subject?

The claim that it does is stunningly implausible. If one performs prudential action and one does so on the basis of reliably prudential motives, this is sufficient for one to be a prudential subject. The ability to engage in critical prudential scrutiny of one's motivations is irrelevant to one's status as such a subject. The principle that *ought implies can* simply does not figure when we are dealing with the "ought" of prudence. To act prudentially, it is sufficient that one is motivated by prudential reasons—even if one cannot subject those reasons to critical prudential scrutiny, and even if one is "at the mercy" of those motivations. Nevertheless, there is an "ought" of prudence, just as there is an "ought" of morality. There are certain things that one, as matter of prudence, ought to do, and certain things that one ought not. If critical prudential scrutiny is irrelevant to the status of a motivation as prudent, we must look elsewhere to understand the "ought" of prudence. Finding this understanding will, I think, help us understand an alternative way of thinking about the "ought" of morality.

In other words, there must be another way of explaining the normative grip of prudential motives. This explanation will be a broadly *externalist* one. Roughly, the idea is that a given circumstance might possess certain prudentially salient features: features that impact, for good or for ill, the well-being of the subject. A motivation is prudent when it stands in the correct sort of relation to these features. That is, a motivation is prudent when it tracks the good (in the sense of useful) features of the situation and thus allows the subject to make use of them in furthering his or her ends. For example: It would, let us suppose, be prudent for Jack to give up smoking. The prudentially salient features of the situation are these. First, Jack's lungs are being damaged by his predilection. Jack has a desire to live a long and fulfilled life. Smoke-damaged lungs are incompatible with this desire. Lungs can, to some extent, recover from this sort of damage—and so Jack's abstinence would make a clear difference. Given all these facts, the normative status of Jack's motivation to refrain from further smoking consists in the fact that it is, in this sense, an appropriate response to the prudentially salient features of the situation. That is, his course of action is what the prudentially salient features of the situation require.

To understand the prudential "ought" we do not need to look for a subject's control of his or her motivations, whether or not it is grounded in the ability to engage in effective critical prudential scrutiny of those motivations. Rather, we understand it by looking at the features of the situation in which the subject finds herself, and examining the extent to which the subject's motivations cohere with the prudentially salient features of this situation. This is an externalist account of the prudential "ought." I shall now recommend such an account in understanding the moral "ought."

RECONSTRUCTING NORMATIVITY II:
THE EXTERNALIST ACCOUNT
OF THE MORAL "OUGHT"

Julia Driver has defended a consequentialist and externalist account of moral virtue.[3] A moral virtue, Driver argues, is a character trait that systematically produces good consequences. In rejecting the intellectualist model of moral virtue endorsed by Aristotle, Driver's position is of a piece with the one defended in this book. There are, however, some important differences between both the positions we defend and the arguments we use to defend them. First, Driver's thesis is one that concerns moral virtue. My thesis is one that concerns moral motivation more generally. I argue that moral emotions count as moral reasons for action. But I take no stand on the issue of whether these moral emotions should be regarded as virtues or virtuous—at least not in any technical sense. Second, Driver's arguments turn on what she refers to as the "virtues of ignorance"—virtues such as modesty, blind charity, trust, forgiveness, and impulsive courage. She argues that possession of such virtues is possible only if their possessor lacks knowledge of some specific sort. For example, she argues that possession of the virtue of modesty by a subject requires that the subject lack accurate knowledge of her worth or achievements. This argument presupposes that the subject possesses the sorts of intellectual abilities Aristotle argues are required for virtue, but merely fails—if Driver is right, *must* fail—to exercise those abilities in this instance. A modest person, for example, is the sort of individual that could be made aware or otherwise convinced of the worth of her achievements. If a person is modest, she in fact lacks certain knowledge that she could come to possess—although not, if Driver is correct, without ceasing to be modest. The position I defend is, therefore somewhat more radical.

3. Julia Driver, *Uneasy Virtue* (New York: Cambridge University Press, 2001).

I have argued that at least some moral motivations can be possessed by individuals who lack complex intellectual abilities of the form presupposed by even the virtues of ignorance. Myshkin could not be modest in Driver's sense—he is not the sort of being that could be made aware of his worth or the value of his achievements. Nevertheless, if the arguments of this book are correct, he can be compassionate and sympathetic—he can be *concerned*, broadly understood—where there is no reason for supposing that these are not genuinely moral motivations rather than nonmoral facsimiles.

Nevertheless, despite the divergence of our positions and the arguments we use to support them, my reconstruction of normativity, like Driver's account of virtue, is both consequentalist and externalist. First, consider the consequentialist component. Following Driver, let us distinguish between *subjective* and *objective* forms of consequentialism.[4] According to the former view, the goodness or rightness of an action is a function of subjective states of the agent who performs it. For example, *expectabilism* is the view that an action is right if and only if its agent expects that the consequences of the action will be good. Objective consequentialism, on the other hand, defines a good or right action as one that actually produces good consequences—and the agent's expectations in performing the action are irrelevant to whether the action is right or wrong.[5] Part of the story concerning the normativity of Myshkin's motivations will be an objectively consequentialist one in this sense: the normative status of these motivations is explained, in part, in terms of their actual (and not intended) consequences.

The second distinction is between evaluational *internalism* and *externalism*.[6] According to internalism, as I shall understand it, the

---

4. Driver, *Uneasy Virtue*, pp. xiv and following.
5. Although it will certainly be relevant to the evaluation of the agent as opposed to the action. See Driver, *Uneasy Virtue*, p. xiv.
6. See Driver, *Uneasy Virtue*, pp. 60ff.

moral quality of a person's action or motives—whether they are good or bad, right or wrong—is determined solely by factors internal to a person's agency. Externalism is, then, the view that the moral quality of a person's actions or motives is determined, at least in part, by factors external to the person's agency. Subjective consequentialism is a version of internalism. Objective consequentialism is a version of externalism. The other component of the story concerning the normative status of Myshkin's motivations will be an externalist one in this sense.

In virtue of the (cognitively impenetrable) operations of his (let us suppose) "moral module," Myshkin has a certain *sensitivity*—both to which situations are good and which are bad, and also to what makes them good or bad. The assessment of these situations as good or bad, and their relevant features as "good-making" or "bad-making," is an objective consequentialist one. That is, their status has nothing to do with any expectations or other subjective states possessed by Myshkin. Different moral theories, embodying different accounts of well-being, will provide different answers with regard to what grounds these evaluations. The hedonistic utilitarian, for example, will judge that a situation is a good one to the extent it elevates the overall amount of happiness in the world, and bad to the extent that it diminishes overall happiness. For the hedonic utilitarian, elevation and diminution of overall happiness are, accordingly, the respective good- and bad-making features. The sort of *capabilities approach* developed by Martha Nussbaum and others will begin with a concept of *flourishing*: of what it is for a creature of a certain type to flourish, and then understand the good- and bad-making features of a situation as ones that, respectively, promote or suppress flourishing.[7] There are, of course, many competing accounts of what makes situations good

---

7. See, for example, Martha Nussbaum, *Frontiers of Justice: Disability, Nationality, Species Membership* (Cambridge, MA: Harvard University Press, 2006).

or bad ones—there are as many options here as there are versions of objective consequentialism—and, for our purposes, it is not necessary to adjudicate between them.

Whatever these features are that make situations good or bad ones, the claim is simply that Myshkin is sensitive to them. This does not mean, of course—and here I am merely reiterating earlier qualifications—that Myshkin is sensitive to all or even many of the good-and bad-making features of situations—merely that he is sensitive to some of them. For Myshkin, happiness is the primary good-making feature of a situation, and suffering the primary bad-making feature. This is not to deny that there are other good- and bad-making features of situations—and to these Myshkin is, we can suppose, not sensitive. Nor need we suppose that Myshkin is even sensitive to all the multifarious forms that happiness and suffering can take. He is merely capable of detecting some of these forms, and when he does detect them, those he detects are among the good- and bad-making features of a situation. Finally, we can remain neutral on whether the happiness and suffering that Myshkin detects are intrinsically bearers of value or disvalue (as a view such as hedonistic utilitarianism would maintain) or symptoms of other things that are the intrinsic bearers of value and disvalue (as the capabilities approach would maintain). All that is required for our purposes are the following assumptions. First, it is an objective moral fact—in no way dependent on Myshkin's subjective states—that there are certain features of situations that make those situations good ones. Similarly, there are other features that make situations bad ones. Second, Myshkin is capable of detecting some of these features. The form that Myshkin's sensitivity takes is, of course, experiential. He feels happy when he witnesses the happiness of others and feels sad when he witnesses their suffering. But his experiences of happiness or sadness do not constitute the good- and bad-making features of situations as good- or bad-making ones. Rather, his experiences are the form taken by his detection of features that make a situation good or bad, independently of those experiences and their phenomenal qualities.

When Myshkin sees another happy, he feels happy. When he sees another suffering, he suffers. More than that: he is happy because the other is happy and he sees that she is. He suffers because the other suffers and he sees that she does.[8] The happiness of the other is the intentional object of Myshkin's emotional state. That is, there exists, let us suppose, a certain content—*that* X is happy—and Myshkin entertains this content happily. Conversely, there is another content—*that* X is sad—and Myshkin entertains this content sadly. In both cases we have an intentional directedness toward content and, in Myshkin, this directedness takes an emotional form.[9]

These dispositions, on the part of Myshkin, to entertain certain content happily and certain (other) content sadly, shape the ways in which he behaves toward others. If we assume that X's happiness and suffering are, objectively and respectively, good- and bad-making features of situations, then in his own happiness and suffering Myshkin is sensitive not only to the goodness or badness of situations, but also to the features that make them good and bad. Myshkin, we might say, is *negatively sensitized* to suffering: his witnessing the suffering of another is experientially unpleasant for him. He is *positively sensitized* to happiness: his witnessing the happiness of another is experientially pleasant for him. Having rather attenuated metacognitive abilities, Myshkin is unable to formulate general principles like "suffering is bad" or "happiness is good." Nevertheless, his negative sensitivity to suffering manifests itself in fairly transparent counterfactuals, such as: "Ceteris paribus, if the

8. Thanks to Colin McGinn and Daniel Hampikian (both, in conversation) for requiring me to clarify this point.

9. There are, of course, a multitude of competing accounts—both naturalistic and nonnaturalistic—concerning in what, precisely, intentional directedness consists. I am not forced to choose one of these accounts here.

situation did not involve suffering, then Myshkin would not have unpleasant experiences and so would not feel compelled to try to change the situation." His positive sensitivity to happiness manifests itself in counterfactuals of the same general form. The expression "ceteris paribus" is intended to cover the absence of any other states to which Myshkin is, in this way, negatively or positively sensitized.[10]

The way I have described Myshkin's detection of good- and bad-making features of situations—as taking the form of pleasant or unpleasant experiences respectively—might suggest to some that we are not dealing with moral sensibility or behavior on the part of Myshkin at all. Rather, Myshkin is merely subject to a form of emotional contagion, and his subsequent behavior is the result of the purely selfish desire to alleviate his own unpleasant experiences and have more of the pleasant ones. But, as I mentioned in chapter 1, this argument embodies a well-known error. It is an error familiar to philosophers: one that often manifests itself, repeatedly, in undergraduate ethics courses. "We always act selfishly," some or other student will almost certainly say, "because we always do what we want to do." The error here is to suppose that whether an action counts as selfish is a function of its motivation rather than its content. Suppose someone says, "Saint X—how selfish he was! All he wanted to do was help other people, and he spent his life doing just that. He spent all his time doing exactly as he pleased—and that is the mark of selfishness." Saint X might, indeed, have been acting selfishly. If the goal of his seemingly altruistic behavior had been to get his soul into heaven, then his behavior was certainly self-interested. However, the mere

10. These counterfactuals can, of course, be used to avoid the complications of scenarios in which, for example, Myshkin is given $100 every time he sees someone happy. Appropriate specification of the counterfactual dependencies will allow us to rule out that Myshkin is happy because of the $100 he receives rather than the other's happiness. This is, of course, implicit in the claim that it is the other's happiness that is the intentional object of Myshkin's emotional states.

fact that a person always does what he wants—if it is a fact—does not mean that he is acting selfishly. Whether or not a person's action counts as selfish is *not a matter of whether the action is one that he wants to do, but of what it is he wants to do.* The fact that Saint X wanted to spend all his time helping other people, by itself, shows that he was not selfish. The selfishness or otherwise of Saint X is a matter of the *content* of his desires, and not a matter of whether he acts on his desires.

The same point is clearly true of Myshkin. The fact that he experiences suffering in the face of the suffering of another, and happiness in the face of another's happiness, does not show that his motivations and subsequent actions are selfish ones. In the attempt to promote another's happiness or mitigate another's suffering, Myshkin is indeed doing what he wants to do. However, the content of Myshkin's sensibility, and subsequent desires, is one that concerns the welfare or well-being of other people. His emotional responses to the happiness or suffering of others are expressions of his *concern* for these others. This is why these responses should be regarded as moral emotions rather than selfish reactions. Myshkin detects the good- and bad-making features of situations. And when he does so, the mode or manner of his detection is emotional. Or, to put the point in adverbial terms, Myshkin detects the morally salient features of situations *emotionally*. That is, the emotional nature of Myshkin's motivations does not characterize the *content* of those motivations but their *character*. Myshkin is emotionally directed toward moral content. And this content consists in the objectively good- and bad-making features of situations. Thus, we might compare Myshkin with an emotionless counterpart— Manu—who detects the good- and bad-making features of situations purely rationally. This does not alter the content of Manu's detections—at least not in all cases (and that is sufficient for my purposes). Rather, in some cases at least, Manu can be directed toward the same content as Myshkin. He is, however, directed toward this content *rationally*—an adverbial modifier that qualifies the manner in which he is aware of content and not the content itself.[11]

This aside completed, let us now return to the advertised reconstruction of normativity. Myshkin's sensitivity is directed toward objectively good- and bad-making features of situations. It is this that makes his emotions—the experiential expressions of this sensitivity—the sort of things that can be normatively assessed. That is, his emotional responses to situations are ones that can be judged as correct or incorrect. In effect, Myshkin's emotions *track* the good- and bad-making features of situations, and this tracking is the sort of thing that can be successful or otherwise. Myshkin can make mistakes. His emotional response is the sort of thing that can be appropriate or inappropriate—correct or incorrect. Myshkin does not just feel happiness or sadness in the face of a good- or bad-making feature of the situation that presents itself to him: he is, or at least can be, *right* to do. He is right to be motivated to promote certain features of situations and mitigate other features. The reason is that it is an objective moral fact that the features in question make the situations in which they are present good ones or bad ones. The correctness or incorrectness of Myshkin's emotional response is a matter of whether it accords with the moral facts. It is this possibility of accord or discord that underwrites the normative status of Myshkin's motivations.

In chapter 5, I took an initial step in this externalist/objectivist direction by invoking, in the form of Marlow, the concept of an ideal moral spectator. This was done as a way of providing Myshkin with external reasons for action—the first step in converting Myshkin

---

11. I introduce Manu only for expository purposes. I take no stand on the issue of whether it is possible for there to be an entirely dispassionate moral subject.

(M1) into Myshkin (M3). The arguments of this section have merely made explicit what was implicit in that invocation. The concept of an ideal moral spectator presupposes that the good- and bad-making features of situations are objective ones. If they were not, no sense could be given to the idea that the moral spectator is an ideal one— any spectator would be as good as any other.

To sum up the story so far: Myshkin is sensitive to (some of the) objectively good- and bad-making features of situations. And because these features are objectively good- and bad-making ones, Myshkin's sensitivity can be normatively assessed. For ease of exposition, I shall contract this to the claim that Myshkin has a *normative sensitivity* to (some of the) good- and bad-making features of situations. This sensitivity is expressed in the form of emotions, and these emotions, thereby, have normative status. They are correct or incorrect responses to morally relevant features of situations.

There is one further feature possessed by Myshkin's normative sensitivity to morally relevant features of situations, and this should not be overlooked. His sensitivity is *reliable*. It is not simply that his sensitivity is describable in normative terms—as correctly or incorrectly exercised on any given occasion. Rather, Myshkin's sensitivity must be exercised correctly a significant portion of the time. It is, presumably, not possible to specify, precisely, what counts as "significant" in this context. But the underlying idea is clear. If Myshkin were, for example, to "get it right" only once in his life, this would cast serious doubt on whether Myshkin is, in fact, a moral subject. Getting it right a significant proportion of the time—exhibiting the correct emotional response to a given good- or bad-making feature of the environment—presumably amounts to getting it right some percentage of the time that lies between once and always. There is almost certainly no precise line here. Nevertheless, Myshkin's emotional response must dispose him to promote the good-making and mitigate the bad-making features of situations in a relatively systematic, although (of course) not necessarily error-free, way.[12] I have captured this systematicity in terms of the idea that the mechanism responsible for producing Myshkin's emotional responses to morally salient features of situations—his, for want of a better expression, "moral module"—is a reliable one.

Thus, suppose that hedonistic utilitarianism turned out to be true. Myshkin's "moral module" must be reliable enough to dispose him to feel happiness in the face of another's increase in happiness, and sadness in the face of her decrease in happiness, a substantial proportion of the time. The objectivity of the good- and bad-making features of situations ensures that Myshkin's emotional responses to these features can be normatively assessed. The reliability of the operations of his "moral module" ensures that his emotional responses are not mere accidents or flukes. This is important because it is required to make true the very descriptions that underwrite the claim that Myshkin is sensitive to morally salient features of situations—let alone that he is normatively sensitive to them. As described earlier, these descriptions will consist in counterfactual statements of the form: "Ceteris paribus, if the situation did not involve suffering then Myshkin would not have unpleasant experiences and so would not feel compelled to try to change the situation." The truth of these counterfactuals is grounded in the reliability of the operations of Myshkin's "moral module."

Putting these various strands together, the profile of what we might think of as a *minimal moral subject* looks like this:

X is a *moral subject* if X possesses (1) a sensitivity to the good- or bad-making features of situations, where (2) this sensitivity can be normatively assessed, and (3) is grounded in the operations of a reliable mechanism (a "moral module").

12. Driver also emphasizes the importance of systematicity in development of her consequentialist virtue ethics. According to Driver, a moral virtue is one that *systematically*—rather than occasionally or accidentally—leads to good consequences.

The idea of sensitivity is understood in the intentional sense explained earlier. Moral subjects are ones who are sensitive to the good- and bad-making features of situations in the sense that they entertain intentional content emotionally. Thus, (1)–(3) collectively amount to the claim that X entertains intentional content emotionally, where this emotional mode or manner of entertaining content can, in specific cases, be normatively assessed and is grounded in the operations of a reliable mechanism, or "moral module."

This is intended as a *sufficient* condition for an individual to qualify as a moral subject. If the individual satisfies these three conditions, then she is a moral subject, irrespective of any other perceived lacks or deficiencies. It is not intended as a necessary condition: there may be other ways of being a moral subject—this possibility is left open by the above conditions. Note also that the definition is neutral with respect to the type or mode of sensitivity involved. I have presented Myshkin's sensitivity as a fundamentally emotional one, since this accords best with the dialectical purposes to which I have put Myshkin (that is, to establish that animals are moral subjects). However, Myshkin's purely rational counterpart, Manu, would also satisfy the above definition.

Myshkin satisfies these conditions and therefore, if the arguments of this book are correct, qualifies as a moral subject—a subject capable of acting for moral reasons.[13] The extent to which animals satisfy these conditions is, of course, an empirical matter. It is a matter of the extent to which a large and growing body of evidence that apparently shows animals acting on the basis of moral emotions should be understood as indicative of their satisfaction of these three conditions. If animals do satisfy these conditions, they

---

13. We might also imagine an evil version of Myshkin—Bizarro Myshkin, if you like—who delights in the suffering of others and feels repulsion at their happiness, where these emotional responses are also systematic because grounded in the operations of a reliable "moral module." Bizarro Myshkin is also a moral being, merely a morally evil one.

are moral subjects. And I think it is likely that the growing body of empirical evidence does support the attribution of this sort of profile to animals. Indeed, it is difficult to imagine what other general profile would be capable of explaining this body of evidence. Therefore, I think it very likely that some animals will turn out to be moral subjects.

Most humans—adults and children—satisfy these conditions. Therefore, they are moral subjects. The reconstruction of normativity, therefore, allows us to see why both humans and, pending the likely resolution of certain empirical matters, at least some animals are moral subjects. In their moral decisions and actions, humans can, of course, do many things that animals cannot, and have recourse to abilities that animals do not. If the arguments of this book are correct, these additional elements that humans bring to the table are not relevant to the issue of whether humans are moral *subjects*—of whether they can act for moral reasons. However, they are deeply relevant to the issue of whether humans are moral *agents*. It is to this issue that we now turn.

RECONSTRUCTING AGENCY I: THE DIALECTIC OF PEACE

Wittgenstein once claimed that "The real discovery is the one which enables me to stop doing philosophy when I want to. The one that gives philosophy peace, so that it is no longer tormented by questions which bring *itself* into question."[14] A useful way of thinking about the idea that we can ground control in effective critical scrutiny is as an exemplar of a particular type of temptation that we might think of as a desire for peace—a desire to find a place where all our conceptual

14. Wittgenstein, *Philosophical Investigations*, sec. 133.

troubles and travails will come to an end. So we are faced with a class of items—motivations—that are perceived to be in some way problematic. Specifically, nothing intrinsic to them ensures they have the property of being under a subject's control. So we look for control in what is extrinsic to them: effective critical scrutiny. This is where we can find peace: the place where what was problematic is no longer so. Put in these terms, the arguments of this book seek to show that there is no shelter here. Effective critical scrutiny provides no resting place. What was problematic in our original class of items—motivations— is simply reiterated in the new class of items that we thought would bring us peace—effective critical scrutinizings. We might refer to this as the *dialectic of peace*.

The debate between compatibilists and incompatibilists on the nature and status of moral responsibility is a dialectic of peace in this sense. Incompatibilism, of course, comes in two forms: incompatibilist determinism and incompatibilist voluntarism. The incompatibilist determinist argues that humans are not morally responsible for what they do because being responsible would require meeting a certain condition or conditions that humans do not, in fact, meet— and perhaps could never meet. Precisely what this condition is can vary depending on the particular incompatibilist in question. Galen Strawson, for example, has argued that responsibility for our actions, including moral responsibility, requires that we be capable of a form of "self-creation" that is ultimately incoherent.[15] Strawson insists that this general point is quite independent of the issue of universal causal determinism. Robert Kane has argued that we must meet an "ultimacy" condition on responsibility that is not possible to meet in a causally deterministic world.[16] In a similar vein, Saul Smilansky has argued that responsibility for our actions requires that we be the

---

15. Galen Strawson, *Freedom and Belief* (Oxford: Oxford University Press, 1986).
16. Robert Kane, *The Significance of Free Will* (Oxford: Oxford University Press, 1996).

"source" of these actions in a way that a causally deterministic world rules out—in anything other than a "shallow" sense.[17]

In the dialectic of peace, incompatibilist determinists are those who deny that there is any shelter to be found. "Self-creation," "ultimacy," and "sourcehood" denote mere illusions. Whenever we look for these, we merely find reiterations of the same old problems. The incompatibilist voluntarist, on the other hand, has faith that there is a place where our problems will stop. Roderick Chisholm provides a useful—if, or perhaps because, intentionally exaggerated—account of what this place might look like:

> If we are responsible for what we do, and if what I am trying to say is true, then we have a prerogative which some would attribute only to God; each of us, when we act, is a prime mover unmoved. In doing what we do, we cause certain events to happen, and nothing—or no one—causes us to cause those events to happen.[18]

We are having difficulty in understanding how an item—an action, choice, or decision—could possess a certain property: the property of being free. There is nothing intrinsic to our actions, choices, and decisions that ensures they have this property, and so guarantees that they are the sorts of things for which we are responsible. Therefore, the incompatibilist voluntarist looks for freedom and responsibility in what is extrinsic to these things: if it is to be free, an action, choice, or decision must be caused by *me*—and nothing must cause me to cause it. My unmoved movement is the place where my problems with freedom come to an end.

17. Saul Smilansky, *Free Will and Illusion* (New York: Oxford University Press, 2000).
18. Roderick Chisholm, "Human Freedom and the Self," in G. Watson ed., *Free Will*, 2nd ed. (New York: Oxford University Press, 2003), pp. 26–37. Chisholm did not defend a conception of free will as extreme as this.

In terms of the dialectic of peace, we might identify the compatibilist position with the movement of synthesis. Doing so does not necessarily commit us to the claim that it is superior to the other positions. That might be true if we assumed a Hegelian conception of the dialectic as essentially progressive. But if our conception of the dialectic were more gloomy—more, as we might put it, "Schopenhauerian"—this would not follow. I take no stand on the issue of whether the dialectic is Hegelian or Schopenhauerian. The compatibilist movement of the dialectic consists in rejecting the picture of shelter or peace presupposed by the incompatibilist. That is, it involves arguing that (1) the incompatibilist is committed to a specific picture of what responsibility would involve or entail, and (2) this picture is, in one way or another, implausible. The idea that responsibility requires self-creation, ultimacy, or sourcehood, compatibilists will argue, forms no part of our ordinary understanding of what responsibility is, and of what is required to be responsible for one's actions. In place of what they see as this erroneous conception of freedom, compatibilists urge that we instead think in terms of choice mechanisms that translate beliefs about our alternatives, coupled with our desires, into plans of action that are designed to realize these desires. For the compatibilist, being produced in this way by the appropriate choice mechanism—a mechanism that is *responsive* to our reasons—is precisely what it is to be free.[19]

I have argued that the concept of control is problematic. This claim should be treated with care: it is not a blanket denial of the legitimacy of the concept of control. For the purposes of this book, the key issue is not whether the idea of control over motivations is, in general, spurious, but whether there is a nonspurious conception of control that humans can plausibly be thought to have and animals

---

19. The work of John Martin Fischer is a good example of this type of compatibilist strategy. See especially his *The Metaphysics of Free Will* (Oxford: Blackwell, 1994).

can plausibly be thought to lack. I have focused much of my effort on the idea of effective critical scrutiny of motivations. This idea has provided the principal historical support for the claim that animals cannot act morally. The reasons for this are clear. The ability to effectively critically scrutinize one's motivations is one that animals can plausibly be thought to lack. Thus, if this ability does provide the basis for an individual's control over its motivations, there would be a clear rationale for claiming that humans can be the subjects of normative reasons whereas animals cannot. But to deny a specific conception of control is, of course, not to deny control in general. Suppose, however, we opt for another conception of control—for example, the compatibilist conception of control as residing in choice mechanisms of a certain sort. Then, it is far from clear that animals do not possess control over their motivations in this sense. That is, there is no reason to suppose that animals cannot possess choice mechanisms that translate beliefs about alternatives, coupled with desires, into plans of action. In short, if we are looking for a conception of control that could underwrite the idea that humans can act morally whereas animals cannot, it seems we are left with the idea that control over motivations is grounded in the ability to critically scrutinize those motivations. This conception of control, I have argued, is spurious.

Control, in this sense, is the equivalent of "self-creation," "sourcehood," or "ultimacy." This, therefore, is tantamount to rejection of the (incompatibilist voluntarist) idea that we can find control—and, hence, peace—in effective critical scrutiny. So I am left with two options. The first (incompatibilist determinist) option is to deny there is a place of shelter. If there is no control, there is no responsibility. And, given that I have defined moral agency in terms of the idea of responsibility, this means that there is no moral agency. If this is the case, then animals lack nothing that humans have. However, it is a conclusion that many will find unpalatable. The purpose of the remainder of this chapter is to argue that it is not a conclusion to which this book is committed. There is a broadly compatibilist way of reconstructing the idea of agency according to which the absence of control does not entail the absence of agency. Moroever, this account will accommodate the idea that moral agency is something that humans have and animals do not. Instead of locating agency in the concept of control, the compatibilist reconstruction is predicated on the idea of *understanding*.

RECONSTRUCTING AGENCY II: AGENCY AND UNDERSTANDING

Let us return to consideration of the differences between Myshkin and Marlow. Marlow has something that Myshkin lacks: the ability to effectively critically scrutinize his motivations and actions. I have argued that this is not the sort of ability that could elevate a motivation from the status of nonmoral to moral. If it does so, it does so through the medium of control. But effective critical scrutiny of motivations does not supply this control. Nevertheless, it would be a non sequitur to suppose that Marlow's additional abilities bring nothing new to the table.

First of all, it is unclear that Myshkin is able to make qualitative distinctions between the states to which he is negatively and positively sensitized. Thus, while Myshkin is negatively sensitized to a plethora of states that might fall under the general rubric "suffering" or "distress," it is not clear that he distinguishes kinds within this general category. Can he distinguish suffering from, for example, anxiety or nervous anticipation? While it is plausible to suppose that Myshkin is sensitive to quantitative differences of distress—he can, for example, distinguish someone who is suffering greatly from someone who is only mildly inconvenienced (assuming there is no dissembling involved)—it is not easy to see how he could be in a position to make qualitative distinctions among the states to which he is negatively and positively sensitized. To do so would require scrutiny of each of these types of emotion, analyzing both their phenomenological profile and their eliciting causes. And these abilities are beyond Myshkin. So the ability to make fine-grained distinctions between types of emotional states is one that Marlow—in virtue of his metacognitive abilities—has, but Myshkin lacks.

Second, and more important, Marlow can possess a type of moral knowledge that lies outside the abilities of Myshkin. Marlow can know moral *facts*. Myshkin's "moral module," and resulting profile captured by (M3), gives him sensitivity not only to which states of affairs are good or bad, but also to (some of) the things that make a state of affairs good or bad. His motivations reflect these sensitivities. However, what Myshkin does not have is knowledge *that* a motivation is a good or bad one. Being unable to reflect on his motivations, he is unable to represent to himself a motivation as being a good or bad one. This, in itself, might be enough to make his moral profile substantially different from that of Marlow. Marlow, for example, is able to deliberate as follows: "I am inclined to act according to motivation M. But I am going to resist this because M is wrong." The exclusion of a range of motivations and behaviors on the simple grounds that they are wrong—perhaps identifying these motivations as items that are not even to be brought to the table of consideration—is not something that is possible for Myshkin, but is for Myshkin.[20] And so there are at least some patterns of moral reasoning that are available to Marlow but not Myshkin.

Third, and more important still, Marlow is also able, to some extent, to understand *why* something is right or wrong. Perhaps Marlow is a Kantian, for example, and so thinks that the impossibility

20. My thanks to Brad Cokelet (in conversation) for pointing this out.

of universalizing his motivation, M, is what makes M morally improper. Or perhaps he is a contractualist, and so thinks that the failure of others to rationally endorse M renders it a morally improper motivation. This ability requires being able to scrutinize a motivation and examine its compatibility, or lack of compatibility, with a preferred moral theory. If we assume that there is a correct moral theory, and if we assume Marlow is capable of understanding this theory, then Marlow's metacognitive abilities bring with them the ability to understand the basis of moral facts expressible in sentences like "M is wrong."

Fourth, given that he understands the basis of moral facts, he has a grasp of the moral principles that underwrite them. If he understands why M is wrong, he will understand what makes it wrong—the principle of principles that determine the wrongness of M. But given that he has a grasp of moral principles, he is in a position to assess these principles. He can examine their mutual consistency. He can assess their scope and application. Are they being applied correctly, and to all the things to which they are supposed to be applied? On the basis of the answers he gives to questions such as this, he can modify or even reject principles he has antecedently adopted. Moral development or progress is possible for Marlow in a way it never could be for Myshkin.

In these four ways at least, Marlow differs from Myshkin, and he differs because of his metacognitive abilities. Myshkin is sensitive to what is good and bad and also to some of the factors that make a situation good and bad. Marlow has more than this: he has knowledge of moral facts and, if he is a sufficiently skilled thinker, an understanding of the principles that provide the bases of these facts. That is, Marlow has both knowledge *that* a given course of action is wrong and also, potentially, knowledge of *why* it wrong. More than this, he has the ability to scrutinize these principles and, if they are found wanting, to replace them with better ones. These differences are all ones of *understanding*. Therefore, if it is true that Marlow is a moral agent whereas Myshkin is not, then what demarcates moral subjects from moral agents, it seems, is a kind or level of understanding. If this is correct, it is to the concept of understanding rather than control that we need to look to reconstruct the idea of moral agency.

This idea is, of course, a familiar one, and plausible on independent grounds. Our folk conception of responsibility seems to involve two distinguishable elements. On the one hand, there is the idea of control: a person should not be held accountable for what she does if she had no choice, or could not have done any differently.[21] On the other hand, there is the idea of understanding: a person should not be blamed for an action if she did not understand what she was doing (or the consequences of what she was doing). I have argued that the idea of control—at least when understood in terms of effective critical scrutiny of motivations—is a spurious one. But this still leaves intact the second component of our folk conception of agency: understanding. And this provides all the materials necessary for the advertised reconstruction of agency.

According to this reconstruction, the extent to which one is an agent is the extent to which one understands what one is doing, the likely consequences of what one is doing, and how to evaluate those consequences. Agency, on this view, comes in degrees—because this sort of understanding comes in degrees. The typical child is less of an agent than the typical adult—and even in the case of adults the level of agency possessed will vary, perhaps dramatically. Responsibility can be diminished to the extent that the actor's mind is sufficiently disturbed that she can be said not to understand the consequences of her actions. Responsibility can be entirely absent, as in the case of the proverbial baby who finds herself in possession of a loaded gun.

---

21. Although, of course, Frankfurt cases provide well-known problems for the "couldn't have done otherwise" formulation.

Whether agency is present, and if so to what degree, tracks the level of understanding of the purported agent. The degree of agency varies from person to person and, often, from action to action.

When agency is understood in terms of control, it comes in degrees. It should be thought of as a spectrum rather than simply something one has or one does not. Adult human beings, blessed with generous levels of phronesis, would be bunched toward one end of the spectrum. Young children, and some less fortunate adults, would congregate toward the other end. Animals would also be found at the far end of this spectrum. Are they agents or are they not? The question is no longer a legitimate one. If we think of agency as a spectrum whose left-hand side corresponds to the low, and runs to high on the right, then animals might be thought of as occupying a position on the far left, with normal, adult humans clustering toward the right. It is all a matter of degree, and in the case of animals, the degrees involved are small enough that, if we were thinking in all-or-nothing terms, we would be inclined to say they are not agents.

Myshkin can be motivated by moral reasons, and so qualify as a moral subject, without being a moral agent. The reason is that Myshkin does not exhibit sufficient understanding of what he is doing to be held responsible for it, and so to be praised or blamed for it. Understanding, however, is rarely an all-or-nothing matter. And so we may think of the distinction between a (mere) moral subject and a moral agent as one of degree rather than kind. The concept of control has been taken out of the picture. But the more a subject understands what he is doing—understands what counts as moral fact and what makes it a moral fact—the more that subject qualifies also as an agent. Full moral agency may be an ideal to which we can aspire but which few, if any, of us ever really attain. If one does not wish to reject the idea of agency altogether, then this is the best way of thinking about the model of agency required by this book.

THE LOGICAL INDEPENDENCE OF MORAL SUBJECTS AND MORAL AGENTS

There is an obvious objection to this account of agency—or, more precisely, to the idea that it is an account I can afford to endorse. Why not make this level of understanding—the sort of understanding exhibited by Marlow but not Myshkin—a condition of qualifying as a moral subject? The short answer is that this claim is implausible. The long answer is found by reminding ourselves of the dialectical situation that led to this account of agency. Driving the argument—and the denial of the status of moral subject to animals—was the SCNM schema. Scrutiny is required for control, control for normativity, and normativity for morality. However, I have argued that the S-C stage of the explanation is untenable. I still need to account for normativity, and I did so by way of the idea of normative sensitivity grounded in the operations of a reliable mechanism: that is, systematic normative sensitivity to morally salient features of situations. The rationale behind the SCNM system was to account for the normativity of motivations, and via that their moral status. But S and C have gone, and I have offered a different account of normativity. So there is no reason to deny that Myshkin's motivations are normative ones. And their perceived failure to count as normative was the primary reason for their perceived failure to count as moral. But they are normative, and so there is no reason remaining for us to deny that they are moral motivations. In other words, once we have normativity, we can implement the distinction between moral subjects and moral agents. An individual counts as a moral subject to the extent his or her motivations satisfy the normativity requirement.

The extent to which an individual counts as a moral agent, on the other hand, is the extent to which she understands her actions, their consequences, and how to evaluate them. Satisfaction of the two conditions is now a logically independent matter, in a way that it was not on the SCNM schema. Therefore, there is no reason to suppose that one must satisfy the agency condition in order to satisfy the subject condition. Any individual who exhibits systematic normative sensitivity to morally salient features of situations is a moral subject. At least, given the demise of the SCNM schema, it is grossly implausible to suppose that he is not.

Myshkin is a moral subject because of his normative sensitivity to morally salient features of situations—a sensitivity that is grounded in the operations of his reliable "moral module." Marlow is a moral subject also—and for *precisely* the same reasons. However, Marlow is also more than a moral subject. He is a moral agent—or, at least, can be thought of as a moral agent by those inclined to believe in such things. What makes him a moral agent is the type of understanding that his additional intellectual capacities bring. Marlow understands *that* certain motives and actions are right and he understands *that* others are wrong. More: he also understands, at least to some extent, *why* some motives and actions are right and some are wrong. Agency is a function of understanding. Since understanding comes in degrees, so too does agency. Marlow is certainly more of an agent than Myshkin, and Myshkin is an agent to such a small extent that, if we were to think of agency as a categorical matter—either you are an agent or you are not—then we would almost certainly say he is not an agent at all. This, I suspect, is the case with those animals that are moral subjects.

10

A Cognitive Ethologist from Mars

WHY DOES IT MATTER?

We might imagine a cognitive ethologist from Mars, arrived to study a strange species of hairless ape. The goal of his[1] research is to work out whether or not these apes are moral beings: if they are or are not the sorts of creatures that can act for moral reasons. Many—perhaps most—of his fellow Martian academics are skeptical of the worth of this project, and this skepticism takes one of two forms. The first form is particularly prevalent among the Martian scientists. Many of them doubt the possibility of uncovering evidence that could decide the matter one way or another. The existence of moral action in these apes is massively underdetermined by the available empirical data. And it is difficult to imagine discovering additional data that would bridge the evidential gap. These scientists do not deny that the apes sometimes give the impression of acting for moral reasons (although at other times they give the opposite impression). And, of course, they claim, it is *possible* that these apes act for moral reasons: that they act on a sense of morality or justice. But, they say: we are scientists. And, in science one must present evidence that a certain relationship is true and no plausible alternative is possible.[2]

---

1. Yes, I am imagining the ethologist as a "him." In fact, as I type these pages I am picturing an individual who looks very much like Marc Bekoff—except with a cone head.
2. Compare, once again, Bernstein, "The Law of Parsimony Prevails," p. 33.

The Martian ethologist has a ready response to this line of argument. In fact, he has two of them. First, standards of plausibility are notoriously difficult to identify, and are often clouded by the antecedent expectations one brings to the table. His fellow scientists have antecedent expectations aplenty, many of them grounded in a strange form of empiricism to which the Martian psychological sciences inexplicably became attached in the not too distant past. While now widely discredited, this empiricism still plays an important role in shaping the expectations of Martian scientists in their dealings with other fauna. Second, the idea that the goal is to establish that no other plausible explanation is even *possible* is far too stringent. Many things are possible, and more than a few of them may be plausible. The goal of science is to find out whether the apes, as a matter of fact, act for moral reasons, not to establish whether it is possible that they do not. After all, some Martian sociobiologists have claimed that even Martians do not engage in moral action. When Martians act for apparently moral reasons, their actions are really performed with the selfish aim of propagating their genes or motives of that ilk. It may seem to Martians as if they are acting morally, but they are really puppets whose strings are pulled by their biological nature. It is certainly possible that this hypothesis is true, and in some ways the hypothesis is quite plausible, but it has attracted a distinctly limited number of adherents. Most Martians now recognize that biology and morality are not opposed in this way. Martian morality is not a veneer imposed on unruly biology, and the moral sense of Martians is not akin to a gardener who must continually strive to keep his garden free of weeds. On the contrary, the morality of Martians has its roots in their biology. It is natural—biologically natural—for Martians to have certain emotions in given circumstances. Failure to have these emotions is a sign that something has gone wrong on a basic biological level. These emotions often have identifiable moral content. The morality of Martians may, to a considerable extent, be grounded in their biology. But when they act, they are often doing precisely what it seems to them they are doing: they are acting for moral reasons. Therefore, the assumption that matters *must* be different in the case of the hairless apes seems, to the ethologist, to be merely an unjustified prejudice.

If the first form of skepticism was prevalent among Martian scientists, the second form is, to a considerable extent, the preserve of their philosophers. Suppose we could, these philosophers say, discover evidence that allows us to determine that these apes do act for moral reasons. What does it matter? We already know enough about these apes to establish that they feel and have experiences more generally. They can suffer, they can enjoy. We are moralists. We understand that this capacity that they possess is sufficient to place significant restrictions on the way we deal with these creatures. When we invade their planet—and we will—we shall make sure we treat them in ways that reflect and respect their capacity to feel pleasure and pain. It is notable that in doing this we are already showing them a courtesy greater than that they show other fauna on their planet, for which the evidence also overwhelmingly supports the attribution of sentience and the resulting capacity to suffer and enjoy. It is true that some of our more excitable colleagues have speculated that these apes might actually possess a language—a language that takes the form of sounds emitted from their facial cavities. But we doubt this is, in fact, the case: everyone knows that real language must be telepathic. But even if it were the case, it would not change the situation one bit. The question is not, "Can they reason?" Nor is it, "Can they talk?" The question is, "Can they suffer?" Whatever moral entitlements these apes possess will be determined by their sentience and not by any more complex intellectual abilities such as those involved in thought and language. So even if they turn out to be capable of acting for moral reasons, it really does not matter one bit: it does not change the way we deal, or interact, with these creatures.

WHY IT MATTERS: A FIRST STAB

The cognitive ethologist muses that the question of whether Martians can act for moral reasons is, of course, an important question—for Martians. Most Martians never could quite take seriously the idea that what they thought of as their moral action had, in reality, quite other, nonmoral, causes: that they were all mere puppets of their essentially amoral nature. However, if they had taken this idea seriously, any reaffirmation of their status as moral subjects would, presumably, have come as a great relief to them. So if the question matters when asked of Martians, why does it not matter when asked of the hairless apes? The likely answer, the ethologist realizes, is that the question matters *to* Martians. It does not matter to the hairless apes, because they are not, as far as we can tell, the sorts of creatures to which it *could* matter. It is possible that things might be otherwise—that these apes are more psychologically complex than Martians have been willing to admit— but this, at least, is the way most Martians understand the situation. It matters to Martians because they have a certain self-image: an understanding of what they are and their place in the grand scheme of things. The discovery that they are not, in fact, moral subjects, not creatures that act for moral reasons, would be a blow to this self-image. They would discover themselves not to be the sorts of things they had taken themselves to be: they would discover themselves to be, in a relatively clear sense, *less* than they had taken themselves to be. But possession of the sort of self-conception required to make sense of this discovery requires complex intellectual powers. While the study of the hairless apes is in its infancy, and relevant evidence is extremely sparse, it is not yet clear that they possess the necessary intellectual capacities. If this initial assessment is borne out by further evidence, then there is a clear difference between Martians and the apes: the question of what I am and what I can do matters to a Martian in a way that, all the evidence suggests, it cannot matter to an ape.

Nevertheless, the Martian ethologist is struck by the thought that even if it does not matter to the apes, it matters to *him*. Indeed, he is tempted by the thought that even if the question does not matter to the apes, it nevertheless matters *objectively*. The question is: "Why?" I am in the business of discovering truth, the ethologist says to himself. That is what we philosophers and scientists do. I am trying, in effect, to locate the hairless apes in moral space. There is already enough evidence to suggest they are moral patients—the legitimate objects of moral concern. I am trying to work out if they are more than this. If it is a truth that they are more than this, I am in the business of uncovering such things.

There is nothing wrong with this thought. But as soon as he has thought it, the ethologist realizes that it is only part of what is at issue. The Martian moral philosophers claimed that the discovery that the hairless apes acted for moral reasons would change nothing in the way Martians interact or deal with them. The ethologist is now beginning to suspect that is not the case.

A MATTER OF RESPECT

The widespread Martian belief that, with respect to the hairless apes, what is important is not whether they can reason, and not whether they can talk, but whether they can suffer is not, the ethologist begins to understand, normatively harmless. Implicit in it is a certain conception of the essence of the hairless ape. This is not its biological essence but its moral essence. The place the ape occupies in moral space is determined simply by its capacities to suffer and enjoy. A life is going well for an individual hairless ape when the quantity of enjoyment it experiences outweighs the quantity of suffering. To the extent Martians have moral obligations to the hairless apes, these will be the negative one to not inflict unnecessary suffering on the hairless apes and, possibly, the positive one of promoting their enjoyment, assuming this can be done without too much cost to the Martians. In other words, the parameters of the Martians' obligations to the hairless apes are fixed by the apes' ability to suffer and enjoy and by nothing else. Of course, if a Martian were raised in accordance with such parameters—in such a way that his entitlements simply amounted to feeling more pleasure than pain, more enjoyment than suffering—it is likely that his life would be little more than a sad waste. A fulfilled life, for a Martian at least, would be one lived exercising the full gamut of one's proclivities, talents, and abilities. The ethologist is at a loss to see why things should be any different for the hairless apes. It all depends on precisely what proclivities, talents, and abilities the apes turn out to possess. If this is the case, the assumption that the quality of the life of a hairless ape can be captured simply in terms of the relative amounts of pleasure and pain contained in it amounts to nothing more the assumption that their proclivities, talents, and abilities number no more than the ability to suffer and enjoy—or, at the very least, that whatever other proclivities, talents, and abilities they possess are insignificant compared to these. This, the ethologist begins to suspect, is an unwarranted, and potentially baleful, prejudice.

Underpinning this idea, the ethologist suspects, is a general principle, one that concerns the idea of *respect*.[3] But the specific content of this idea, as it applies to a given individual, is a function of the natural or characteristic abilities of that individual. To respect an individual is, fundamentally, to respect it as the kind of individual it is. To treat a Martian as if the quality of its life were simply a matter of the relative amounts of pleasure and pain contained in it would be to

---

3. If the ethologist had been familiar with the work of human philosophers, he might recognize this as a consistent theme in the animal rights work of Tom Regan. See, especially, *The Case for Animal Rights*. The fundamental right possessed by animals, Regan argues, is the right to be treated with the respect one is due as the kind of individual that one is.

fail to respect it—because it is to fail to treat it as the kind of thing it is. It is much more than a receptacle of pleasure and pain. The kind of thing an individual is—at least from the perspective of the respect it is due—is a matter of the natural proclivities, talents, and abilities that it possesses. That is, what counts as treating an individual with respect depends on the abilities or *capabilities* of that individual. Any individual will possess certain capabilities that are natural to, or characteristic of, it. That an individual is permitted to exercise such capabilities is essential to its flourishing.[4] So to treat a hairless ape with respect—the fundamental moral injunction—requires that one understand its capabilities, and treat it in such a way that it is able to exercise those capabilities, and so live a flourishing life.

The capacity to act morally is a natural capability in this sense. So whether or not the hairless apes possess it is, it turns out, a rather important question after all. Perhaps it is not important to the hairless apes in the sense that they are not *interested in it*. But it is important to them in the sense that it is *in their interests* for the others with whom they must deal to ask and answer this question correctly.

PRAISE, ADMIRATION, AND RESPECT

In thinking through these issues, the Martian ethologist has an advantage. The moral vocabulary of Martians is a rich one, and incorporates a tripartite distinction between concepts that some other cognitively advanced species have tended to run together. This is the threefold distinction between *praise, admiration,* and *respect.*

Praise is an attitude (and resulting behavior) directed only at an individual that is responsible for what it does. In some cultures, praise is

---

4. Again, familiarity with the work of human philosophers would enable the ethologist to recognize the position described here as that of Martha Nussbaum. See, for example, her *Frontiers of Justice.*

regarded as, specifically a *speech act*. This is not the case for Martians: for them, praise is, fundamentally, an attitude.[5] Praise can be both moral and nonmoral. In its nonmoral form, praise might, for example, be directed at an artist who is praised for the quality of his creation, or to the athlete who is praised for the quality of his performance. In its moral form, praise is appropriate only for moral *agents*. Thus, one might praise someone for doing the right thing. Or one might condemn the individual for doing otherwise—condemnation is the negative counterpart of praise, and thus is also only properly applicable to moral agents.

In the Martian evaluative vocabulary, *admiration* is appropriately directed only at things that do not act at all. One might admire the creation of the artist, but one does not praise it. One might admire the selfless act of another, but one does not, strictly, praise it. Of course, admiration might provide the basis of praise. One might praise the artist on the basis of his work. One might praise the moral actor on the basis of the selflessness of his act. Nevertheless, one admires the work and praises the artist; one admires the act and praises the actor.

Respect, in the Martian vocabulary, is directed only at things that act, but incorporates both things that are responsible for their actions and things that are not. That is, respect is something that can be appropriately applied both to moral agents and to moral subjects. Respect comes in two forms—moral and nonmoral. In the nonmoral sense, one might, for example, respect the athlete for his sporting prowess. In the moral sense, one might respect a person because she is good or virtuous. So, just as one might praise a person in both moral and nonmoral senses, one can also respect persons in both senses. Both praise and respect can be—indeed, typically are—grounded in admiration for the works or actions of others. Respect differs from praise only in

5. The Martians are, after all, telepathic, and so the distinction between attitudes and speech acts is not as marked in them as it is in the case of creatures that communicate by nontelepathic means.

the sense that it is a broader category that applies to both agents and subjects, whereas praise applies only to agents.

Armed, as he is, with this tripartite array of concepts, the ethologist understands the question of whether the hairless apes can act morally is important because the answer he gives to that question determines whether they are the sorts of things that are worthy of a certain kind of respect. If we assume that the apes are not moral agents, then praise would be an inappropriate attitude to bear toward them.[6] One can certainly respect the hairless apes in nonmoral ways, just as one can respect other fauna on this richly populated planet. Indeed, the ethologist might have been interested in the efforts of one long-forgotten hairless ape to express a kind of aesthetic respect he had for his wolf companion:

> My realization was fundamentally an aesthetic one. When we were running, Brenin would glide across the ground with an elegance and economy of movement I have never seen in a dog. When a dog trots, no matter how refined and efficient its gait, there is always a small vertical vector present in the movement of its feet... and this movement of the feet will transmit itself to the line of its shoulders and back.... A wolf uses its ankles and large feet to propel it forwards. As a result there is far less movement in its legs—these remain straight and move forwards and backwards but not up and down. So, when Brenin trotted, his shoulders and back remained flat and level. From a distance, it looked like he was floating an inch or two above the ground. Brenin is gone now and when I try to picture him it is difficult to furnish this picture with the details necessary to make it a concrete and

6. Of course, it might be *useful* to engage in speech acts that involve praise (or blame) if, for example, one discovers that the hairless apes can be trained or otherwise coerced into behaving in certain (from the Martian perspective) desirable ways by way of such acts. Utility is, of course, not what I mean by "appropriate" here.

living representation. But his essence is still there for me. I can still see it: the ghostly wolf in the early-morning Alabama mist, gliding effortlessly over the ground, silent, fluid and serene.

The contrast with the noisy, puffing and leaden-footed thudding of the ape that ran beside him could not have been more pronounced or depressing. I wanted to be able to lope. I wanted to glide across the ground as if I were floating an inch or two above it. But no matter how good at running I became—and I became very good—this was always going to escape me … If you want to understand the soul of the wolf—the essence of the wolf, what the wolf is all about—then you should look at the way the wolf moves. And the crabbed and graceless bustling of the ape, I came to realize with sadness and regret, is an expression of the crabbed and graceless soul that lies beneath.[7]

This passage expresses a form of aesthetic respect. The wolf[8]—Brenin—cannot be *praised* for the way he runs. He has no say in the matter, but simply does what he does. Nevertheless, running *is* something he does. Therefore, to describe this as merely aesthetic *admiration*—the sort of attitude one might bear to a work of art—is also inappropriate. The attitude in question is respect, and the mode it takes, in this case, is aesthetic. One might sum up the attitude of the ape author in these terms: it is a good thing—aesthetically—that the world contains an individual that is capable of moving in this way. The world is a better place, aesthetically speaking, for containing an individual capable of acting in this way. That, roughly, is the content of the author's aesthetic respect for Brenin, the wolf.

However, there is another important form that an attitude of respect can take: the moral form. If someone is a moral agent, it is

7. This passage is, in fact, from Mark Rowlands, *The Philosopher and the Wolf* (London: Granta, 2008), pp. 85–86.
8. Or, quite possibly, wolf hybrid.

possible to legitimately praise her for her actions, or for adopting the principles that gave rise to her actions. It is not possible to similarly praise someone who is merely a moral subject. Nevertheless, it is possible to respect the person and to do so morally. The content of this respect can be explained in a way that is at least roughly analogous to the content of aesthetic respect. If we assume that the moral subject, in this instance, acts in a way that is good rather than evil, then we can say it is a good thing—morally speaking—that the world contains someone who acts in this way. The subject is not responsible for its actions, and has no say in whether or not it performs them. Nevertheless, because of what the subject does, the world is— temporarily, perhaps even momentarily—a better place. It is, therefore, a good thing that the world contains a subject like this, an individual who acts in this way. This is not moral praise, of the sort one might give to an agent, responsible for its actions. Nor is it moral admiration of the sort one might have for something that cannot act—an illuminating moral work of some sort. Rather, this is the sort of attitude one bears to something that can act, and acts for the good, but is not responsible for what it does. This is moral respect. If animals can, and sometimes do, act for moral reasons, then they are worthy objects of moral respect. That is why it matters.[9]

9. If animals are worthy of respect, then further avenues of exploration appear. If an individual is the sort of thing worthy of respect, then might it also be the sort of thing that is worthy of friendship—the sort of thing with which one might be friends? This is a question for another time, although my preliminary thoughts on this matter can be found in my paper "Friendship and Animals: Reply to Fröding and Peterson," *Journal of Animal Ethics* 1.1 (2011), 70–79. See also my "Friendship and Animals, Again: Response to Fröding and Peterson," *Journal of Animal Ethics* 1.2 (2011), 190–94. As their titles suggest, these papers are replies to Barbro Fröding and Martin Peterson, "Animal Ethics Based on Friendship," *Journal of Animal Ethics* 1.1 (2011), 58–69, and also to their reply to me, "Animals and Friendship: A Reply to Rowlands," *Journal of Animal Ethics* 1.2 (2011), 187–89. Some even more preliminary thoughts on why the question of moral action in animals is often assumed to be unimportant can be extrapolated from the idea of a *morality for strangers* that I develop in my paper "Responding to Animals," *Common Knowledge* 16 (2010), 351–60. This paper is also a reply to another paper, Emilie Hache and Bruno Latour, "Morality or Moralism: An Exercise in Sensitization," *Common Knowledge* 16 (2010), 311–30.

INDEX